The Mobile Internet:

How Japan dialed up
and the West disconnected

by
Jeffrey Lee Funk

www.isipublications.com

Copyright © 2001 Jeffrey Lee Funk

ALL RIGHTS RESERVED. No part of this publication may be reproduced, stored in a retrieval system, or transmitted in whole or part, in any form or by any means, electronic, mechanical, photocopying, recording, or otherwise, without the prior written permission of the publisher.

Any questions or comments regarding this publication should be forwarded to ISI Publications at the following addresses:

The Zurich Centre
90 Pitts Bay Road, Pembroke
HM08, Bermuda
Tel: (1 441) 292 5666
Fax: (1 441) 292 5665
E-mail: info@isipublications.com

9/F Carfield Commercial Building
75-77 Wyndham Street,
Central, Hong Kong
Tel: (852) 2877 3417
Fax: (852) 2877 0942/0914
E-mail: ianh@isipublications.com

25 Mount Ephraim Road
Royal Tunbridge Wells
Kent, TN1 1EN, UK
Tel: (44) 1892 548881
Fax: (44) 1892 515892
E-mail: johnb@isipublications.co.uk

ISBN: 962-7762-69-5

This book is available at special quantity discounts for use as premiums or for sales promotions, in corporate training programs, or for academic institutions.

www.isipublications.com

To my daughters Augusta and Luisa

Contents

Preface

Chapter One: How Success Begins with Simplicity *1*

1.1 Network Effects and Reinventing the Wheel
1.2 New Business Models
1.3 New Services
1.4 New Content
1.5 Young People are *Initially* the Main Users
1.6 New Portals and Search Engines
1.7 New Phones and Compatible Devices
1.8 Returning to Network Effects
1.9 Why Japan Got it Right and the Rest Haven't

Chapter Two: The Japanese Mobile Internet Market Explodes *19*

2.1 The Origins of the Mobile Internet
2.2 i-mode's First Year: Slow Growth, But a Few Very Happy Customers
2.3 The Second Stage of i-mode: New Handsets and Content
2.4 The Third Stage of i-mode: Growth in Traffic to Unofficial Sites
2.5 Killer Application: Entertainment
2.6 Killer Application: News
2.7 Killer Application: E-mail
2.8 Key Initial Users: They're Young
2.9 The Result of Positive Feedback: Increased Revenues

The Mobile Internet

Chapter Three: Mobile versus Fixed-Line Content 47

3.1 The Traditional Trade-off between Reach and Richness
3.2 The New Trade-off between Reach and Richness
3.3 Reach and Richness Explain Traffic Patterns and Ages in the Japanese Mobile Internet
3.4 Youth and Entertainment in the Fixed-Line versus Mobile Internet
3.5 US and European Companies are Overemphasizing Richness

Chapter Four: Mobile versus Fixed-Line Business Models 63

4.1 Service Provider and Manufacturer Business Models
4.2 Content Provider Business Models: Paid Content
4.3 Mobile Shopping
4.4 Transaction-Based Business Models
4.5 Information-Loading Models
4.6 Discount Coupons, Dynamic Pricing, and Auctions
4.7 Advertising
Appendix: Alternative Micro-Payment Schemes

Chapter Five: Mobile versus Fixed-Line Information Strategies for Content Providers 93

5.1 Reach is Critical in the Mobile Internet
5.2 On-Line Stock Trading
5.3 Concert Tickets
5.4 Navigation Services
5.5 News
5.6 Entertainment

Chapter Six: Mobile versus Fixed-Line Portal Sites and Search Engines 117

6.1 Basic Differences between Fixed-Line and Mobile Portals and Search Engines
6.2 Japanese Mobile Portals and Search Engines
6.3 Expanded Reach through New Services
6.4 Expanded Reach through Greater Breadth of Sites
6.5 Expanding Richness

Contents

Chapter Seven: Multi-Channel Convergence *133*

7.1 Fixed-Mobile Convergence
7.2 Phones and Other Mobile Devices
7.3 The Mobile Internet and Televisions
7.4 The Mobile Internet and the Print Media
7.5 Clicks and Mortar: Convenience Stores
7.6 Clicks and Mortar: Virtual Shopping Malls
7.7 Clicks and Mortar: Music and Video Stores

Chapter Eight: Mobile versus Fixed-Line Content: The Future *151*

8.1 Greater Richness through Advances in Semiconductor Technology
8.2 Greater Richness through Higher-Speed Services and Phones
8.3 Greater Reach of Car Navigation Systems
8.4 Greater Reach of PDAs
8.5 Wearable Computing
8.6 Navigation and Location-Based Services
8.7 Mobile Intranets
8.8 Business-to-Business Webs

Chapter Nine: The Challenge for the Rest of the World *173*

9.1 Mistake #1: Initial Use of Complex Technologies and Business Models
9.2 Mistake #2: A Focus on Existing Users
9.3 Mistake #3: Modular Improvements to the Existing System
9.4 Mistake #4: Lack of Openness
9.5 A Proposal for Creating Positive Feedback in the Rest of the World

Chapter Ten: The Challenge for Japan *191*

10.1 Phone Manufacturers
10.2 Content Providers
10.3 Service Providers
10.4 Portal Sites and Search Engines
10.5 Mobile Virtual Network Operators
10.6 Regulators
10.7 Creating the Mobile Economy

Preface

The mobile Internet is the most exciting research that I have been involved with since becoming a graduate student at Carnegie Mellon University in 1980. And my involvement in this research is partly luck, since I just happened to be in Japan and studying the mobile phone market when the mobile Internet exploded in early 2000. I first came to Japan in 1985 and I have lived here on a continuous basis since 1996. I started doing research on the mobile phone industry in 1993 and it became my full-time research project in 1996. While writing my first book on the mobile phone industry (*Competition Between and Within Standards: The Case of Mobile Phones*, London: Palgrave, 2001), in 1999 and 2000 the Japanese mobile Internet exploded. Thus, the first book kept me from pursuing further research on the Japanese mobile Internet until mid-2000, since which time it has become an almost full-time project.

The fast-moving pace of the industry makes it difficult to write a book that is up to date on publication. New content, business models, phones, portals/ search engines, and complementary technologies appear on almost a daily basis. Although I believe that many of these new technologies will reinforce the concepts presented in this book, some are harder to predict. Thus, I am also a victim of the positive feedback that I write about in this book!

Many people helped me with my research on the mobile Internet, including more than 50 Japanese firms and innumerable Westerners. Two service providers (NTT DoCoMo and KDDI) and many content providers in the financial services (DLJDirect Securities, Daiwa Securities), entertainment (Bandai, Dwango, Index), concert tickets (Lawson, Pia), navigation services (Toshiba, Mitsui Bussan, Matsushita Communications, Increment P), music

The Mobile Internet

information and sales (Tsutaya, Cyber Wing), employment, rentals, and restaurant information (Recruit, PA, Chintai, Guru Navi), news (Impress, Asahi, WNI), travel (Open Door), virtual shopping malls (Net Price, Rakuten), and book sales (Kinokuniya) granted me interviews and provided me with information. Portals and search engines (Yahoo! Japan, Digital Street, K-tai.net, Excite, Starts Publishing, and M-Star), technology providers (Asahi TV Data, Access, Oracle, 104.com, Japan Communications), micro-payment providers (Bit Cash, NTT Communications, Japan Net Bank, Bit Wallet), advertisers (Value Click and D2C), a publisher of mobile-related magazines (Media Works), and more than 10 phone manufacturers also granted me interviews and provided me with information.

Many Westerners supplied information about their firms and their mobile Internet services through my presentations and related activities at mobile-Internet-related conferences in Dublin, Istanbul, Washington D.C., Hong Kong, and London. This information was supplied to me through feedback on my presentations, in informal conversations, and in presentations that I attended at these conferences. In particular, I would like to thank George Huitema for reading a partial draft of the book. Finally, I would like to thank Carol Bonnett and others at ISI Publications, and Robyn Flemming for her fine editing job. Of course, any errors, including those of omission, over-generalizations, or misconceptions, are completely my responsibility.

Jeffrey L. Funk
Kobe, Japan
July 2001

Chapter One:
How Success Begins with Simplicity

Mobile Internet phones have made little headway in two of the world's three major markets. Why have these phones been such a phenomenal success in Japan, as opposed to lackluster market performance in Europe and the United States? In both of the latter markets the mobile Internet looks like another over-touted technology whose time has not come. In spite of heavy efforts by service providers, content providers, and manufacturers to introduce relevant services, content, and phones, a lack of users has subsequently caused many of these firms to place the mobile Internet and its associated technologies on the back burner. So-called WAP (wireless application protocol) phones, which were supposed to enable users to access a limited version of the fixed-line Internet, were poorly received in the US and Europe when they were first released in 1999 and 2000. This has caused the service providers, manufacturers, and content providers to place less emphasis on these technologies, thus leading to even worse evaluations from users and the media.

This pessimism has spread to third-generation systems, which will be capable of sending two million bits per second in data, or more than 100 times the capability of most current mobile phone systems. Whereas wild bidding drove up prices for third-generation licenses in Great Britain and Germany in mid-2000, interest was much lower in subsequent auctions in Italy, Austria, Switzerland, and France, and other service providers are scaling back their investment plans for third-generation services. Further, concern over third-generation licensing and other investment costs has caused stock prices to fall for those service providers who have aggressively pursued third-generation licenses and investments throughout the latter half of 2000 and early 2001.

The Mobile Internet

This book argues that the problems with WAP and its associated technologies lie in the West's perception of the mobile Internet. Most service providers have focused on business-related content such as banking, travel, location-based services, and news, and have aimed their WAP phones at business users. (They have *always* offered new services and phones first to business users and then to other users.) They have emphasized complex content and technologies, because these technologies are driving the fixed-line Internet. The media has also played its role by constantly comparing the quality, levels of openness, and methods of the mobile and fixed-line Internet.

This book argues that the mobile Internet is very different from the fixed-line Internet, and also from other technologies that have been previously adopted by mobile service providers. The content, users, devices, services, portals/search engines, and business models are all very different on the mobile and fixed-line Internet. The mobile Internet contents must be simple, due to the small screens and keypads found on mobile phones. Young people are the major users of most portable devices, such as portable music players, and they will most likely be the major users (at least initially) of portable — ie, mobile — Internet phones. Service providers must offer packet services, or, at the minimum, charge by the packet as opposed to connection time. Simplicity is also needed in portals and content provider business models, where the small screens make a fixed menu convenient for users. Further, mobile service providers must create a comprehensive business model that encourages content providers, phone manufacturers, and portals/search engines to produce the appropriate content, phones, and portals/search engines for the mobile Internet.

The mobile Internet is also different from technologies that have been previously offered by mobile service providers, such as smaller phones, digital services, and roaming. Most service providers have aimed these new technologies at business users, since these people generally have a higher capability and willingness to pay for these services. A focus on business users is primarily appropriate when the costs of the services and devices are initially very high. Inexpensive mobile phones are common, however, and mobile Internet capabilities add very little marginal costs to these phones. The mobile Internet services also involve very low marginal costs. And as any economist can tell you, industries with high fixed and low marginal costs require volume. US and European service providers need to aggressively push their mobile Internet services to mainstream users, including young people, in order to generate these large volumes.

How Success Begins with Simplicity

1.1 Network Effects and Reinventing the Wheel

The fact that the mobile and fixed-line Internet is very different means that we must "reinvent the wheel." As shown in Figure 1.1, an entire new wheel, or network, of services, users, content, devices (in this case, phones), business models, and portals/search engines needs to be constructed to make the mobile Internet work. Although all of them are not shown, there are of course interdependencies between each of the items in the figure. New mobile services will not work, and users will not subscribe to these services, unless there are appropriate content, phones, business models, and portals. Content providers will not create appropriate content unless there are appropriate services, phones, business models, and portals. Manufacturers will not invest in the development of the appropriate phones unless there are appropriate services, content, business models, and portals. And without users, no one will invest in anything, the wheel will not turn, and positive feedback will not be created in the new network shown in the figure.

Figure 1.1   Key Interdependencies in the Mobile Internet

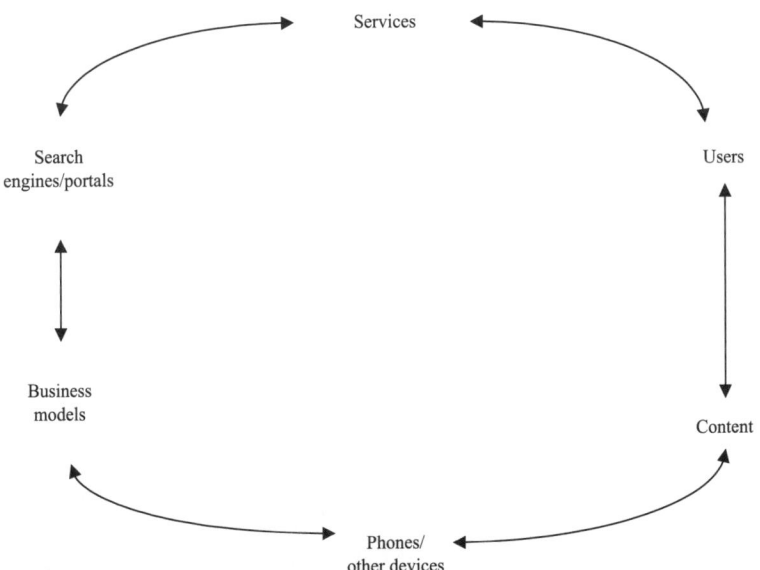

The Mobile Internet

The WAP Forum (see Chapter 2) was supposed to solve this problem. Service and content providers, manufacturers, and portals co-operated to create a robust and powerful standard; a standard that could work in any mobile phone system (eg, Europe's GSM or America's cdmaOne) and any device (eg, phones and personal digital assistants). Although critics claim the technical challenge was too large, and they point to many technical problems with the WAP phones, these technical problems are part of a larger misunderstanding about positive feedback in the mobile Internet.

The positive feedback between the items shown in Figure 1.2 will lead to the evolution of each item. The services, content, users, phones, business models, and portals (critical items) will each evolve from generally simple to more complex and diverse levels as the mobile Internet grows through the positive feedback that is generated between these individual items. The words "evolve" and "simple" are important, since the mobile Internet is really a simplified version of the fixed-line Internet — and it is the evolution of the items shown in Figure 1.2 that is critical.

Figure 1.2   Primary and Secondary Feedback Loops in the Mobile Internet

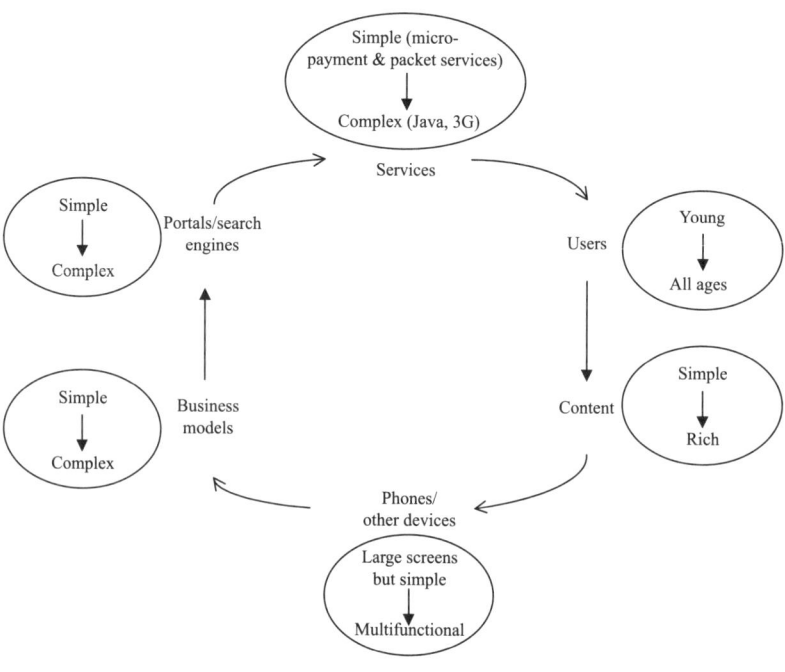

How Success Begins with Simplicity

In particular, without an emphasis on the *initially* appropriate services, content, users, phones, business models, and portals/search engines, positive feedback in the network will not be created; this is what is occurring in the US and Europe. The participants in the current WAP network have been emphasizing the wrong initial content, users, phones, services, and business models, and the resulting slow growth in WAP subscribers has caused everyone in this network to stop innovating. People keep talking about how *new technologies* are needed in order to make *their* contents and other critical items succeed, but it is actually a *new set* of critical items that are needed to make the mobile Internet work with *existing technologies* in the US and Europe.

On the other hand, the opposite is occurring in Japan, where positive feedback is causing the mobile Internet to explode in terms of revenues for all the participants and quickly evolve toward greater complexity and diversity. As discussed in Chapter 2, the Japanese mobile Internet had grown to almost 40 million subscribers and a market of almost US$800 million per month by the end of May 2000.[1] This market includes transmission revenues for the service providers and content revenues for the content providers.

NTT DoCoMo continues to be the leader, with more than 25 million subscribers to its i-mode mobile Internet services, followed by KDDI and J-Phone, each with about seven million subscribers at the end of May 2000. Although NTT DoCoMo has the lion's share of the subscribers and an even larger percentage of the packet and content charges, the other two service providers are actually doing much better than any non-Japanese service provider. For example, KDDI's EZ Web mobile Internet service uses the much-maligned WAP technology, but it has more WAP subscribers than most of the rest of the world combined.

The reason for the greater success of the mobile Internet in Japan is that the Japanese service providers *initially* focused on the *initially* appropriate critical items, and the positive feedback between them caused each of these items to quickly evolve. Whereas the initial content, portals, content providers, business models, and phones were simple and the users were young, they have dramatically evolved through the positive feedback that NTT DoCoMo and other Japanese service providers have created in the Japanese mobile environment (see Table 1.1). All of these evolutions are interacting with each other to produce a successful mobile Internet environment in Japan.

The Mobile Internet

Table 1.1 The Evolution of Critical Items in the Mobile Internet

Item:	**Popular content**
Initially:	Simple entertainment and mail
Current:	Entertainment and mail, plus news, navigation information, remote mail, on-line stock trading
See chapters:	3, 5, 7

Item:	**Users**
Initially:	Young
Current:	Diverse
See chapter:	3

Item:	**Content provider business models**
Initially:	Simple monthly charges
Current:	Simple monthly charges plus advertising, discount coupons, dynamic pricing, multi-channel convergence
See chapters:	4, 7

Item:	**Portals/search engines**
Initially:	Simple
Current:	Complex and varied
See chapter:	6

Item:	**Phones**
Initially:	Large screens, but simple
Current:	Large screens and multifunctional
See chapter:	8

Some people will argue that low fixed-line Internet usage in Japan is a key reason for the success of the mobile Internet in Japan. However, fixed-line Internet usage is higher in Japan than in many European countries. Further, there are more joint users of mobile and fixed-line Internet services than pure mobile Internet users in Japan. This book will argue that the mobile and fixed-line Internet are not substitutes for each other, just as other portable and fixed devices are not substitutes. For example, portable music players and home entertainment systems are not substitutes for each other, just as calculators and PCs — or even mobile phones and fixed-line phones — are not simple substitutes for each other. Most users of these portable devices also own a fixed device, but they use each of them for different purposes. Similarly, the mobile

How Success Begins with Simplicity

and fixed-line Internet are not substitutes for each other; as described in this book, their differences actually complement each other. As part of an overall convergence between multiple channels and media, many Japanese content providers offer integrated fixed-line and mobile services, and this, along with the overall success of the mobile Internet, is raising the awareness of the fixed-line Internet in Japan. Thus, it is likely that the mobile Internet will accelerate the diffusion of the fixed-line Internet in Japan, and if handled properly the opposite could occur in the US and Europe.

Some people also argue that high public transportation usage is a key reason for the success of the mobile Internet in Japan. It is true that public transportation usage is high in Japan, but it is also high in other parts of Asia and in Europe. It is actually the US that is unique here, and not Japan. Further, as is discussed in later chapters, the mobile Internet is appropriate for those people who spend a lot of time away from their home and office. There are many such people in every country in the world. But before going into this, let's look at the necessary components of the mobile Internet network in more detail.

1.2 New Business Models

Mobile service providers need to create a comprehensive business model that encourages content providers, phone manufacturers, and portals/search engines to produce the appropriate content, phones, and portals/search engines for the mobile Internet. Chapter 3 describes why simple content and young users are the initially appropriate content and users. Mobile service providers can increase the number of these and other contents by offering micro-payment services for their "official" content providers, which makes it easier for the content providers to collect content charges and thus make money. As discussed in Chapter 4, they should subsidize mobile-Internet-compatible phones, making them less expensive for young users and thus accelerating the diffusion of these phones. Service providers should allow users to access so-called unofficial content through independent portals and search engines.

The reason why the mobile service providers must create such a comprehensive business model for the mobile Internet is that the service provider plays a much more important role in the mobile than in the fixed-line Internet in creating the necessary positive feedback between the items shown in Figure 1.2. While in the fixed-line Internet, positive

The Mobile Internet

feedback between services, users, content, devices (in this case, PCs), business models, and portals/search engines was created in the US, Europe, and elsewhere in a fairly natural and undirected manner over a number of years,[2] mobile service providers *can* and *must* create the positive feedback in the mobile Internet in a much shorter time period. *They* must create the positive feedback, since they are the ones who will make the most money in the short term through the mobile Internet. For example, NTT DoCoMo receives about seven times more income from the mobile Internet than all of the Japanese content providers put together.

Simplicity is the key word in business models for mobile Internet content providers, just as it is with the content itself. Chapter 4 describes how the most successful content providers in i-mode have made money through simple monthly charges (between $1 and $3) for their content. The small screens, relatively high transmission charges, and short viewing times make a fixed contents menu very practical. This menu provides easy access to content that has been screened by the service provider and thus presumably have high quality.

Some people will argue that many users will be unwilling to pay for content on the mobile Internet, since most content is free on the fixed-line Internet. Although some users will follow this logic, others will realize that they want something to do while they are in transit and don't want to wait until they are home before they look at particular content. Others will realize that they are too busy to wait until they are back in the office. The willingness to pay, plus the ease with which service providers can collect charges through micro-payment systems, will initially make paid contents the key business model for content providers in the mobile Internet.

Service providers may also want to promote alternative payment systems from third parties, which are also discussed in Chapter 4. Truly strong positive feedback between the number of contents and users will overwhelm a service provider's capability to adequately screen contents for its portal site. This has already happened in Japan, and as a result, a number of alternative payment systems are emerging.

In the long run, the positive feedback between the critical items shown in Figure 1.2 will cause the content provider business models to evolve from simple monthly charges to more sophisticated and complex business models such as mobile shopping, transaction-based charges, discount coupons, dynamic pricing, advertising, and multi-channel convergence. An important part of mobile shopping is the alternative

How Success Begins with Simplicity

payment systems that are mentioned above. Discount coupons and advertising are discussed in Chapter 4, and multi-channel convergence is discussed in Chapter 7. Multi-channel convergence involves the convergence of content and strategies in fields such as the fixed-line and mobile Internets, broadcasting, the print media, car navigation systems, and traditional bricks and mortar.

1.3 New Services

Mobile service providers need to introduce a number of new services, such as micro-payment and packet services, in order for the mobile Internet to be successful. As mentioned above, mobile service providers should offer micro-payment systems in order to encourage content providers to develop content for the mobile Internet. Service providers can easily provide micro-payment services, since they already have most of the technologies in place to bill customers each month and to identify customers who are accessing specific contents. The three Japanese service providers all provide micro-payment services and take a percentage of the content charges as a handling fee. Further, NTT DoCoMo's early start of these services is a major reason why it has done better than the other two service providers; these services have enabled NTT DoCoMo to obtain far more co-operation from the content providers than the other service providers.

Mobile service providers also need to introduce packet services. Packet services provide users with an "always on" connection, so that users don't have to wait to be connected. Further, these services are cheaper than existing services, since users only pay for the packets they send and receive, as opposed to the time they spend reading and writing mail messages and surfing the mobile Internet. As of mid-2001, most non-Japanese service providers had not implemented packet services and thus users were required to endure long connect times and to pay by the minute as opposed to the packet. This problem will be solved when US and European service providers complete their introduction of packet services, which, outside of Japan, are called either general packet radio systems (GPRS) or 2.5G (2.5 generation). The term "2.5G" is really just a new name for WAP with a packet service included. However, Western service providers don't have to wait for GPRS to be started before implementing packet charges. Service providers that have excess capacity can charge by the packet as a means of increasing mobile Internet usage. J-Phone, a Japanese service provider with more than seven million mobile Internet subscribers, charges by the packet, although its packet services will not be officially started until the end of 2001.

The Mobile Internet

1.4 New Content

Chapter 3 uses the concept of reach and richness to show how mobile and fixed-line content is different. "Richness" refers to the quality and quantity of information. "Reach" refers to the number of people who can participate in the sharing of that information.[3] Mobile phones have smaller screens and keyboards and thus cannot access the level of rich information that can be accessed with a desktop computer; however, they have higher reach than desktop computers and even personal digital assistants (PDAs). The larger reach of mobile phones comes from their greater diffusion, greater mobility, and faster power-up as compared to desktop computers.

The concepts of reach and richness provide us with one reason why simple entertainment, news, and e-mail dominate the mobile Internet traffic in Japan. These content and applications match the capabilities of the initial and current mobile Internet. As discussed in Chapter 2, these content and applications represent about 70% of the traffic in the Japanese mobile Internet. They have little richness but a great deal of reach, particularly for young people.

Nevertheless, richer and more sophisticated content is already appearing in Japan through the positive feedback that has been generated between the evolving services, content, users, and phones. This comes from better phones, services, and learning by users. The small screens and keyboards require people to learn how to use the mobile Internet, which is another reason why young people, who are always the most open to new ideas, are the initially appropriate users.

Chapter 5 uses the concepts of reach and richness to discuss information strategies for content providers, particularly non-entertainment content providers. In particular, while a focus on richness is very appropriate for content providers in the fixed-line Internet, reach is the critical variable for content providers in the mobile Internet. Content providers need to focus on reach before richness in order to exploit the large potential reach of mobile phones. Mobile content providers can do this by expanding the breadth of the contents and services, of which two key tactics for the latter include mail and site customization services. These two services eliminate many of the complex search activities and thus make it easier for users to obtain the specific information they want. The effective use of these two services is a major reason for the success of non-entertainment content providers in the Japanese mobile Internet.

How Success Begins with Simplicity

1.5 Young People are *Initially* the Main Users

Chapter 3 uses the concepts of reach and richness to describe why young people are *initially* the major users of the mobile Internet. People under 25 generally spend a much larger amount of their time away from home and the office (if they have one), and make greater use of public transportation (buses and trains) and walking, compared to older people. Young people also place less emphasis on richness than older people do, due to the fact that they have less experience and thus lower specialization. This is why portable music devices and calculators are much more popular with young people than people over 30.

The fact that young people are the major users of the mobile Internet is the second reason why simple entertainment is the most popular type of content in the Japanese mobile Internet. Teenagers and young women in their twenties are clearly more interested in simple entertainment such as screen savers with animated characters, ringing tones, horoscopes, and games, than are older business users. These young users were the first people to subscribe to the entertainment content services that drove i-mode in its first year of operation. In particular, they started the positive feedback between the number of users and the quantity of content, both official and unofficial.

This positive feedback between the number of users and content has caused the Japanese mobile Internet to evolve from relatively young users to people of all ages. Although young people are still the major users of i-mode and subscribers to its content services, by mid-2000 most new NTT DoCoMo subscribers and those who were purchasing a new NTT DoCoMo phone were also subscribing to i-mode. This has made the average i-mode and NTT DoCoMo subscriber indistinguishable. The positive feedback between the number of users and the amount of content is also causing many of these older i-mode *subscribers* to become i-mode *users*.

1.6 New Portals and Search Engines

Mobile portals and search engines in the Japanese mobile Internet market have already begun to evolve from simple to more complex portals and search engines. Mobile service providers need to initially offer a simple fixed menu and provide micro-payment services to start the positive feedback in the mobile Internet. A simple fixed menu makes it easy for users to find information, which is why Yahoo! is so popular on the

The Mobile Internet

fixed-line Internet. And just as Yahoo! is not the only way to find information on the fixed-line Internet, multiple portals and search engines are needed to both expand, and respond to the expansion of, positive feedback in the mobile Internet. As described earlier in the discussion about alternative micro-payment systems, truly strong positive feedback between the amount of content and users will overwhelm a service provider's capability to adequately screen contents for its portal site.

This had happened to NTT DoCoMo by late 1999, and by March 2001 there were more than 25 times the number of unofficial sites (more than 40,000) registered on the main search engine for these unofficial sites than there were official sites (1,480) on NTT DoCoMo's set menu. Further, it was estimated that there were more than 20 times the number of pages on unofficial sites than on official sites. This dramatic rise in the number of unofficial sites and pages had caused traffic to these sites to exceed traffic to the official sites by the fall of 2000. The extraordinary growth in the unofficial sites has generated a large number of portals and search engines, which in turn are driving the number of unofficial content and users.

Chapter 6 describes how different capabilities are needed for portals and search engines in the mobile and fixed-line Internets. The small screens, relatively high transmission charges, and short viewing times make screening of contents even more important on the mobile Internet than on the fixed-line Internet. The variety of mark-up languages and screen sizes that are used on phones and PDAs suggests that mobile search engines and portals should be able to adjust the content to the phone's or PDA's appropriate mark-up language and screen size when a user accesses the content through a search engine or portal. The difficulty of inputting information on mobile phones suggests that mobile search engines and portals should enable users to input and store this kind of information (including payment information) for easy sending to content providers. Finally, mobile search engines and portals can provide micro-payment services more effectively than single content providers because they can consolidate users and accounts under a single payment system.

1.7 New Phones and Compatible Devices

The final key aspect of creating positive feedback in the mobile Internet is the mobile-Internet-compatible phone, a phone that at the minimum must be able to access content that is written in the appropriate mark-up language. These phones are mentioned last, since they are in many ways the most important aspect of creating positive feedback between

How Success Begins with Simplicity

phones, users, and content. As mentioned earlier, problems with WAP phones have slowed the growth in WAP users and content, and more importantly, the lack of users has discouraged manufacturers from solving these problems. There have also been problems with Japanese mobile Internet phones, but in Japan the positive feedback between the critical items has caused manufacturers to quickly solve these problems and, in general, to focus heavily on mobile Internet phones. By mid-2000 it was difficult to purchase a phone that *did not* have mobile Internet capabilities.

The phones are also discussed last because they largely determine the advantages and disadvantages of the mobile Internet. As mentioned above, Chapter 3 uses the concepts of reach and richness to show how the appropriate mobile content and users are different from fixed-line content and users. Due to their smaller displays and keyboards, mobile phones provide lower richness but have higher reach than desktop computers and even PDAs.

Large displays are needed on mobile-Internet-compatible phones. The most popular Japanese mobile Internet phones have displays that are larger than two square inches. They first appeared in early 1999, and by late 2000 these display sizes and mobile Internet capabilities had become standard items on almost all Japanese mobile phones. These screens could display as many as 100 Japanese characters in spite of the fact that Japanese characters are far denser than Roman characters. And users could acquire many of these phones for less than $100, even if they were existing, as opposed to new, subscribers.

Further, the positive feedback between phones, users, content, business models, and portals/search engines has caused innovations to flourish in the Japanese mobile phone market. Phones with displays larger than two square inches are getting lighter, while smaller and new functions are constantly being added because the basic electronic devices are becoming smaller. Polyphonic capabilities, a capability that is popular with young people, have evolved from four tones to 128 tones as of early 2001. Color displays had appeared by the end of 1999 and had become the standard for all phones by the end of 2000. Higher-resolution color displays that can display more than 65,000 colors had appeared by the end of 2000 and are expected to become the standard for all phones by the end of 2001. Java is becoming a standard feature on phones; location technologies are just around the corner; and phones compatible with experimental high-speed data services have been available since May 2001. The commercial services are expected to be started in late 2001.

The Mobile Internet

As discussed in Chapter 8, these innovations are causing the trade-off between reach and richness to change. They are enabling users to obtain richer content, albeit the definition of richness is different from that on the fixed-line Internet. Further, we can expect the use of PDAs and other mobile-Internet-compatible devices to increase, thus causing their reach to expand, partly through lower prices but also through expected subsidization of these devices by service providers. The greater richness of phones and the expected greater reach of PDAs will continue to accelerate the positive feedback between the phones/PDAs, content, users, business models, and portals/search engines. Mobile Intranets, navigation and other location-based services, and business-to-business webs are already under development in Japan. These are discussed in Chapter 8.

1.8 Returning to Network Effects

The interaction between the six items shown in Figures 1.1 and 1.2 is critical. While a lack of just one item can seriously slow the diffusion of the mobile Internet, virtually none of them was in place outside of Japan as of the spring of 2001, particularly in the US and Europe. Most US and European firms had not at that time introduced packet and micro-payment services, appropriate entertainment content, low-priced phones for young people, and appropriate business models and portals/search engines. Further, the so-called 2.5G services appeared as if they would only add packet services and not the other critical items shown in Figures 1.1 and 1.2.

On the other hand, the Japanese service providers — in particular, NTT DoCoMo — introduced all of them very quickly, and positive feedback is already causing each of the items in Figure 1.2 to evolve from generally simple to complex and diverse levels. This is why WAP has been a dismal failure in the US and Europe, while not only i-mode but WAP itself is succeeding in Japan. US and European firms need to reinvent the wheel; they need to start over and rethink the appropriate critical items. Unless they do this, it may be many years before the mobile Internet becomes a reality in the West. The failure of the mobile Internet in the US and Europe may also cause third-generation services to initially experience problems in these countries.

As shown in Figure 1.2, third-generation services are just one part, albeit a very expensive part, of the mobile Internet. Although third-generation services will require a whole new set of mobile Internet content, phones, and business models, they will have a very difficult time succeeding

How Success Begins with Simplicity

unless positive feedback is generated between the critical items in the *current* generation of mobile Internet services. The failure to create this positive feedback in the current-generation services may have significant repercussions for those service providers who paid high fees for third-generation licenses, such as in Great Britain and Germany.

However, these service providers are not victims of their environment; they actually *create* their mobile Internet environments. Reinventing the wheel and creating positive feedback between the items shown in Figure 1.2 is not just relevant at the country level; it is also relevant at the service provider level.[4] This is why I argued earlier that the *service providers* must create the positive feedback in the mobile Internet. The aggressive actions taken by NTT DoCoMo and the other two service providers to create this positive feedback are the reason why almost 25% of Japanese people were subscribing to a mobile Internet service within two years of their start, whereas it took far longer to create this level of use even in the US *fixed*-line Internet market. Of course, unlike the fixed-line Internet, NTT DoCoMo and the other Japanese mobile service providers currently are, and likely will be for some time, the major beneficiaries of the rapid growth in the mobile Internet.

The negative side of the aggressive efforts by NTT DoCoMo and the other two Japanese service providers to independently create positive feedback is that they have created multiple, and to some extent redundant, networks of services, content, phones, and portals/search engines. Due to differences in mark-up languages and efforts by service providers to create semi-closed systems, there are multiple networks that compete with each other in Japan, as well as in the US and in each European country. In Japan, the existence of these multiple networks has not prevented growth in the overall mobile Internet, but it has caused problems for some service providers. KDDI and J-Phone have trouble competing with NTT DoCoMo, since NTT DoCoMo has created more positive feedback between the critical items than the other two service providers. This provides NTT DoCoMo with a long-term competitive advantage in the Japanese market.

The media sometimes argue that the existence of the multiple networks is the reason for the lack of diffusion of the mobile Internet outside of Japan. Certainly those few service providers who have created so-called walled gardens and attempt to prevent access by their users to content not on their official menus will not create positive feedback between content and users; thus, they are merely shooting themselves in the

The Mobile Internet

foot. But the greater success of KDDI and J-Phone than of service providers in the rest of the world suggests that multiple networks themselves are not the problem with the mobile Internet in the US and Europe. If Western service providers were doing half as well as KDDI and J-Phone, the US and Europe would have already declared victory in the mobile Internet and no one would care about what is going on in Japan. Further, the existence of multiple networks is a problem that will be solved everywhere through competition and convergence between the networks. Already, this is happening as the technologies that underlay the mobile Internet (eg, the mark-up languages) are converging.

1.9 Why Japan Got it Right and the Rest Haven't

Japan has moved faster than the West to create positive feedback in the mobile Internet for a variety of reasons. At one level, it is a difference of simplicity versus complexity; Japanese firms initially focused on simple entertainment contents, while the US and Europe are emphasizing more complex content, such as location-based services and mobile shopping. This is partly since the US success in the fixed-line Internet has blinded many Americans, and to a lesser extent Europeans, to the possibilities inherent in the mobile Internet. Complex technologies currently play a very important role in the competition in the fixed-line Internet, so it is natural for Americans to assume that complex technologies will also play an initially important role in the mobile Internet. Unfortunately, when the complex services don't work, many Westerners, including the media and commentators, end up criticizing the concept of the mobile Internet as opposed to the specific approaches taken by US and European firms.

Some readers will remember a similar battle in the 1980s when Japan applied simplicity to factories in the form of just-in-time manufacturing and the West applied complexity in the form of computer-integrated manufacturing.[5] Interestingly, in spite of Japan's initial emphasis on simplicity, Japanese firms have ended up being the leading users of automation and computer-integration *because* they eliminated waste in their factories by focusing first on simplicity. It wasn't until Japan started building factories in the US that US firms began tearing out their automation and emphasizing simplicity. Hopefully, it won't take the West so long to understand simplicity this time. In particular, it would be sad indeed if the firms who paid such high prices for third-generation licenses ended up never using them because they were unable to create positive feedback in their current mobile Internet.

How Success Begins with Simplicity

This emphasis on complexity, along with the service providers' historical emphasis on business users, has also caused these service providers to see business applications and users as the key applications and users. It is common for firms to look at new technologies through the filters of their existing customers;[6] many people have pointed this out when they have compared the fixed-line Internet with traditional bricks-and-mortar businesses.[7] But it is also a mistake to look at the mobile Internet through the filters of fixed-line Internet users. It is, of course, difficult not to do this when most executives of the mobile service providers are major users of the fixed-line Internet and, due to their very mobile lifestyles, probably believe they will be the major users of the mobile Internet. If they think that *they* represent the major initial users of the mobile Internet, they may thus make the mistake of thinking that they merely need to ask themselves what content *they* would like to see on the mobile Internet.

Chapter 9 will return to the West's misconceptions of the mobile Internet and how they can be overcome by understanding that these misconceptions are actually common mistakes made by firms when confronted with new technologies. Chapter 10 takes this one step further and discusses the challenges for Japan. There are several aspects of the Japanese mobile Internet that will eventually limit the expansion of positive feedback in the system. Non-Japanese people will also find this chapter interesting, as the West will eventually have to wrestle with the same issues.

Sound Bites

1. **Firms must reinvent the wheel.** The mobile and fixed-line Internet are different, but they are not substitutes. Firms in the mobile phone and fixed-line Internet industries must create a new wheel or network of services, users, content, devices (in this case, phones), business models, and portals/search engines.

2. **Firms must create positive feedback between services, users, content, phones, business models, and portals/search engines.** The positive feedback that has been created in the Japanese mobile Internet is why more than 70% of the world's users and 90% of mobile Internet revenues are in Japan.

The Mobile Internet

3. **Service providers play a much more important role in the mobile Internet than in the fixed-line Internet.** Since they will initially receive most of the benefits from the creation of a successful mobile Internet, service providers must promote the creation of content and phones through micro-payment systems and the subsidization of phones.

4. **Firms must initially focus on simplicity.** The positive feedback in the Japanese market came from a focus on the initially appropriate services, content (which is simple), users (who are young), phones (which have large screens), business models, and portals/search engines (which are both simple).

5. **Positive feedback will cause each element in the wheel or network to evolve.** Japan's creation of positive feedback has caused the content, users, phones, business models, and portals/search engines to evolve from simple and young to more complex and diverse.

Notes:

1. All currency translations are at ¥100 (US$).
2. For example, see Figure 1.2 in Don Tapscott, *The Digital Economy: Promise and Peril in the Age of Networked Intelligence* (New York: McGraw-Hill, 1996), p. 16.
3. See Philip Evans and Thomas Wurster, *Blown to Bits: How the New Economics of Information Transforms Strategy* (Boston: Harvard Business School Press, 2000), Chapter 3.
4. Actually, this concept is relative to a single firm or any group of firms that would like to create an interface standard.
5. The first book to recognize this phenomenon was Richard Schonberger's *Japanese Manufacturing Techniques: Nine Hidden Lessons in Simplicity* (New York: The Free Press, 1982).
6. The first book to describe this phenomenon was Clayton Christensen's *The Innovator's Dilemma When New Technologies Cause Great Firms to Fail* (Boston: Harvard Business School Press, 1997).
7. For example, see M. Modahl, *Now or Never: How Companies Must Change Today to Win the Battle for Internet Customers* (New York: HarperBusiness, 2000).

Chapter Two:
The Japanese Mobile Internet Market Explodes

The Japanese mobile Internet market surprised everyone by exploding in the year 2000. Japan had almost 40 million Internet subscribers by the end of May 2001. The market for mobile content and commerce was $590 million in fiscal 2000 (April 2000 to March 2001), of which more than $400 million was for content; the remainder was for shopping, transactions, and information loading charges.[1] In May 2001 alone, service providers made almost $700 million from monthly and packet/air time charges on the mobile Internet, while content providers made almost $100 million. NTT DoCoMo had more than two-thirds of these subscribers and an even larger percentage of the income from mobile Internet services, and it was expected that NTT DoCoMo would continue to dominate the Japanese market. In all, Japan expected to have more than 60 million Internet subscribers by the end of 2002, and the content and service providers were expected to have sales of at least ¥200 billion and ¥1 trillion, respectively, in fiscal 2001.

Contrast this with the rest of the world, where the number of mobile Internet subscribers (ie, WAP subscribers) was less than four million as of mid-August 2000[2] and probably not more than eight million by the end of that year. Interestingly, the two countries that have done reasonably well are Korea and Taiwan, whose service providers have offered micro-payment systems and simple entertainment content. Outside of these countries it is generally agreed that few WAP subscribers actually use the service, thus placing the market for WAP contents and services outside of Asia at almost zero in late 2000.[3]

This chapter looks at how NTT DoCoMo and the other Japanese service providers created positive feedback between the critical items in the mobile Internet, while the West has not done so. NTT DoCoMo had its packet

The Mobile Internet

service and micro-payment system in place when i-mode services started in February 1999. Low-priced phones and simple entertainment contents started the positive feedback in mid-1999; phones with color displays and compatible contents expanded it in early 2000; and the growth in unofficial contents (through new search engines) further expanded this positive feedback in mid-2000. Key events in each of these three stages are shown in Figure 2.1.

2.1 The Origins of the Mobile Internet

Service providers have long dreamed of making money from data transmission. With the growth in the fixed-line Internet in the late 1990s, many firms saw a natural convergence between the Internet and mobile phones. Service providers dreamed of higher traffic, while infrastructure and phone manufacturers dreamed of selling more expensive infrastructure and phones.

Phone manufacturers saw both the potential of the mobile Internet and the danger in the form of Microsoft and, to a lesser extent, Palm Computing (then part of 3Com). The phone manufacturers were afraid that Microsoft would be able to transfer its dominance of the desktop computer market to the mobile phone, and they did not want to see personal digital assistants become the dominant method of accessing the mobile Internet. Nokia, Motorola, Ericsson, and Psion created the WAP[4] Forum in June 1997, Symbian in mid-1998, and Bluetooth in June 1998 to fight both Microsoft's Windows CE and Palm Computing's operating system and browser. The WAP Forum was charged with creating an open standard for mobile browsers that was based on WML (wireless mark-up language). Symbian was charged with creating an open operating system (called EPOC) for mobile phones and PDAs. Bluetooth was charged with creating an open standard for wireless communication between handsets that are in close proximity. By 1999, most manufacturers and service providers, including those in Japan, had joined these organizations.

WAP has always been the most critical of these three efforts. The WAP Forum released version 1.0 of the protocol in early 1998 and it was posted on the Internet in May of that year. Nokia announced the first WAP-compatible phone, called the 7110, at the 1999 GSM world congress. However, as with announcements by other manufacturers, the release of the phone was delayed several times, including once to update it after version 1.1 of WAP was released in June 1999. The WAP standard was subsequently updated in January 2000, version 2.0 was released in the third quarter of 2000, and an X-HTML version was expected in mid-2001.[5]

Figure 2.1 Key Events in NTT DoCoMo's Creation of Positive Feedback between i-mode Services, Content, Users, Phones, Business Models, and Portals/Search Engines

	2/99	4/99	6/99	8/99	10/99	12/99	2/2000	4/2000
Services	Start of i-mode, micro-payment & packet services							
Users & Revenues	(Subscribers) ——— ¥600/month/subscriber in packet charges ———→ 1 million … 2 million … Number of subscribers reach: 3 million … 4 million … 5 million. Packet charges begin growing at 13% a month							
Official Content		67 firms provide content > 1/3 of i-mode subscribers subscribe to entertainment content		Large jump in entertainments content		Color content emerge		Most relevant content become color
Unofficial Content				Growth accelerates due to popularity of search engine		Growth accelerates due to emergence of ads and i-mode magazines		
Phones		Phones released by: Fujitsu	Prices drop below ¥5,000 first for Fujitsu's phone and then for all of them			2 Color phones released (all have polyphonic capability)		Lighter, large-screen NEC
Business Models		Variety of models exist, but paid contents are main source of revenue for content providers				Advertising begins		Further diversification of business models
Portals/ Search Engines		DoCoMo's official portal Digital Streets search engine		Digital Street's OhNew! becomes popular		Expansion in types of portals and search engines		

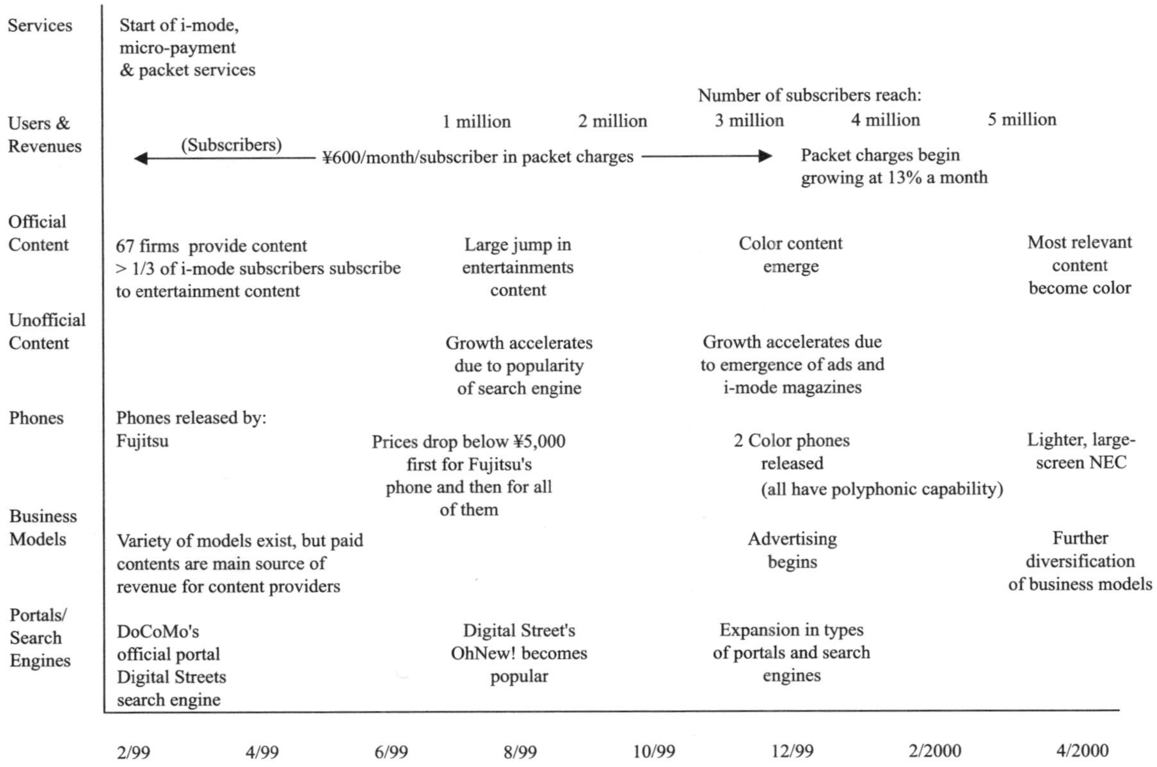

The Mobile Internet

BT Cellnet started the first WAP services in January 2000 following a campaign that many people believe was highly misleading. The tag line "Surfing the BTCellnet" implicitly suggested that its service would provide PC-level quality, which of course it did not. Other service providers used similar advertising campaigns in their rollouts in the year 2000 with similar results. Users were disappointed by the long times (up to 40 seconds) that it took to establish a connection, the poor content, the small displays, the high price tags for the phones, and other problems. By mid-2000, these problems and the resulting slow growth in subscribers had caused anticipation and excitement to be replaced by disappointment. Positive feedback had been replaced by negative feedback, and most firms began hoping that new technologies such as GPRS (packet communication) would bring about a recovery.[6]

Japan Takes a Different Path

In Japan, firms were following paths similar to, but in critical ways different than, the rest of the world. NTT DoCoMo had been working on the creation of a mobile Internet service for many years. Like their foreign counterparts, NTT DoCoMo dreamed of making money from data transmission. Unlike the Western manufacturers, its technological emphasis caused it to introduce a packet communication system called DoPa in 1997, which, like the Western service providers, was aimed at business applications. NTT DoCoMo initially saw little growth in data traffic, and it is quite likely that this would have continued if it had not been for the vision of Senior Vice President Keiichi Enoki and the success of a competitor's messaging service.

Mr. Enoki recognized that there was a potentially large market for a mobile-phone-based consumer information service and in mid-1997 hired Mari Matsunaga from one of Japan's largest media companies, Recruit. She hired Takeishi Natsuno, an executive with an Internet company, and several other people and together they created the i-mode concept. They were helped by the success of J-Phone's (the third-largest service provider in Japan) short messaging service (SMS), which was superior to the other messaging services, including NTT DoCoMo's service. As in Europe, this messaging service was a major hit with young people from the day of its introduction in October 1997 when young people had already become the leading users of mobile phones in the Japanese market. This caused J-Phone's share of young subscribers to skyrocket; in fact, it still had the highest market share among college students even as late as mid-2000, more than a year after the introduction of i-mode. Further, the popularity of J-Phone's messaging service with young people caused J-Phone's share of overall *new* subscribers to jump into the number two spot, where it has remained almost continuously

The Japanese Mobile Internet Market Explodes

since then. J-Phone jumped past KDDI,[7] in spite of KDDI's introduction of cdmaOne, which now provides data services of 64 kilobits per second, or more than six times faster than those of NTT DoCoMo or J-Phone, at 9.6 kilobits per second.

The success of J-Phone's SMS provided Mari Matsunaga and Takeishi Natsuno with additional ammunition in their battle with those who preferred a focus on business users and a "rent-based portal." For example, an outside consulting firm strongly recommended that NTT DoCoMo charge firms for a position on the i-mode portal and let them be responsible for the collection of fees. Mari Matsunaga and Takeishi Natsuno opposed these ideas and instead proposed the introduction of a micro-payment system. They also worked hard to convince Japanese and foreign firms to participate in the portal, and 67 firms were initially providing information for the service.

The Start of Mobile Internet Services in Japan

NTT DoCoMo started i-mode in February 1999; it was followed by other service providers, so that by the end of 1999 all Japanese service providers were offering mobile Internet services. KDDI and the fourth-largest service provider, Tsuka Cellular, started EZ Web in April and December 1999, respectively, and J-Phone started J-Sky in December 1999. Each of these services utilized a different mark-up language to write their content. NTT DoCoMo's i-mode service uses c-HTML (compact-hyper text mark-up language), EZ Web uses WML, and J-Phone uses MML (mobile mark-up language). c-HTML is a compact form of HTML, which is the mark-up language that is widely used in the fixed-line Internet. WML is the mark-up language for WAP, and MML is very similar to c-HTML.

NTT DoCoMo had an official menu and packet and micro-payment services in place from the beginning of its i-mode services; the other service providers were much slower to introduce packet and micro-payment services. Its official menu was, and still is, divided into nine categories and multiple sub-categories, and these sub-categories and contents are basically organized by the amount of access (ie, traffic) to them. Users can also access so-called unofficial contents by inputting URLs (universal resource locators) or by creating bookmarks, much like in the fixed-line Internet world.

In the micro-payment system, NTT DoCoMo collects content charges for these official content providers and takes 9% of these charges as a handling charge. Its official content providers are allowed to charge between $1 and $3 per month for their contents. KDDI did not introduce packet services until the end of 1999 and a micro-payment service until the spring of 2000.

The Mobile Internet

J-Phone introduced micro-payment services in mid-2000 and they were not expected to introduce packet services until late 2001. However, J-Phone has been charging customers by packets as opposed to time.

2.2 i-mode's First Year: Slow Growth, But a Few Very Happy Customers

Initially, there was very little growth in i-mode and the other mobile Internet services. As shown in Figure 2.2, the number of i-mode subscribers increased from 4,500 a week in March 1999 to 24,000 a week in June 1999, 75,000 a week in September 1999, 135,000 a week in January 2000, 250,000 a week in mid-2000, and 350,000 a week in late 2000, around which level it has remained since then. The growth in mobile Internet subscribers for the other two service providers took even longer to accelerate due to their initial lack of packet and micro-payment services and appropriate phones and contents.

Figure 2.2   Number of Mobile Internet Subscribers
by Service Provider

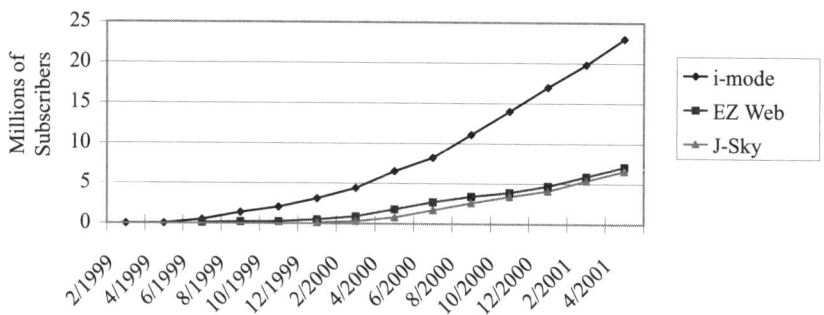

The Japanese Mobile Internet Market Explodes

The first acceleration in i-mode growth occurred after multiple phones were available. Fujitsu's phone was the only one available in the first six weeks of the i-mode service. In March 1999, Mitsubishi and NEC, and in April, Matsushita, released i-mode phones. Although these phones were initially priced at more than $350 to new and existing NTT DoCoMo users, by June, users could buy the Fujitsu and Mitsubishi phones for less than $200 and by August for less than $100. This caused the number of subscribers to increase from 4,500 per week in March 1999 to 24,000 per week in June of that year, with increased growth rates throughout the summer.

The falling prices for the phones from NEC and Matsushita caused this growth to accelerate to 75,000 subscribers a month by the fall of 1999. NEC's phone was relatively heavy at 115 grams, but it had a screen size of 2.2 square inches and it could display more than 100 Japanese characters. With Matsushita's phone, it was easier to download animated characters and use them as screen savers than with the other phones.

The third and most important event was when the number of NTT DoCoMo's official content providers jumped in September 1999 (see Figure 2.3) through the sudden increase in entertainment contents. This increase in entertainment content was brought about by the early success of the few entertainment content providers in existence at that time. At the start of i-mode services in February 1999, entertainment sites made up only 9% of i-mode's 67 official sites, versus 47% for banking and other financial services.[8] Few entertainment companies were interested in i-mode at that time, the general view being that it was "ridiculous to have small pictures on a tiny cell-phone screen."[9] It was only by chance that a few companies such as Bandai, Index, Giga Networks, and Cybird were interested in i-mode in early 1999.[10]

Screen savers, ringing tones, and horoscopes were the so-called killer applications that caused young people to subscribe and actually become "very happy" i-mode users. For example, about 20% of the early i-mode subscribers subscribed to Bandai's screen saver service, and content providers such as Index (horoscopes) and Giga Network (ringing tones) were also able to acquire a large number of young people. About 8% and 5% of the early i-mode subscribers also subscribed to their services, respectively.[11]

Other entertainment-related companies noticed this phenomenon and quickly applied to become i-mode content providers, thus causing the sudden jump in content providers in September 1999 that is shown in Figure 2.3. The increase in the number of these entertainment content providers naturally led to a rise in the number of i-mode subscribers, which caused more entertainment-

Figure 2.3 Number of Firms Providing Content on the i-mode Official Menu 1999-2000

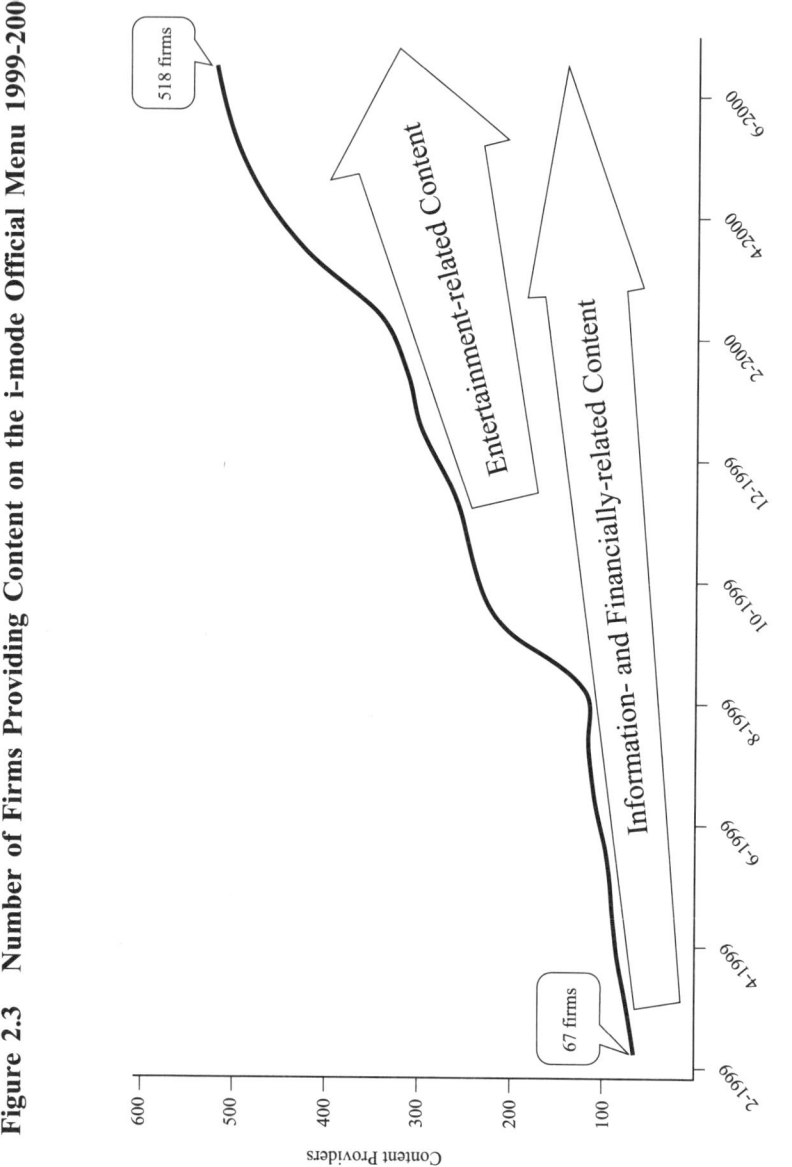

Source-NTT DoCoMo

The Japanese Mobile Internet Market Explodes

related firms to apply to become i-mode content providers. These entertainment-related firms first applied to i-mode and not EZ Web (in spite of its higher data capabilities), since i-mode offered a micro-payment system and had more subscribers than EZ Web.

The falling prices of phones, the success of certain content providers, and the entry of new content providers enabled NTT DoCoMo to begin creating positive feedback between users, content, and phones in its i-mode service. Once started, this positive feedback is easy to perpetuate and actually very difficult to stop. NTT DoCoMo started it through heavy subsidization of phones and the existence of a few critical entertainment contents. One wonders, though, how long it would have taken for NTT DoCoMo to start this positive feedback if those entertainment contents had not been available in early 1999.

2.3 The Second Stage of i-mode: New Handsets and Content

The second stage of i-mode growth started in late 1999 and early 2000 with the introduction of new phones that contained new technologies and content that made use of these technologies. For example, color handsets from Mitsubishi and Fujitsu made screen savers that contained cartoons, pictures, and other animated characters even more popular. Some 30% of the people who purchased these color phones in early 2000 also subscribed to Bandai's $3 a month color screen saver service. Game, horoscope, and other entertainment-related content providers also upgraded their contents to color. NEC's new phone still had the largest display, but it was now 20 grams lighter, weighing less than 100 grams. Further, all of these new phones had improved sound quality on the ringing tones due to the use of "polyphonic" capability that was based on Music Instruments Digital Interface.

These new phones and contents saw the number of new i-mode subscribers reach between 120,000 and 150,000 each week in the late winter and early spring of 2000. By mid-2000, 250,000 new people were subscribing to i-mode each week, a rate that had increased to 350,000 by the end of 2000. Further, by the end of 2000, subscribers could buy more than 50 different phones from more than 10 different manufacturers that could be used to access the mobile Internet. Large screens, some as large as 2.8 square inches with the capability to display as many as 100 Japanese characters, had become the standard. Color displays had also become the standard, and higher-resolution color screens that could display more than 65,000 colors had appeared and were expected to become the new standard by the end of 2001. Best of all, new subscribers could buy most of these phones for less than $100 and many of them for less than $50.

2.4 The Third Stage of i-mode: Growth in Traffic to Unofficial Sites

While the early growth in i-mode came from traffic to i-mode's official contents, by the fall of 2000 there was more traffic to the so-called unofficial sites than to the official sites (see Table 2.1). Learning was a critical part of this trend. The official i-mode menu made it easy for users to learn to use the small keyboard and screens, and to overcome the other idiosyncrasies associated with the mobile Internet. They then began to venture beyond the official i-mode menu where the number of unofficial sites was growing rapidly.[12] They used the mail function to send the addresses of interesting sites to their friends, thus accelerating the rise of popular unofficial sites.

Table 2.1 Traffic to Official versus Unofficial Contents in i-mode

Date	Official Contents	Unofficial Contents
March 1999	91%	9%
September 1999	83%	17%
March 2000	72%	28%
September 2000	50%	50%
February 2001	45%	55%

Source: Takeshi Natsuno, *i-mode Strategy*, p. 187.

Growth in Unofficial Sites
The reason for this growth in unofficial content was that NTT DoCoMo does not allow some types of content on its official site (eg, dating services); more importantly, it could not keep up with the large number of applications to become an i-mode site. The surge in the number of official content providers in the summer of 1999 caused the time taken to process an i-mode contents application to increase dramatically. There was a six-month backlog in applications for the i-mode official menu by early 2000 and this had increased to a year by the end of 2000. Further, many content providers

The Japanese Mobile Internet Market Explodes

were upset about the strict [13] and often unclear criteria according to which NTT DoCoMo chose — and still chooses — its official sites.

Figure 2.4 shows the growth in the number of unofficial sites that are registered with Digital Street's Oh! New? search engine, which has been the leading i-mode search engine since the start of i-mode services. As shown in the figure, the growth in these unofficial sites began to accelerate first in the fall of 1999. This acceleration was a result of the growing popularity of the Oh! New? search service. Although Digital Street had initially looked for sites, by the end of the summer of 1999, the sites were coming to Digital Street. And as the sites began to recognize that Digital Street was the leading search engine, positive feedback was started between content providers and users. The existence of this search engine made it easier for unofficial content to be found by users, and the users' knowledge of its existence encouraged content providers to register on the search engine.

Figure 2.4   Number of Unofficial i-mode Sites

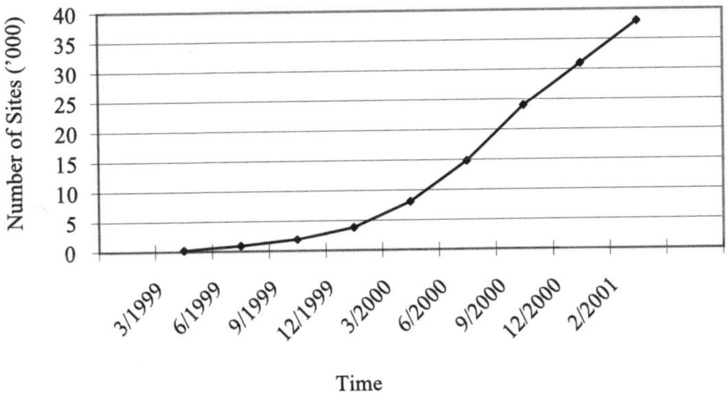

The second acceleration in the growth of these services came about through the start of advertising on i-mode unofficial sites. Advertising, which is one example of the continuing diversification and creation of positive feedback in mobile Internet business models, makes it easier for unofficial contents to obtain revenues and thus encourages the creation of unofficial sites. For example, Value Click Japan started sending two-line by eight-character advertisements to i-mode sites in early 2000, and by July 2000 it was sending about one million advertisements to about 180 sites.

The Mobile Internet

The Media's Role in Promoting Unofficial Content

The media have also played a role in the growth of these unofficial content sites. The growth in i-mode subscribers, content, and, in particular, subscribers to the entertainment content has received a great deal of favorable press in Japan. By late 1999, consumer products magazines had begun reporting on mobile Internet services, content, and phones. By early 2000, magazines that cater specifically to i-mode had also appeared. These magazines described and evaluated official and unofficial sites, thus promoting the growth in unofficial sites and to some extent serving as search engines for these sites.

However, it is not just the growth in unofficial sites that is interesting; the number of home pages accessible through i-mode has seen even more explosive growth. There are probably at least 15 times more pages accessible from an i-mode phone than there are unofficial sites. For example, a site called Magic Island offers a very popular home-page creation service. It had more than 320,000 pages as of mid-January 2001, and 650,000 as of mid-March, on its home-page creation site. Individuals who most likely have little interest in making money have created almost all of its pages. As the number of i-mode subscribers approaches the total number of NTT DoCoMo subscribers, a more interesting measure of i-mode popularity may become the percentage of i-mode subscribers who have created and maintain i-mode sites.

2.5 Killer Application: Entertainment

Entertainment content and e-mail are the two killer applications in the mobile Internet. As shown in Table 2.2, traffic can be divided into e-mail and access to official and unofficial content where the latter is dominated by entertainment contents (see Tables 2.3 and 2.4). Further, entertainment actually became more popular during 2000, rising from 55% of total access from the main i-mode menu in February to 64% of access in August, and to 72% of accesses in March 2001. Screen savers, ringing tones, games, and horoscopes dominate these accesses from the main menu.

The Japanese Mobile Internet Market Explodes

Table 2.2 Composition of i-mode Traffic

Category	Feb 2000	Sept 2000	March 2001
Access to official menu	43%	32%	25%
Access to unofficial menu	17%	32%	34%
E-mail	40%	36%	41%

Source: DoCoMo Kansai and Natsuno (February 2000); www.nttDoCoMo.co.jp/ir/index.html (September 2000 and March 2001).

Table 2.3 Percentage of Access to NTT DoCoMo's Official Menu

Type of Content	Feb'00	Aug '00	Sept '00	Mar '01
Entertainment	55%	64%	70%	32%
Screen savers & ringing melodies Games & horoscopes Other entertainment			32% 19% 19%	35% 18% 19%
News & weather	14%	19%		
Tickets & living	11%	5%		
Financial	6%	4%		
Administrative information	5%	2%		
Tools	5%	4%		
Travel	3%	1%		
Restaurants & recipes	1%	1%		

The Mobile Internet

Source: Personal communication with NTT DoCoMo (February 2000); "Jouhou saito kyuuhouchou-pasokon kawari ni kensaku, kattei saito 2manken (i-mode, the growth in information sites — more than 20,000 unofficial sites can be found with a mobile phone search engine)," *Nikkei Shinbun*, August 24, 2000; www.nttDoCoMo.co.jp/ir/index.html (September 2000 and March 2001).

Table 2.4 Types of Unofficial i-mode Content by Registration and View Data

Genre	By Registration	By View
Individual sites	15%	
Communication/dating sites	15%	20%
Ringing tones	7%	20%
Phone information	7%	
Games	5%	
Restaurants	5%	
Screen savers		13%
Adult entertainment		11%
Other	46%	36%

Source: Search engine (Giga Flops).

Simple entertainment content also make up the majority of i-mode subscribers to content services. Of the 1,480 firms that managed official sites in early 2001 on the i-mode menu, more than 400 of them charged a monthly fee to view some or all of their contents and/or to use their mail service. Only 50% of these sites had more than 10,000 subscribers. Most of the sites were entertainment; the second most popular category consisted of news and weather services. Only a handful of the sites had more than one million subscribers at the end of 2000, of which these were only simple entertainment contents (see Table 2.5). For example, in total there were more than 10

The Japanese Mobile Internet Market Explodes

million subscribers for ringing tones, 2.5 million for screen savers, 1 million for music and video information, 600,000 for horoscopes, and 350,000 for games at that time.[14] Of the top 17 content providers, 13 provided entertainment, two provided news (WNI Weather and Asahi News), one provided navigation services (Toshiba), and one provided a remote mail service (Net Village).

Table 2.5 Leading Content Providers as of Late 2000

Content Provider	No. of Subscribers	Main Content
Bandai	3.1 million	Screen savers
Xing	2.5 million	Ringing tones
Giga Networks	2.3 million	Ringing tones
Cybrid	2.1 million	Various entertainment
Index	1.5 million	Horoscopes
Yamaha	1.2 million	Ringing tones
Sega Communications Network	1 million	Ringing tones

Source: Firms or Nikkei Electronics.

Entertainment is even more popular in the unofficial than in the official contents. Table 2.4 shows the percentage of i-mode unofficial content in terms of the number of registered sites and the percentage of page views. Individual and communication/dating sites, ringing tones, games, characters (screen savers), and adult content can be considered entertainment, while phone information and restaurants can be considered non-entertainment. The entertainment sites represent 42% of the registered sites and 64% of the page views versus 12% and 0%, respectively, for the non-entertainment sites. In other words, of the sites that can be classified, 77% of the registered sites and 100% of the page views are entertainment-related sites.

What is also interesting is that two of the most popular unofficial categories are also popular as official contents. Ringing tones and screen savers are popular as both unofficial and official contents. Although some of the unofficial

The Mobile Internet

sites do offer original songs, which differentiate them from the official sites, many of them are able to survive by not paying copyright fees and offering their services to users for free. As of late 2000, it was expected that copyright violators would be shut down sometime in 2001.

Both communication/dating sites and adult entertainment would most likely be popular official i-mode contents if NTT DoCoMo allowed them to be on their official menu. Although adult entertainment is not allowed on the EZ Web or J-Sky official contents, communication/dating services are allowed and are the most popular sites on their official menus. These communication sites are very similar to the bulletin boards that drove much of the early traffic in the fixed-line Internet. The sites cater to a large variety of needs, including communication between special interest groups such as volunteers, people with physical impediments, and unemployed people. But people looking for partners are the largest users, and in this group of users, young people are clearly the major users.

2.6 Killer Application: News

News is the second most popular type of official contents. Like the entertainment category, it is simple news — such as WNI's weather site, Mainichi's sports and entertainment news, Asahi News, and Yomiuri News — that is popular in terms of traffic, as opposed to special business news. For example, the most popular information on Asahi News's site is sports news. It provides 10-minute updates on baseball and soccer games on both its PC and mobile sites, and it is the mobile site that attracts the most traffic in the evenings. Many people access these sites just to see the scores. This interest in sports also has an effect on the number of its subscribers. The number of Asahi News subscribers rose at the start of the baseball and soccer seasons in both 2000 and 2001 and then dropped again at the end of these seasons. The other factor that drives subscribers and traffic for Asahi News is news on natural disasters such as earthquakes and volcanic eruptions.

Many of the other leading providers of news on i-mode are actually classified under entertainment. There are many sites that provide news about a specific baseball team, a sport such as surfing, skiing, or fishing, the entertainment industry as a whole, or even a specific entertainment figure. Thus, a significant proportion of the accesses shown under "other entertainment" in Table 2.3 are actually for news about the entertainment industry. Since this category represents almost 20% of total accesses from the i-mode menu, it is likely that news and weather represent more than 25% of all accesses from the i-mode menu.

The Japanese Mobile Internet Market Explodes

On the other hand, leading providers of business and technology news on the Japanese fixed-line Internet, such as Nikkei, BizTech, and Impress, have much lower amounts of traffic and subscribers, since their service does not as yet match the high reach and low richness of mobile phones as well as the typical i-mode user. However, they are trying to match their services to these young users, as described in Chapter 5.

2.7 Killer Application: E-mail

E-mail is the second killer application in the Japanese mobile Internet. As shown in Table 2.2, it has represented between 36% and 41% of i-mode traffic through 2000 and early 2001. Although e-mail is also a killer application on the PC Internet, e-mail on the mobile Internet differs in two main ways.

E-mail is an Important Part of Content Services

The first major difference between mobile and fixed-line e-mail is that e-mail is a very important part of the services offered by mobile content providers. For example, screen savers, which typically include various cartoon characters, are sent in e-mail. With more than 2.5 million subscribers for this kind of official service, there are more than 2.5 million of these e-mails sent every morning from the content providers to their subscribers. Further, there are many entertainment services that enable users to add these cartoon characters along with photos, ringing tones, and, in the future, video clips to their e-mail. Thus, the popularity of e-mail is being driven to some extent by the popularity of entertainment contents.

Non-entertainment content providers also send a lot of e-mail as part of their information services. As discussed in Chapter 5, these content providers offer mail services since they have found that it is easier for users to acquire information through mail than by searching through a menu with the small keyboard and screen. Chapter 5 describes how these mail services are an important way in which content providers are realizing the full potential of the reach of mobile phones.

Mobile E-mail: What Are You Doing Right Now?

The second key difference between fixed-line and mobile Internet e-mail is that the latter tends to concern what people are doing at the immediate moment, or a recent event, such as what they did the night before, because the higher *reach* of mobile phones enables them to do this. Messages such as "It's pretty hot today. How's work? When do you get off? How was your date last night? What are you doing tonight?" are common messages during

The Mobile Internet

the day. At night, "What are you doing right now? Where are you? Who are you with?" are common messages. These types of messages are less common in fixed-line e-mail messages, since by the time people receive a response to such an e-mail message on the PC, they have forgotten much of the event.

The peak time for e-mail traffic demonstrates this point. The peak time is just before 10pm, when the main dramas end. When the main dramas end, many young people fire off e-mails to their friends asking them what they thought of the drama and what they did that day. In spite of the fact that these people are in their homes and some of these homes have PCs, they use the mobile phone because they can do it from their couch while watching television.

Young people also often use e-mail as a way to initiate a voice conversation. People often respond to the above types of daytime e-mail messages with such messages as "I'll call you later" or "Last night's date was terrible. I'll tell you about it later." E-mail is, of course, less obtrusive than voice calls and thus can be used to gauge another person's interest without embarrassing yourself with a phone call. This is particularly important at night, when young people want to initiate a conversation or a meeting at night. A fast and lively response signals interest, while a delayed or less interesting response signals less interest.

The high reach of mobile e-mail also enables people to stay in contact with a larger number of people than does fixed-line e-mail. And young people place a much higher emphasis on maintaining a large number of friends and making new friends than do people over 30, who are often married and have children. Young people are often still looking for partners, starting new hobbies, and wanting to meet different people, whereas married couples have a much more limited number of people they interact with or want to interact with.

2.8 Key Initial Users: They're Young

Young people have played a very important role in the evolution of the Japanese mobile Internet. This is true both in the e-mail that was just described and in the entertainment content, which make up a large percentage of the accesses. Young people were the people who subscribed to the services offered by Bandai, Index, and Giga Networks in the spring of 1999 that caused other entertainment companies to begin offering i-mode content. They were the people who continued subscribing to the screen saver, ringing

The Japanese Mobile Internet Market Explodes

tone, game, and horoscope services that these new content providers offered in the second half of 1999, and to their color versions that were introduced in early 2000. They are also the people who are accessing many of the unofficial sites, such as those that provide communication/dating services, ringing tones, screen savers, and adult entertainment. They started the positive feedback between content, users, phones, and other key elements of the mobile Internet.

Young people represent a disproportionate share of i-mode subscribers and an even more disproportionate share of actual i-mode users. As shown in Table 2.6, people under 30 represented 50% of the i-mode subscribers in April 2000 and 48% in November 2000. These shares increase when we consider who actually uses i-mode. In surveys conducted by Hakuhodo Institute of Life and Living, it found that young i-mode subscribers were more likely to use i-mode than older subscribers. Using this data and the data on subscribers from NTT DoCoMo's advertising arm, D2C, we can calculate the percentage of users that are represented by each age category. As shown in Table 2.6, people under 30 represented 67% and 63% of the users in April and November 2000, respectively. This suggests that the representation by young people is dropping, as people under 30 may have represented more than 75% of the users in mid-1999.

Age data from content providers also confirms the importance of young people. For example, about 70% of the subscribers to Index, a leading provider of horoscopes and ringing tones, were less than 30 years old in early 2001. The subscribers to Tsutaya Online, a provider of information on music and videos (see Table 2.6), are even younger. As of late 2000, some 24% of its subscribers were less than 20 years old, 57% were less than 25, and 81% were less than 30; clearly, young people are their key customers.

Interestingly, younger people also make up a larger percentage of Tsutaya Online's mobile Internet subscribers than its fixed-line Internet subscribers. The average age of their mobile Internet subscriber is 21, while the average is over 30 for their fixed-line service. This is also true for other types of content, such as concert tickets and even on-line trading. The average age of subscribers to Pia's concert ticket service is early twenties for the mobile service and early thirties for the fixed-line service. The percentage of subscribers who are less than 40 years old is 56% for the mobile version of DLJ Direct's on-line trading service and about 44% for the fixed-line version. Nevertheless, in spite of the importance of young people in creating positive feedback in the Japanese mobile Internet, this positive feedback is now causing people of all ages not only to subscribe to, but also to use, i-mode. As shown in Table 2.7, people over 30 make up a large percentage of the

Table 2.6 Age and Gender of Subscribers and Users

Age Group and Gender	Percentage of i-mode Subscribers		Percentage of Each Group That Use i-mode		Actual Percentage of i-mode Users	
	4/2000	11/2000	4/2000	11/2000	4/2000	11/2000
18-29, Male	28%	27%	13%	16%	32%	31%
18-29, Female	22%	21%	18%	21%	35%	32%
30-49, Male	24%	24%	11%	13%	23%	22%
30-49, Female	15%	16%	4%	10%	5.3%	12%
50-74, Male	8%	8%	4%	6%	2.7%	3.6%
50-74, Female	4%	4%	0%	0%	1.5%	0%
Total	100%	100%	NA	NA	100%	100%

Source: D2C and Hakuhodo Institute of Life and Living, "NTT DoCoMo's i-mode business enters second phase," *AsiaBizTech.com*, March 26, 2001.

The Japanese Mobile Internet Market Explodes

subscribers to many content services. For example, about 50% of the subscribers to news-related content are aged over 30. The same holds true for restaurant guides and other popular services, such as Toshiba's navigation service.

Table 2.7 Percentage of Subscribers Who Are Less Than Specific Ages

Service/content	<20	<25	<30	<40
i-mode	7%	31%	48%	70%
Entertainment				
Horoscopes & ringing tones			70%	
Music info	24%	57%	81%	97%
TV info	22%	45%	68%	94%
Prize guide	13%	34%	59%	90%
News				
Sports	4%	29%	55%	79%
General	5%	27%	50%	75%
Technical	3%	22%	49%	80%
Weather	10%	38%	59%	77%
Restaurant guide	3%	27%	55%	80%

Source: D2 Communications and company data.

The number of users aged over 30 will most likely increase as the positive feedback between contents and users increases. In this case, it is the interaction between users who are over 30 years old and contents that have been created for those people that is critical. Overall, as more sophisticated phones, business models, and content emerge, i-mode users will diversify and the number of over 30-year-old users will continue to increase.

The Mobile Internet

2.9 The Result of Positive Feedback: Increased Revenues

Positive feedback between the critical items in the mobile Internet has not only caused the number of subscribers to grow in leaps and bounds, but it has also caused the average revenues per subscriber to grow. NTT DoCoMo charges i-mode subscribers $3 a month and 0.3 cents per packet of information, and it takes 9% of the charges it collects for content providers through its micro-payment system. While the monthly charges have grown proportionately to the number of subscribers, the other two revenue streams have also increased on a per-subscriber basis throughout the life of i-mode, and similar trends exist with EZ Web and J-Sky. Average packet charges were about $7 per month and per subscriber throughout 1999, but from the beginning of 2000 they had risen in a linear fashion to three times that amount by September 2000 (about 13% a month). This was due to non-using subscribers becoming users, and users becoming bigger users. For example, the percentage of subscribers who had accessed contents in a typical week rose from 51% in March 2000 to 87% in September 2000. [15]

A related trend involves increased content charges incurred per month and per i-mode subscriber, which is good for both NTT DoCoMo and the content providers. This increase is due both to a greater number of content subscriptions per i-mode subscriber and to increases in the average fee per content subscription. For example, the ratio of paid content to i-mode subscribers rose from 0.66 in December 1999 to 0.96 in April 2000 and 1.07 in August 2000. As part of this trend, the percentage of i-mode subscribers who were also subscribing to at least one paid content service rose from 34% in December 1999 to 45% in April 2000 and 49% in August 2000. [16] The fees that people were charged, and apparently were willing to pay, for this content also rose as the content was improved through color, polyphonic, and other new capabilities. While most entertainment content charges were $1 per month in 1999, they rose to $3 per month in 2000 for the phones with color screens and polyphonic capabilities.

The growth in average charges per subscriber is another example of the positive feedback that NTT DoCoMo has created between the critical items in the mobile Internet. One reason I use the term "users" instead of "subscribers" is that the positive feedback between these items is causing more subscribers to become users and more users to become bigger users. For example, as the number and quality of content increases, subscribers have more reasons to actually use i-mode phones to access and subscribe to contents. This causes the average packet and content charges to rise over time.

The Japanese Mobile Internet Market Explodes

Packet Charges Are Larger Than Content Charges

Another conclusion from the growth in these revenue streams is that packet charges are clearly more important than content charges. Packet charges were more than six times the content charges as of February 2001, and many content and service providers argue that Japanese subscribers attempt to regulate their packet charges through content subscriptions. By canceling a content subscription, mobile Internet subscribers believe they will use the phone less and thus incur lower packet charges. As discussed in Chapter 5, users are applying the same logic to mail services. Further, users appear to be more aware of content charges than packet charges. There is a great deal of churn in content subscriptions, particularly at the end of the month when subscribers cancel their subscriptions before the next month's charge is applied to their bill.

The greater importance of packet charges as compared to content charges suggests that service providers should minimize handling charges on their micro-payment services in order to promote the creation of contents. For example, even if NTT DoCoMo were to increase its micro-payment handling fee from 9% to 50%, which some European and US service providers are apparently considering doing, NTT DoCoMo would still make 12 times more money from packet charges than from content charges. But the implementation of a 50% handling fee would have a dramatic effect on the income of content providers, thus providing them with less incentive to offer content for mobile services. In the battle to create positive feedback between content, users, and the other items, stingy policies toward content charges are a poor strategy for service providers.

Should Service Providers Share Their Packet Charges with Content Providers?

In fact, it may even make sense for service providers to give a portion of their packet charges to the content providers in order to promote the creation of content. This is a particularly reasonable strategy if you are losing the contents battle to another service provider, as EZ Web and J-Sky are experiencing in their battle with i-mode. NTT DoCoMo's i-mode service has succeeded far more than the other mobile Internet services because it has created stronger and earlier positive feedback between the critical items in the mobile Internet.

This success has caused NTT DoCoMo's share of the Japanese mobile phone market to soar. NTT DoCoMo obtained 69% of new subscribers in 2000 and forced KDDI to introduce a 50% discount plan for college students in late 2000. KDDI had completed a nationwide cdmaOne network in early

The Mobile Internet

1999 in order to compete as the high-quality service provider and had aimed its service at business users. Its discount plan for college students clearly represented a 180-degree change in strategy; it was now competing as the low-cost provider for these students, not business users.

Things may get even worse for KDDI, and perhaps for J-Phone, since they have far fewer official and unofficial content than NTT DoCoMo has. Their lower number of mobile Internet subscribers and content provides less positive feedback than that of NTT DoCoMo. This may doom EZ Web and J-Sky to a marginal position in the Japanese mobile phone market, much like Apple Computer occupies in the PC market.

One way to jump-start the positive feedback between content, users, and the other items in the EZ Web and J-Sky services is for their supporters (KDDI, Tsuka, and J-Phone) to provide content providers with a bigger piece of the revenue stream than NTT DoCoMo is providing. Like NTT DoCoMo, these service providers currently take about 9% of the content charges as a handling fee. They could eliminate this fee, thus increasing the revenues for the content providers. More importantly, these service providers could give the content providers a portion of their packet charges in proportion to the traffic that the content providers generate for the service providers. This would provide additional incentives for content providers to create content for EZ Web and J-Sky.

As of early 2001, these service providers did not plan to do this and were hoping that the convergence of c-HTML (i-mode), WML (EZ Web), and MML (J-Sky) into X-HTML would eliminate the differences in content numbers. Beginning in mid-July, EZ Web subscribers could access images in addition to the text in unofficial i-mode content, while J-Sky subscribers could access only text. However, NTT DoCoMo continues to stay one step ahead of its rivals by introducing Java and other technologies that enable content providers to offer content that is not accessible by EZ Web and J-Sky subscribers. Further, even if its rivals come close to NTT DoCoMo in terms of contents, NTT DoCoMo has created a strong brand image that will be difficult to overcome. [17]

The Japanese Mobile Internet Market Explodes

Sound Bites

1. **Low-priced phones and simple entertainment content are critical.** They, along with the packet services and micro-payment systems, started the positive feedback between phones and users in the first six months of the i-mode service.

2. **The early success of simple entertainment content led to an increase in the number of entertainment content providers.** This key entertainment content included screen savers, ringing tones, and horoscopes.

3. **Young people played a key role in the creation of this positive feedback.** Young people were the ones who subscribed to these simple entertainment content.

4. **Search engines, magazines, and advertising have driven the rise in unofficial content and traffic to these sites.** Traffic to unofficial sites represented more than 55% of the total traffic to mobile Internet sites in early 2001.

Notes:

1. The mobile commerce included $50 million in travel products and $25 million in CDs and books. "Dai2bu erite-ru kakumei tokushu — keitai netto hansoku ni iryoku, 2chouen shijou he (The second e-commerce revolution — the power of the mobile Internet)," *Nikkei Distribution*, March 6, 2001, p. 5.
2. "China and Japan seen as key drivers for new-generation Internet access," *South China Morning Post*, September 19, 2000.
3. K. Chan, "Mobile Internet hits bumps but next year looks better — despite flaws WAP is set," *Dow Jones Newswire*, September 25, 2000.
4. WAP was created in June 1997 by Ericsson, Motorola, Nokia, and Unwired Planet. It is not a standards body; it submits its specifications for adoption by appropriate standards bodies. It is independent of the air-interface standard and thus can be used with cdmaOne, GSM, DAMPS, cdma2000, and W-CDMA. It is also independent of the handset and thus can be used with any multiple displays, devices, input methods, transports, and applications.

The Mobile Internet

5. See Mike Hibberd, "How it all began," *Mobile Communications International*, December/January 2000/2001, pp. 41–43 and other articles in the same issue entitled "WAP: On fire or burnt out?"
6. Ibid.
7. KDDI is a recent merger between two mobile service providers, DDI Cellular and IDO, and Japan's largest provider of international phone services, KDD. The two mobile service providers and Tsuka Cellular (which is also owned by DDI Cellular) have combined their mobile Internet services into one nationwide service. Before the merger, DDI Cellular and IDO did not have nationwide licenses, and thus only offered nationwide services through collaboration between the two firms. They announced a merger in the summer of 1999, as well as the acquisition of Tsuka Cellular who was also a regional operator.
8. Initially, 47% of the 67 official sites were banking and other financial services, 12% were travel, 10% were news, 9% were entertainment, and 21% were other. Takeshi Natsuno, *imo-do sutorateji (i-mode Strategy)* (Tokyo: Nikkei BP, December 2000), p. 98.
9. Takashi Koyama, "Bandai puts bad times behind it on road to success," *Nikkei Weekly*, April 16, 2001, p. 1; quote from Toshiki Hayashi, Bandai Networks' chief executive officer.
10. Bandai accidentally became involved with providing screen savers for the i-mode service. It had lost large amounts of money in 1997 and 1998 and was looking for a way to connect its Wonder Swan game with mobile phones. The man responsible for this, Mr. Hayashi, accidentally visited the wrong section at NTT DoCoMo, which was looking for a partner to provide cartoon characters for NTT DoCoMo's phones. Takashi Koyama, "Bandai puts bad times behind it on road to success," *Nikkei Weekly*, April 16, 2001, p. 1. Other content providers such as Index and Cybird became involved with i-mode early due to their previous work with providing entertainment contents for Japan's Personal Handyphone System (PHS).
11. The number for Index is from Index, while the numbers for Bandai and Giga Networks are from "Pokemon wo oi bunka no kabe ni idomu (Challenging the cultural barrier on the back of Pokemon)," *Nikkei Electronics*, January 15, 2001, pp. 132–137.
12. I am indebted to Stephen Walker of Value Click Japan for this insight.
13. NTT DoCoMo requires its sites to have 24-hour phone and e-mail service. This is rather expensive, but NTT DoCoMo believes it is a necessary condition to create positive feedback between contents and users.
14. Source: various content providers.
15. See Chapter 1 of Takeshi Natsuno, *imo-do sutorateji (i-mode Strategy)* (Tokyo: Nikkei BP, December 2000), in particular, pp. 38 and 45.

The Japanese Mobile Internet Market Explodes

16. Ibid., in particular, p. 56.
17. For example, see *Mobile Media Japan Weekly Headline Service*, July 6, 2001, Vol. 46.

Chapter Three:
Mobile versus Fixed-Line Content

The Japanese mobile Internet has grown much faster than its US and European counterparts because Japanese service providers — in particular, NTT DoCoMo — have created stronger positive feedback between the appropriate services, content, users, phones, and business models (critical items) than has been achieved in the West. They did this by focusing on the *initially* appropriate critical items and portals/search engines. These included packet and micro-payment services, simple entertainment contents, young users, low-priced phones with large screens, and simple paid contents and simple portals.

Simple entertainment content and young people played an important role in creating the initial positive feedback. Many young people subscribed to simple entertainment content such as Bandai's screen saver service, Index's horoscope service, and Giga Network's ringing tones service in the first six months of the i-mode service. This caused other entertainment providers to begin offering similar types of entertainment content, which created positive feedback between the amount of content and users. Phones with large displays, and later large color displays, also played a role in creating and expanding this positive feedback in 1999 and 2000. The availability of phones with large color displays caused color content to appear, thus creating positive feedback between users, color content, and phones with color displays.

This chapter looks at why these simple entertainment content and young users are initially the appropriate content and users in the mobile Internet, and thus why they have played an important role in creating the positive feedback in the Japanese mobile Internet. It uses the concepts of reach and richness to show that high-reach and low-rich content such as simple

The Mobile Internet

entertainment are more appropriate, at least initially, for the mobile Internet than are more sophisticated and rich content for the business user. "Reach" refers to the number of people who participate in the sharing of that information. "Richness" refers to the quality and quantity of information, as defined by the user. This includes accuracy, bandwidth, timing, customization, interactivity, relevance, and security,[1] of which bandwidth may be the most important aspect of the trade-off between fixed-line and mobile-Internet applications. "Bandwidth" refers to the amount of information that can be moved from sender to receiver in a given time. In the Internet, it is a function of the transmission times, screen sizes, and types of images where the images could range from text to video.

3.1 The Traditional Trade-off between Reach and Richness

Figure 3.1 shows the trade-off between reach and richness in the traditional or pre-Internet economy. Firms could provide *either* reach or richness in their information services, but *not* both of them. For example, general-interest newspapers reach a large number of people and thus enable a large number of people to share in that experience. However, the information contained in newspapers is clearly not as "rich" as the information contained in special-purpose magazines or journals that do not have as large a "reach" as the general-purpose newspapers. Many of these special-purpose magazines and journals have not only been traditionally difficult to obtain; it has often been difficult even to identify them due to their limited circulation. Traditionally, only specialists are familiar with these magazines and journals, and it is difficult to identify and contact these specialists. Thus, there has traditionally been a strong trade-off between richness and reach.

Many people argue that the fixed-line Internet enables firms to provide both more reach and more richness, thus causing the trade-off between reach and richness to change. As the number of Internet users increases, the reach of information provided over the Internet also increases. By one definition, the reach of Internet newspapers will probably soon surpass that of paper-based newspapers, since the number of Internet users will soon exceed the number of newspaper readers in the US and elsewhere. Further, the links between home pages make it possible for users easily and simultaneously to obtain rich information on the Internet, often from these very same "high-reach" sites. For example, many general-purpose newspapers that operate on the Internet provide links to related articles, corporate home pages, and other sites, thus providing access to both rich and high-reach information. Thus, the Internet is creating new trade-offs between reach and richness.

Mobile versus Fixed-Line Content

Figure 3.1 The Trade-off between Richness and Reach

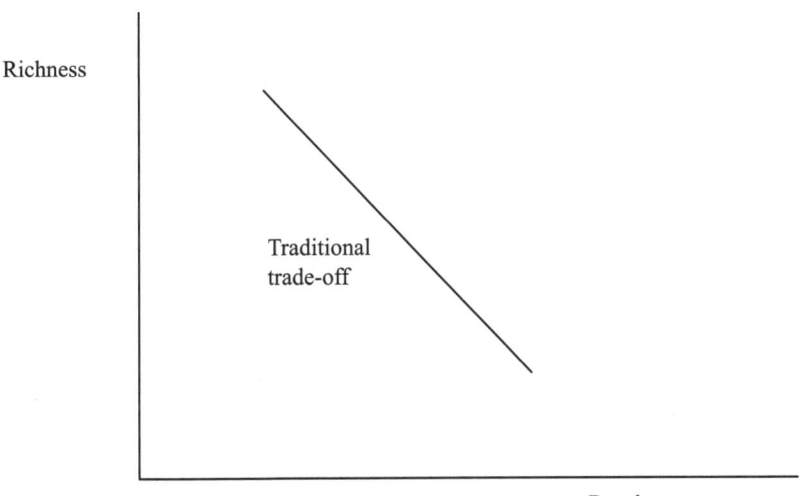

Reprinted by permission of *Havard Business Review*. From "Strategy and the New Economics of Information" by Evans & Wurster, September - October 1997. Copyright © 1997 by the Harvard Business School Publishing Corporation, all rights reserved.

Many people also argue that content providers primarily compete on the basis of richness in the fixed-line Internet. For example, Philip Evans and Thomas Wurster argue that the on-line businesses of Charles Schwab and Dell Computing have largely succeeded through their emphasis on richness. After Charles Schwab expanded the reach (at the expense of richness) of its brokerage services over fixed-line telephones, it expanded richness through the use of the Internet. Charles Schwab added financial data, portfolio tracking, and personalized advice to its basic trade execution services. Similarly, after Dell Computer expanded the reach (again at the expense of richness) of its computer sales over fixed-line telephones, it expanded richness through the use of the Internet. It added multiple price combinations, technical support, and individualized configurations to its basic computer sales services. As we shall see in this and subsequent chapters, competition among content providers in the mobile Internet focuses on reach as opposed to richness.

The Mobile Internet

3.2 The New Trade-off between Reach and Richness

Figure 3.2 shows the trade-off between reach and richness in the new or Internet economy. This new trade-off involves a number of devices, such as PCs, car navigation systems, PDAs, phones, and watches. Mobile devices (car navigation systems, PDAs, phones, and watches) provide the highest reach, but they are less suited than desktop computers to handling rich information. As we move from PCs to watches in Figure 3.2, the devices become smaller and lighter; thus, they are easier to carry and provide higher reach. The shorter power-up times of PDAs also increase the reach of these devices; mobile phones and PDAs can be used within seconds of turning them on, compared with the several minutes required for desktop computers. On the other hand, as we move from PCs to watches in the figure, screens and keyboards become smaller and thus devices cannot access the level of rich information — in particular, the levels of bandwidth — that can be accessed with a desktop computer.

Figure 3.2 The New Trade-off between Richness and Reach

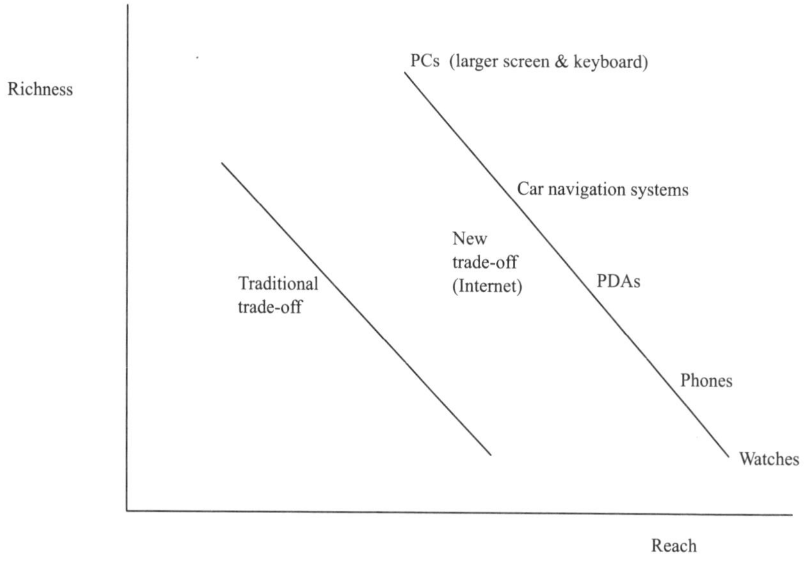

Source: Tracking and Transformation E-commerce and the Terms of Competition in Industries, by the BRIE-IGCC E-conomy Project, published by the Brookings Institution, copyright 2001.

Mobile versus Fixed-Line Content

It should be emphasized that Figure 3.2 represents only the *potential* reach of these devices, since actual usage determines the real reach and some of the devices shown in the figure cannot currently be used to access the Internet. Watches clearly have the highest diffusion in most countries of the world, although (other than some rare examples) they are not currently capable of accessing any kind of information from the Internet. Phones have the second highest rate of diffusion in the world among these devices, including in Japan and many countries in Europe, but they still lagged behind PC usage in the United States as of early 2001.

More interestingly, the diffusion rates for PDAs and car navigation systems are very low as compared to that of PCs, particularly in the US. Thus, although PDAs and car navigation systems have a higher *potential* reach than PCs due to their lower weight, and thus higher mobility, this reach will not be realized until the diffusion of these devices increases substantially. Interestingly, Japan has the highest diffusion rate in the world for car navigation systems, with more than five million devices (7.5% of automobiles) in use as of February 2000. No other country in the world has a diffusion rate of over 1%. Further, Internet browsers became standard items on most car navigation systems in Japan beginning in late 2000.[2]

Figure 3.2 also explains why the fixed-line and mobile Internets are not simple substitutes for each other. PCs, car navigation systems, PDAs, mobile phones, and watches each provide different levels of reach and richness and thus different types of services. As will be described in Chapters 5 and 7, many people are using these devices as complements, where rich information will be handled on PCs (and perhaps, in the future, on car navigation systems) and less-rich information will be handled on PDAs and mobile phones. Thus, it is important for content providers to provide services that make it easier to use these devices as complements; this is already a major area of competition in the Japanese mobile Internet.

However, in spite of the fact that these devices are more complements than substitutes, there will still be competition between some of them. Mobile phones will always have a larger reach than desktop computers, and even PDAs, due to their lighter weight and lower costs. The challenge for phone manufacturers is to increase the capability of phones to access rich information. As discussed in Chapter 8, manufacturers of mobile phones, and even PDAs, are attempting to do this by increasing display size and quality, as well as memory and processing power, and by improving input methods either through larger keyboards or new technologies such as voice recognition. Manufacturers of PDAs are attempting to reduce the costs, and thus prices, of these devices in order to increase their reach. Further, we

The Mobile Internet

will eventually see the emergence of "wearable computing." Manufacturers will "deconstruct" mobile phones and PDAs into a number of smaller devices that can be incorporated into people's clothing. All of these efforts will cause the trade-off between reach and richness to change.

3.3 Reach and Richness Explain Traffic Patterns and Ages in the Japanese Mobile Internet

Figure 3.2 and the trade-off between reach and richness explain the traffic patterns and importance of young people in the Japanese mobile Internet. In particular, the trade-off between reach and richness explains both why simple contents are the most widely used contents in the Japanese mobile Internet and why young people have been the early users of the mobile Internet. For example, it is not just entertainment that has been successful in the Japanese mobile Internet; it is *simple* entertainment, such as screen savers, ringing tones, games, communication and dating services, and horoscopes. These simple applications require very low levels of bandwidth.

Interestingly, the downloading of ringing tones is one of the most popular short messaging services (SMS) in Europe; this makes it hard for people to argue that the popularity of ringing tones and other entertainment services in Japan is due to cultural differences. If European operators were to offer such a service on the mobile Internet, it would be much easier for people to choose and download these ringing tones than it is for them to do so with SMS services. Further, screen savers are just another type of phone personalization service, and horoscopes and games are popular the world over with young people.[3] The popularity of entertainment in Japan is not about culture, it is about reach and richness and the implications that these concepts have for mobile Internet contents and, as we shall see later in this chapter, for users.

Simplicity is also the rule in categories other than entertainment. Weather and general news receive far more traffic than business and information technology news. For example, as of late 2000, the WNI weather information service had three times more i-mode traffic than the *Mainichi* newspaper, which is the most popular newspaper in Japan. Further, *Mainichi*'s service had more than 20 times the traffic of any technical news services such as BizTech News or Impress, which were the most popular i-mode sites for business and information technology news in late 2000. In the tickets and living category, sites offering concert tickets and information about music and videos generate far more traffic than those that provide employment

Mobile versus Fixed-Line Content

services, car sales, or rental information. In the travel category, most of the traffic is from a simple train navigator tool rather than map or sophisticated location-based services.[4]

Figure 3.2 and the trade-off between reach and richness also explain the importance of young people in the Japanese mobile Internet. In most countries, young people place a greater importance on reach and a lower importance on richness than older people do. The reason is that younger people are more mobile than older people, and, due to their having less experience, they place less value on rich information than older people do. High-school and college students, and even people who have just entered the workforce, generally spend a much larger amount of their time away from home and the office (if they have one) and use public transportation (buses and trains) more than older people. Students spend a great deal of time in class, the library, moving around on campus, and in bars and restaurants. People who have just entered the workforce also spend more time away from home in bars, restaurants, and friends' homes than do married couples, particularly those who have young children.

Young people also place less emphasis on richness than older people do. Less experience causes them generally to have less specialization and a wider variety of interests than people who are over 30. This is not a criticism of young people, but, rather, a comment on their overall educational stage in life. It would be a waste if high-school and college students focused all of their interests on the rich information available in a single highly specialized field.

The greater emphasis placed by young people on reach than on richness, and the appropriateness of high-reach and low-rich content for the mobile Internet, is why simple entertainment is so popular in the Japanese mobile Internet. Youth and simplicity explain the popularity of simple entertainment contents such as ringing tones, screen savers, horoscopes, communication and dating services, and games. Young people will be more interested in these kinds of entertainment services than will people over the age of 30. The combination of simplicity and age also explains why concert tickets and other music-related products are the most popular form of mobile shopping.

Of course, the mobile Internet is not the only example of portable devices where young people are the major users; they are also the major users of portable music players and calculators. Many high-school and college students regularly carry both of these devices with them while they are

The Mobile Internet

away from home, in spite of the fact that they also have non-portable counterparts. For example, many college students spend a substantial part of their income on portable music players, high-quality music equipment for their rooms, and music that can be used on both devices. Many students also regularly carry portable calculators in spite of having access to spreadsheet software and other calculating capabilities on their PCs. These young people use these devices as complements, not as substitutes. The mobile and fixed-line Internets will probably also play a similar complementary role in the lives of these young people.

Some people will argue that young people are not the major users of some portable devices such as laptop computers, and were not the major users of mobile phones in the early days of the industry. But this was due to the high cost of these devices and the emphasis on business use for laptop computers. Once the cost of owning a mobile phone had decreased to the low levels that we have seen over the last five years, young people became the biggest users of mobile phones in Japan and Europe, and to a lesser extent in the US. Laptops and PDAs will probably see the same trends as prices decline and these devices become more entertainment-oriented. Through positive feedback between devices and users, firms will create more entertainment-related applications, such as viewing movies or video clips on laptops and PDAs, as the price of these devices and the age of the users decline.

3.4 Youth and Entertainment in the Fixed-Line Versus Mobile Internet

Interestingly, young people and entertainment also play an important role in the fixed-line Internet. Forester Research Inc. found in the US that, in addition to annual income, technology optimism also drives PC and Internet usage and that young people are more optimistic than older people about new technologies. It found that high-income optimists were 1.4, twice, and three times more likely to own a PC, use the Internet, or shop on-line than were high-income pessimists, respectively.[5] It also found that people under 25 are the most optimistic about new technologies, with technology optimism declining in a linear fashion from 70% for under-25s to 35% for over-65s.[6] People under 25 are 50% more optimistic than people in their forties, and twice as optimistic as people aged over 65.

Further, entertainment is the primary reason why these young people go on-line. Some 55% of people under 25 gave entertainment as their primary reason to go on-line, versus 17% for family reasons and 28% for career

Mobile versus Fixed-Line Content

reasons. Of course, the importance of entertainment as an on-line motivator declines with age. Less than 30% of the respondents aged between 35 and 54 cited entertainment as their primary reason to go on-line, versus 31–32% for family reasons and 39–40% for career reasons.[7]

However, in spite of the common importance of young people to both the fixed-line and mobile Internet and the importance of entertainment to young people in both mediums, there are still major differences between the mobile and fixed-line Internet for young people. The simplicity of mobile content was already discussed.

The second key difference between the fixed-line and mobile Internet content for young people involves the importance of personalization with mobile phones. Users personalize their phone screens with animated characters and other pictures that are available from screen saver content providers. They have their pictures loaded on to the Internet through services offered by convenience stores to be viewed and used as screen savers on their mobile phones. Beginning in December 2000, Japanese users could take pictures with a simple camera that is embedded in the back of some phones and then use the picture as a screen saver. As it becomes easier to load and view photos on the mobile Internet, and also to take them with their mobile phone, it is quite possible that printed photos will decline in usage.

Users can also personalize the ringing sound of the phone with ringing tone services. Japanese manufacturers have steadily improved the sound quality of phones with respect to these ringing tones. Users can also add these ringing tones, pictures, and animated characters to mail. As users begin to transfer music and video clips from their PC to their mobile phone, or to download them from the mobile phone network, they will use the clips to personalize their phones and the mail they send with their phones.

The third key difference between the fixed-line and mobile Internet content for young people involves the act of "killing time." The greater mobility of young people means they often spend time waiting for classes, trains, buses, friends, and other people and things during their typical day. While some people would like to see these young people reading books and doing other forms of studying, the mobile Internet may be more interesting to them and phones easier to carry than books. Many young people would rather read their horoscope, play a game, read the sports page or gossip column, look for the latest concert or music by their favorite artist, or check out the snow or surfing conditions at their favorite ski or surfing spot than spend 10 minutes reading their assigned economics text before their next class. In fact, a casual

The Mobile Internet

look around any Japanese train, bus, or train station, or in or outside a classroom, in early 2001 would have found many young people doing the former. Further, survey data suggest that the average session time is far less than 10 minutes.[8]

Similarly, working people who commute by train and bus, travel extensively, or spend a lot of time waiting for people in hotel lobbies, restaurants, and other places also often have time to kill. Many of them might prefer, and would probably find it easier, to do many of the same things mentioned above on their mobile phones than read a book or a newspaper, since these devices are harder to hold than mobile phones while standing on or waiting for a train. The content might be slightly different, but the need to kill time while commuting by train, bus, ferry, or plane is a common situation for many people. The goal for content providers is to come up with more interesting contents so that users can find more interesting and useful ways to occupy that time.

3.5 US and European Companies are Overemphasizing Richness

Figure 3.3 summarizes the differences between the Western and Japanese approaches to the mobile Internet. In Japan, the early success of simple entertainment content caused the number of these entertainment-related content providers to increase, thus creating positive feedback between content and users. Simple content in non-entertainment areas such as news have also played a role in creating this positive feedback. As will be discussed in Chapter 5, the most successful content providers have already come close to realizing the potential *reach* of mobile phones, and they are now turning their attention to *richness*. Continued positive feedback between new services such as Java, phones with color displays, and a diversification of users and business models will make it even easier for these content providers to add richness to their content.

The US and European service and content providers and manufacturers are approaching the mobile Internet from a different direction. They are trying to add reach to the successful applications and contents that exist on the fixed-line Internet in order to leverage the successful fixed-line Internets in the US and elsewhere. They are trying to use complex technologies to do this, because these complex technologies are driving the fixed-line Internet. Further, service providers and phone manufacturers are focusing on applications and content for business users, such as banking, travel, and

Mobile versus Fixed-Line Content

news, because they have always introduced new services and phones first to business users.

Figure 3.3   Japanese versus US and European Approaches to the Mobile Interent

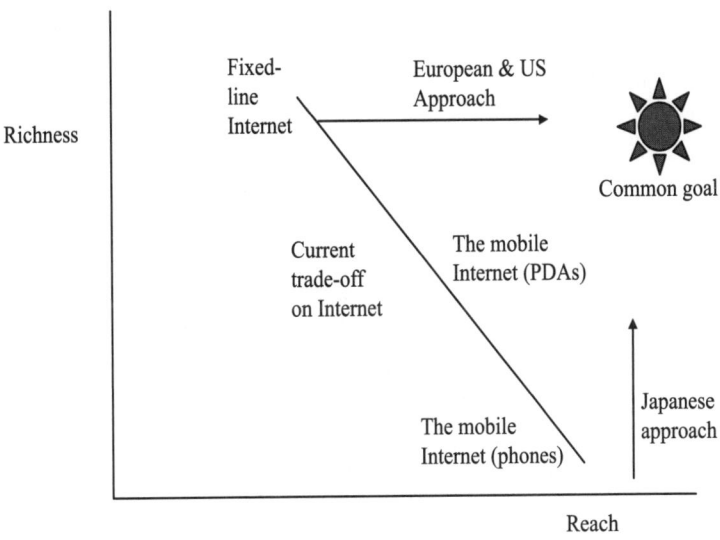

Source: Tracking and Transformation E-commerce and the Terms of Competition in Industries, by the BRIE-IGCC E-conomy Project, published by the Brookings Institution, copyright 2001.

Location-Based Technologies Are Too Complex

For example, a popular application with these Western service providers, manufacturers, and content providers is location-based services. These location-dependent services include travel services (eg, airlines, hotels, and rental cars), more-general navigation services, and information on local stores, restaurants, and bars. Some of these services, such as those that sell airline tickets and reserve hotels, are already highly developed on the fixed-line Internet. And business people are major users of these services. Mobile Internet services that enable business and other people to make or change these kinds of reservations and to look for information on stores, restaurants, and bars while they are on business trips would be very useful.

The Mobile Internet

Further, many people have suggested that these services should recognize the person's location and then inform the user of the hotel, car rental agency, store, restaurant, or bar closest to him or her. This would enable the user to avoid inputting information about his or her location and thus only input information on the types of information/reservations that he or she desires. Others have suggested that such information should be sent in the form of an advertisement where users would merely "opt-in" to such advertisements. These advertisements could then be sent to users through the mobile phone network or with short-range wireless technologies such as Bluetooth when users were passing a specific store or restaurant. Still others have suggested that these services should be incorporated with car navigation systems, in spite of their still-low diffusion rates in the US and Europe.

Location-based services exist to some extent in the Japanese mobile Internet. Users can reserve hotels, airline seats, and rental cars, search for restaurants, bars, and video rentals, determine the optimal set of trains to take, and access and exchange maps on their mobile phone. Further, some firms have attempted to simplify the highly successful car navigation systems for PDAs and mobile phones in the form of simple maps.

However, complex forms of location-based services that are being considered in the West are not yet successful in Japan. Services that recognize a person's position are not popular with users, although one Japanese service provider is offering such a service. Nobody is asking for or providing location-based advertisements, partly since, as the leading Western provider of advertising services in the Japanese mobile Internet argues: "they would require enormous capabilities in real-time, third-party (advertiser) data and transaction management, far exceeding current carrier billing models."[9] Further, car navigation systems still play almost no role in the Japanese mobile Internet in spite of efforts by NTT DoCoMo to do so and the enormous success of car navigation systems in general in Japan. And attempts to simplify these car navigation services for PDAs and mobile phones have not yet succeeded.

Positive Feedback Will Lead to the Emergence of Appropriate Complexity

As opposed to complex location-based services, Japanese content providers are using a much simpler set of technologies to provide people with these location-based services. Toshiba provides the most popular navigation service; its service enables users to determine the optimal trains to ride in order to go from station A to station B. As described in Chapter 5, Toshiba and other content providers have used mail and other services to simplify

Mobile versus Fixed-Line Content

searches for information. And because these techniques have enabled content providers to realize the full potential of the mobile phone's reach, they are now turning their attention toward adding richness.

Thus, these Japanese content providers will eventually utilize the more sophisticated location-based technologies that the West is now considering. But the use of these technologies in Japan will be a result of the positive feedback that has been created between services, users, content, phones, and business models in the Japanese mobile Internet. The West's early focus on these complex technologies may likely prevent the positive feedback from being created and probably cause Japan to be the earlier user of these complex technologies. Just as the early emphasis on simple inventory reduction and quality improvement activities by the Japanese manufacturers enabled them to implement automation and computer-integrated manufacturing faster than the Western manufacturers, in spite of the West's earlier emphasis on automation, Japan's earlier emphasis on simplicity will probably result in its implementing the complex location-based technologies before the West does.

The US and European service providers should first focus on content that match the medium and the early users. These are low-rich and high-reach content for young people; this content includes simple entertainment and news. A focus on this simple content and young people will create the positive feedback that is needed in the West's mobile Internet. Once this feedback is created, there will be a natural progression toward richer content. As part of this progression, content providers must offer the mail and other customization services that will realize the potential reach of the mobile Internet. But before we discuss these issues, we will consider business models in the next chapter.

Sound Bites

1. **The concepts of "reach" and "richness" explain the differences between mobile and fixed-line contents.** "Reach" refers to the number of people who participate in the sharing of that information. "Richness" refers to the quality and, in particular, the bandwidth of information.

The Mobile Internet

2. **Mobile content has higher reach and lower richness than fixed-line content.** Mobile phones provide higher reach due to their smaller size and weight, faster power-up times, and greater diffusion, but provide lower richness due to their smaller screens and keyboards than desktop computers.

3. **Mobile users emphasize reach over richness.** Young people emphasize reach over richness, since they are more mobile and less specialized than older people. This is also why young people are the major users of portable music players and calculators.

4. **Simplicity and youth explain the patterns of traffic in the Japanese mobile Internet.** Simple entertainment drives traffic in the Japanese mobile Internet because it matches the high reach and low richness of the mobile phone and the type of people (ie, mostly young people) who emphasize reach over richness.

5. **Key words in mobile entertainment content are "simplicity," "personalization," and "killing time."** In addition to simplicity, successful entertainment content enable users to personalize phone screens, ringing sounds, and phone mail. Much of the traffic in the mobile Internet is, and will continue to be, driven by people killing time while commuting or waiting for something or someone.

6. **US and European firms are overemphasizing richness.** US and European firms are attempting to modify popular business fixed-line content for the mobile phone. While many of these "location-based services" will eventually play a role in the mobile Internet, they are too complex to be the applications that start the positive feedback in the mobile Internet.

Notes:

1. See Philip Evans and Thomas Wurster, *Blown to Bits* (Boston: Harvard Business Press, 2000), p. 25.
2. In some ways, car navigation systems can provide access to even richer information than PCs, due to their use of digital video disks (DVDs) as a storage medium. DVDs can store more information and access the information faster than CDs or floppy disks. Of course, this storage and access capability raises the price of the DVD-based car navigation systems, with many of them costing more than $3,000, or twice the price of desktop PCs.

Mobile versus Fixed-Line Content

3. Alcatel, Motorola, Siemens, and Ericsson are expanding the capabilities of SMS to allow users also to download screen savers and images. "Cell phone makers to cooperate: Companies aim to create instant messaging standard," *MSNBC*, Technology section, May 29, 2001.
4. These observations are based on page view data from D2 Communications, an advertising company that is 51% owned by NTT DoCoMo, and on positions in the menu. NTT DoCoMo organizes categories and sites by traffic, with the high-traffic categories and sites placed higher in the menu.
5. M. Modahl, *Now or Never: How Companies Must Change Today to Win the Battle for Internet Consumers* (New York: HarperBusiness, 2000), p. 13, Figure 5.
6. See ibid., p. 8, Figure 2.
7. See ibid., p. 15, Figure 6.
8. For example, see Jamie Cattel, "M Research in Japan: The Mobile Internet Revolution and its Implications for Research," Working Paper, Research International.
9. Stephen Walker, Senior Manager, International Business Development, Value Click, "Mobile Click: A Wireless Advertising Case Study, Performance Advertising Network for i-mode," presented at an i-mode seminar, Furama Hotel, Hong Kong, March 19, 2001.

Chapter Four:
Mobile versus Fixed-Line Business Models

Different business models than those used in the fixed-line Internet have played an important role in creating the positive feedback between phones and users in the Japanese mobile Internet, and it is expected that these models will also play an important role in the mobile Internet outside of Japan. The biggest difference is that since mobile service providers will likely be the initial beneficiaries of the rapid growth in the mobile Internet, they need to create a comprehensive business model that encourages co-operation from content providers, phone manufacturers, and portals/search engines. Key aspects of this comprehensive business model include subsidizing phones, offering micro-payment services, and maintaining an open policy toward portals and search engines.

The heavy subsidization of phones by the Japanese service providers has made it very easy for users to acquire high-quality and inexpensive mobile-Internet-compatible phones. With prices for most phones falling below $200 within three months, and below $100 within six months, of the start of i-mode services in February 1999, it quickly became very inexpensive for everyone, including young people, to acquire phones. Subsidies have also fueled the replacement market for phones, which in turn has encouraged phone manufacturers to continually introduce new models with advanced technologies such as high-resolution color screens. Even the most popular phones have not remained on the market for much longer than a year.

The micro-payment services offered by service providers help content providers collect fees and thus encourage them to create contents for the mobile Internet. One study of mobile commerce in Japan estimated that these paid contents, which are primarily entertainment, represented 68% of the mobile commerce market in Japan in fiscal 2000. While this study

The Mobile Internet

probably underestimates the overall size of mobile commerce in Japan, since only 393 firms participated in the study, the percentages are probably reasonable. As shown in Table 4.1, the major markets in mobile commerce are entertainment (which primarily involves paid contents), travel (including hotel reservations and airline tickets), financial (on-line trading and banking), and services (eg, reservations at restaurants and bars).

There are at least three reasons why simple paid content and, in particular, fixed-term paid subscriptions are the initially important business model in the mobile Internet. First, the small screens on mobile phones make other business models such as mobile shopping, more expensive transaction-based business models, and advertising difficult to conduct. Although this is changing as mobile phones evolve, it means that these business models in Japan, and eventually elsewhere, play a role in expanding, but not in creating, the initial positive feedback in the mobile phone network of contents, users, phones, and business models. Further, these business models will probably be implemented in a different manner on the mobile Internet than on the fixed-line Internet. For example, discount coupons and dynamic pricing will probably play a more important role in the mobile Internet than in the fixed-line Internet.

Second, users will probably be more inclined to pay for mobile than fixed-line contents. As described in previous chapters, the small screens, along with the relatively high transmission charges and short viewing times, make a fixed contents menu very practical, since users can access contents that have been screened by the service provider and thus presumably have high quality. It is the relatively closed nature of this set menu that makes it easier for content providers on the set menu to charge for their content.

Third, fixed-term content subscriptions are appropriate for the simple contents that are most relevant in the initial stages of the mobile Internet. Theoretically, content providers could charge by the transaction and service providers could collect these charges for them. But the transmission charges for informing the user of the content transaction fees would probably equal the actual content transaction fees in many cases. For example, in a world where content providers charged content transaction fees, game providers would be forced to charge once-a-day users $0.10 a day and far less than that for each time they played a game! In a related issue, governments that require service providers to inform their users of the costs associated with every transaction will be doing users a big disfavor.

Table 4.1 Mobile Commerce in Japan

Segment	Market Size ($ million)	Percent of Mobile Commerce (%)	Percent of Total E-Commerce (%)	Main Business Model
Entertainment	420	71	71.5	Paid contents
Travel	50	8.4	12.7	Paid contents & transactions
Financial	30	5.1	6.8	Transactions
Books & music	25	4.2	12.7	Shopping
Services	20	3.3	6.5	Various
Electronic products (eg, digital cameras)	10	1.6	1.1	Shopping
Other	35	5.9	0.9	Various
Total	**590**	**100**	**7.2**	

Paid content was $400 million.
Source: Accenture (www.meti.go.jp/report/whitepaper/).

The Mobile Internet

4.1 Service Provider and Manufacturer Business Models

Figure 4.1 summarizes the basic business model used by mobile service providers the world over. Mobile service providers pay activation commissions to retail outlets in return for the acquisition of subscribers. Retail outlets use these monies to purchase phones, to cover the procedures associated with signing up subscribers, and to advertise their services. Of course, mobile service providers also sign up subscribers themselves, and in this case they still designate some monies for the subsidization of phones. The mobile service providers cover these subsidies with the monthly charges that they collect from users.

Figure 4.1 Overall Business Model in the Mobile Phone Market (US$ amounts are approximate amounts for Japan)

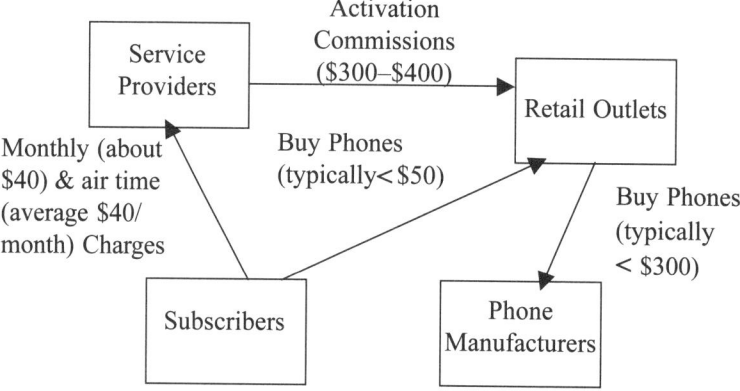

Japanese Service Providers

Figure 4.1 also shows the typical amounts of money that are involved in this business model in Japan. The Japanese service providers are currently paying activation commissions of between $300 and $400 for new subscribers and a somewhat lower amount for the upgrading of existing subscribers.[1] The retail outlets, on average, pay $300 for a phone that they sell to users for an average of $50. This provides the retail outlets with an average profit of $100 per subscriber.

Of course, the prices paid by users and by retail outlets to phone manufacturers vary considerably depending on the phone's newness and the manufacturer.[2] Although most manufacturers sell their phones for less than $200, they are able to sell the most popular phones for much more in

Mobile versus Fixed-Line Business Models

the first few months the phones are available on the market. NEC's and Matsushita's phones typically command the highest prices, since they contain more of the latest technologies.[3] Users must typically pay more than $300 for these phones when they first come out, but prices begin dropping after about three to four months. The prices for phones made by other manufacturers begin dropping quickly and they can be typically acquired for less than $50 within four months of their release.

The amounts involved in the rest of the world vary considerably. But $100 per subscriber is a common activation commission, and manufacturers sell many of their low-end phones for less than $100. This enables retail outlets to sell the phones for $50 and to make more than $50 per subscriber. Higher-priced phones have typically commanded higher subsidies, since business users usually purchase these phones and they typically incur higher monthly charges than other users.

The different subsidies paid by service providers in Japan and elsewhere have had a dramatic impact on the mobile phone market. The high activation commissions paid in Japan are one reason why Japanese use the smallest phones in the world.[4] There is basically one mobile phone segment in Japan where the mobile phone manufacturers competed primarily on the basis of weight until the mobile Internet market exploded in early 2000. Now they compete on the basis of screen size and quality, other new features, and weight. Contrast this with the rest of the world, where multiple price segments exist. For example, Nokia's 8810 still commanded a premium price more than two years after its release.

These high activation commissions also have an obviously dramatic impact on the financial situation of service providers. It takes between four and six months for the Japanese service providers to recoup their initial outlay on an individual subscriber[5] and as long as 16 months to actually make money on an individual subscriber.[6] These high activation commissions are also why between 24% and 30% of the service providers' sales are activation commissions.[7] Thus, roughly speaking, the elimination of these commissions would enable them to reduce their monthly and airtime charges by 24–30% and still maintain the same profits. However, NTT DoCoMo and the other service providers have historically believed that these high activation commissions are necessary to attract new subscribers and retain existing ones, because they believe that subscribers want the latest phones.[8]

Because Western service providers pay lower activation commissions than Japanese service providers, they are able to offer lower-price services. For

The Mobile Internet

example, while in Japan it may cost users $0.30 for a minute of airtime on top of a basic monthly fee, it is easy to receive 15 or 30 minutes in free airtime in a $15 or $30 per-month package in the US. It also takes much less time for a Western service provider to break even on a new subscriber. A US service provider who is paying $100 to acquire a subscriber will break even after 2.5 months, since income from an average subscriber is about $40 per month.

Western Service Providers

Western service providers should increase their activation commissions in order to spur growth in the mobile Internet, but they should not increase them to the extent that the Japanese service providers are paying. It would be a mistake for Western service providers to sacrifice their low-priced services for greater mobile Internet usage. Even if Western service providers do not implement these high activation commissions, they can create positive feedback in their mobile Internets by offering low-priced services and low-priced appropriate phones. In fact, the ability of Western service providers to offer lower-priced *packet* services than Japanese service providers could make the mobile Internet *eventually* more successful in the West than in the Japan.

Western service providers should, however, pay higher activation commissions for mobile-Internet-compatible phones than for regular phones, since they potentially can command higher monthly incomes. If they begin offering the type of mobile Internet services that I am recommending in this book, I believe they will be able to increase their average revenues per subscriber by 10–30%, just as the Japanese service providers have done.

There are a variety of ways for service providers to charge users for these mobile Internet services. Although the Japanese service providers typically charge users separately for basic monthly, airtime, packet, and content charges, it is possible to include a certain amount of airtime, packet, and contents in a single flat monthly charge. The critical issue is to encourage experimentation by users. Rate structures that confuse the user, or that charge them for obtaining access to contents outside of the service provider's "walled garden," will not encourage usage and thus the creation of positive feedback.

Further, Western service providers can implement a more sophisticated scheme for subsidizing upgrades than that used by Japanese service providers. The Japanese service providers currently subsidize upgrades for people who have been users for longer than a year and have not received a subsidized upgrade in the previous year. A more sophisticated and useful method is to introduce a point scheme that is similar to the mileage programs that are

Mobile versus Fixed-Line Business Models

used by airlines. Subscribers can accumulate points as they incur monthly and airtime charges and use these points to acquire a new phone or a related device such as a PDA. Chapter 8 discusses this proposal in more detail for both phones and PDAs.

Higher activation commissions and more sophisticated schemes for subsidizing upgrades will cause low-priced mobile-Internet-compatible phones to appear, thus helping create positive feedback between phones and users outside of Japan. A critical part of creating this positive feedback for Western phone manufacturers is to produce low-priced mobile-Internet-compatible phones that have large screens and are popular with young people. Technologically, this is not difficult, since mobile Internet compatibility doesn't add large costs to phones. Further, the phones don't need to be as small or light as the Japanese phones and thus can be much cheaper to produce than the Japanese phones.

Western Manufacturers

One of the biggest barriers to providing low-priced phones is the changes that are needed in the business models used by Western manufacturers. Unlike the Japanese market where the high activation commissions have caused a single market segment to emerge where competition has been focused on weight and size, the European and US markets have multiple phone segments where price erosion occurs over a much longer time span than in the Japanese market. For example, the past and current high price of Nokia's 8810 is not because it costs so much more than other phones to manufacture, since Nokia uses many common parts (eg, integrated circuits and discrete components) in their high-, middle-, and low-end phones. It is because Nokia and the other manufacturers subsidize the low-end phones to keep out the Asian producers and make their money on the high-end phones where aesthetic design, long battery life, and advanced features are considered important.[9]

The Western manufacturers have been positioning, and it appears that they will continue to position, the mobile-Internet-compatible phones as high-end phones. For example, the new 2.5 G phones, which are old WAP phones with packet capability, are expected to cost users between $300 and $500, or about twice as much as conventional GSM phones.[10] The high price of these 2.5 G phones has little to do with higher costs, since the marginal costs of adding mobile Internet capability such as browsers and additional memory are very low. The manufacturers set these high prices because they have always set high prices for phones with new capabilities, since business users have a higher willingness to pay than other users. And they don't want to set lower prices for these phones because they believe this would cause

The Mobile Internet

the high end of the phone market to collapse. What they need to do is offer a wide range of mobile-Internet-compatible phones in which the high-end phones have better mobile Internet compatibility (eg, better displays and keypads) than the low-end phones. This would enable them to maintain their business model and create a successful mobile Internet market.

4.2 Content Provider Business Models: Paid Content

The most successful business model for content providers in the Japanese mobile Internet is monthly paid content subscriptions. Japanese consumers paid $400 million for content in monthly content subscriptions versus $190 million for other forms of mobile commerce on the service providers' official menus in fiscal 2000.[11] In May 2001 alone, content providers made more than $100 million from their mobile content, or more than $2 per mobile Internet subscriber in Japan.

Official Sites
NTT DoCoMo and the other service providers collect most of these fees through the micro-payment systems they offer for their official content providers. NTT DoCoMo's micro-payment system allows its official content providers to charge between $1 and $3 per month for their content. It does not collect transaction-based fees or monies from the sale of products or other services. As discussed earlier, when users subscribe to a specific content service, this information is transmitted to NTT DoCoMo and the charge appears on the user's monthly bill. NTT DoCoMo takes 9% of these monies as a handling charge and sends the rest to the content provider.

Table 4.2 shows the number of content providers on NTT DoCoMo's official menu and the number of them that charge for their content for a number of categories and sub-categories of content. Even if a content provider's content is partially free, they are shown as paid contents in Table 4.2. For example, many content providers offer their content for free but charge for mail services. Almost all of the entertainment and news-related content providers charge for their content or a portion of them. As discussed earlier, 13 of the largest 17 content providers in terms of content subscribers provide entertainment, while two provide news. The leading news providers are Asahi Shimbun and WNI's weather site. The few entertainment and news sites that don't charge for their content either plan to do so once they generate a sufficient number of subscribers, or they use the sites to promote their businesses. In the entertainment area, the TV and radio stations offer sites for both of these reasons.

Mobile versus Fixed-Line Business Models

Table 4.2 Number of Total and Paid Sites for Selected Sub-Categories as of 12/2000
(Categories and sub-categories organized roughly by traffic)

Category	Sub-Categories	Number of Sites	Number of Sites w/ Monthly Fees
Entertainment	Melody downloading	24	24
	Character downloading/visual	35	33
	Games	71	71
	Horoscopes	22	22
	Sports/outdoor	25	21
	Music & movie information	12	8
	Prizes & horse racing info	14	11
	TV & radio information	52	6
	Magazines	13	11
	Entertainment personalities	20	19
Newspapers/ Information	General newspapers	13	9
	Regional newspapers	21	20
	Foreign newspapers	5	1
Tickets/Living	Tickets	3	2
	CDs, games, & books	11	2
	Employment	4	3
	Cars	6	0
	Rentals	4	0
	Education	7	5
	Other	8	0
Financial	On-line trading	7	
	National banks	10	
	Regional banks	89	
	Other savings & loan Associations	201	
	Postal savings	75	
	Credit cards	8	
	Insurance	7	
Dictionaries/ Tools	Dictionaries	5	3
	Delivery services	9	0
	Phone manufacturers	5	0
Travel	Train navigation	3	2
	Airlines	4	0
	Hotels	7	0
	Rental cars	2	0
	Traffic information	2	1
	Maps	2	2
Food/Recipes	Restaurant Information	7	3
	Recipes	2	0
Other	Local information	9	7

Source: NTT DoCoMo

The Mobile Internet

There are also a number of other sites that charge for their content. These include providers of concert tickets, music information (also in the CDs, games, and books category), employment information (mail concerning new job openings), educational information, dictionaries, train navigators, traffic information, and map services. Many of these sites initially offered their content for free in order to promote trial usage, but as demand increased for the contents, they began charging for some or most of the content or mail. For example, one of the 17 leading content providers is Toshiba, which provides a train navigation service (in the travel category). Although it has been offering its navigation service from the start of i-mode services in February 1999, it was not until April 2000 that it began charging for its service. It had 400,000 subscribers by the end of March 2001.

Unofficial Sites

As discussed in Chapter 2, unofficial sites represent more than 50% of the Internet traffic with i-mode users, and entertainment represents an even greater percentage of the traffic to unofficial sites than to official sites. Although these unofficial entertainment content providers would like to utilize NTT DoCoMo's micro-payment services, NTT DoCoMo was not making these services available to them as of May 2001.[12] Becoming an official NTT DoCoMo content provider typically requires a six-month wait, and many content providers are refused. Thus, some of them have attempted to survive by using alternative micro-payment schemes or advertising (see below).

A number of potential alternative micro-payment schemes have emerged in response both to difficulties in becoming an official content provider with NTT DoCoMo or the other service providers and to the restrictions that these service providers place on their official content providers. As mentioned earlier, NTT DoCoMo allows its official content providers to charge only between $1 and $3 per month and restricts advertising. Many of these official content providers would like to charge higher rates per month, charge by the view or transaction, or use more advertising.

The appendix at the end of this chapter describes a number of these alternative micro-payment schemes that are currently used in Japan. A common aspect of these schemes is that the content provider indirectly provides free advertising for the payment schemes. When users attempt to access content that is aligned with a specific payment system, the content provider informs the user of the appropriate payment system or systems.

Mobile versus Fixed-Line Business Models

These schemes use bank transfers, credit cards, pre-paid cards, fixed-line telephone accounts, and portal sites. Bank transfers are the most common in spite of their relatively high commissions. Credit cards are widely used, but they also have commissions too high for micro-payments. Pre-paid cards have lower commissions, but they are not widely used and thus are difficult to obtain. Fixed-line telephone accounts are obviously widespread, but many young people, particularly in Japan and Europe, don't have them because they live with their parents and/or they only subscribe to a mobile phone service. Portal sites, fixed-line service providers, and search engines can also offer these services in co-operation with a number of content providers and financial institutions.

Service providers benefit when these alternative payment schemes succeed, since they promote positive feedback between contents, users, and new business models, and thus increased traffic. One option is for service providers to make their micro-payment system available to all content providers. The Japanese Government was pressuring NTT DoCoMo to do this as of March 2001. While in some ways this is in NTT DoCoMo's best interest, since it will increase its traffic, most service providers don't want to provide a micro-payment service to a content provider unless they have had the opportunity to inspect the contents. And inspecting all content providers is a very troublesome project, which most service providers would prefer to avoid. One alternative to being overwhelmed by applications to your official menu is to promote the creation of portals and alternative micro-payment systems. Service providers can support the creation of low-commission credit cards and bank transfers, standard pre-paid cards, and other schemes that are summarized in this chapter's appendix.

4.3 Mobile Shopping

Mobile shopping was still a very small market in Japan in early 2001, as the concepts of richness and reach suggest. The screens and keyboards on mobile phones are too small to conduct sophisticated searches or to order products. Mobile shopping probably represented less than 10% of the Japanese mobile commerce market in fiscal 2000. [13]

The concepts of richness and reach also tell us something about the early products that will be sold on the mobile Internet. These concepts suggest that the initial mobile commerce sites will be those that sell simple items to young people. This is certainly the case in the mobile Internet in Japan,

The Mobile Internet

where concert tickets, music, and music-related products are the most popular items of mobile commerce. These items are simple to describe on a home page and they are of interest to young people. Further, as discussed in Chapter 7, the most successful providers of mobile shopping are effectively combining their mobile Internet services with fixed-line Internet and/or bricks-and-mortar capabilities.

For example, as of the end of 2000 about 10% of concert tickets were being sold over the Internet, and a large percentage of them were being sold over the mobile Internet. Pia is the leading seller of concert tickets overall in Japan, but Lawson has overtaken it in the mobile Internet. As discussed in Chapter 7, Lawson is combining its nationwide chain of convenience stores and its mobile Internet site to sell concert tickets. People can make ticket reservations with their mobile phones and then pick them up and pay for them at one of the many convenience stores that are located next to train stations. This is very convenient for young people, many of whom don't have credit credits and are big users of trains. Both Lawson and Pia charge a monthly fee for the use of their ticket reservation services and also receive a commission from the concert promoters for each ticket they sell.

Tsutaya Online is even more successful in mobile commerce, with more than $7 million in sales in fiscal 2000 and more than 90% of this coming in the second half of the year. Tsutaya initially succeeded in the mobile Internet by creating synergies between its nationwide chain of video and CD stores and its music information site (also described in Chapter 7). It has been able to attract more than a million subscribers to its content and mail services. Although they are primarily free, these services have increased the number of visitors and sales at its stores.

Further, Tsutaya Online has been able to use the success of its content and mail services to sell entertainment-related products such as CDs, DVDs, game software, and artist-related products over the mobile phone. Many of these mail services provide information on a specific artist, and young devotees often buy everything available for the specific artist. For example, a pop group called Morning Musume ("girl" in English) was very popular in late 2000, and many of its fans bought all of the Morning Musume products that Tsutaya Online was selling at that time. About half of these products were paid for by credit cards, while the other half were paid with cash on delivery (COD), as of early 2001.

Mobile versus Fixed-Line Business Models

4.4 Transaction-Based Business Models

There are clearly a large number of transactions that could be more effectively carried out on the Internet. These include auctions, on-line stock trading and banking, hotel, restaurant, and airline reservations, as well as employment, automobile, and home/apartment searches. All of these applications are very successful in the US fixed-line Internet.

The reach and richness model tells us that some of these applications may be appropriate for the mobile Internet. The concepts of reach and richness suggest that the initial mobile commerce sites will be those that don't require rich information and that cater to young people. As with mobile commerce, this is certainly the case in the mobile Internet in Japan, where on-line photo-loading services, communication/dating services, and stock trading are very successful. None of these examples require rich information, and young people are primarily the users of the photo-loading and dating services.

Photo Net Japan had acquired almost one million users for its photo-loading service as of early 2001. Users pay between $3 and $4 to have several pictures loaded on an i-mode-compatible home page. The places and methods by which these pictures are loaded on to a home page are described in Photo Net Japan's official but free i-mode site. Within three days of making an application at one of these places, users receive e-mail with the site address and instructions on how to create a home page that contains their photos. Thus, the actual procedures to be carried out on the phone are simple, and ther photo-loading service clearly appeals to young users more than older ones. As discussed in Chapter 7, a key element of Photo Net's success is its alliances with several bricks-and-mortar companies. Users can apply to have their pictures loaded at almost 10,000 different places in Japan, including Kodak and Plaza Create's (the major owner of Photo Net Japan) film processing outlets and Lawson's and Family Mart's convenience stores.

Communication and dating services are some of the most popular types of unofficial i-mode contents and official contents for the other service providers. NTT DoCoMo does not allow these sites on its official menu and thus does not provide them with its micro-payment systems. Most of these sites provide on-line posting and mail services where both women and men post messages to a notice board and exchange mail. The i-mode services are generally free for women, but men are charged to read mail ($0.10), send mail ($0.50), and post messages to the notice board ($1). The i-mode services do this by using a point system where users purchase points with credit cards and bank transfers. Interestingly, the banks inadvertently support these

The Mobile Internet

services because they require users to input their telephone numbers when they transfer money. This makes it easy for the dating services to verify the users when they access the sites. It is quite possible that young people paying for points to be used in these dating services are performing the majority of bank transfers on i-mode.

On-line stock trading on mobile phones is also fairly successful in Japan. On-line trading on both mobile phones and PCs began to increase once the Japanese Government deregulated trading commissions in November 1999. As expected, there have been continual reductions in the commissions, which have caused the amount of on-line trading to rise dramatically. As of early 2000, about 30% of the trades were carried out on-line for one of the leading providers of both on-line and traditional trading, Daiwa Securities. Of the on-line trading, more than 20% is done with i-mode. Similar percentages for i-mode versus PCs are reported by DLJ Securities, a firm that only does on-line trading and completes more than 2,000 trades a day that have been requested from mobile phones.

The reason for the success of on-line trading on mobile phones (and, for that matter, on the PC) is that it doesn't require rich information . Rich information is needed to make good investment decisions, but the act of trading doesn't require a great deal of information to define a trade. Users only need to input the name of the stock, the number of shares to be bought or sold, and, if they so desire, the price at which they are willing to buy or sell. This takes about three pages in the PC and seven to eight pages in the mobile phone services. Further, as discussed in subsequent chapters, the on-line trading companies offer ways of reducing the number of pages needed to make a trade on a mobile phone. They are also integrating their PC and mobile services, and are working with banks to make it easier to use bank deposits when buying stocks.

4.5 Information-Loading Models

Information-loading models are a primitive form of business model that is a carryover from the printed world where companies pay to have information about their product or service loaded on newspapers and magazines. This type of business model dominates several categories of NTT DoCoMo's official sites shown in Table 4.2. This includes the rental, employment, and car sites in the tickets/living category, the hotel sites in the travel category, and the restaurant sites in the food/recipes category.

Mobile versus Fixed-Line Business Models

As shown in Table 4.2, since these sites are located fairly far down the menu in fairly low-traffic categories, most of them probably have fairly low traffic. This is in spite of their emphasis on young people. For example, rentals are of greater interest than new homes to young people, the employment sites emphasize part-time as opposed to full-time work, and the car sites emphasize used as opposed to new cars. One reason for their low traffic is that most of these types of transactions require fairly rich information. People want to see rentals and cars, and desire lots of information about jobs, before they will make a decision. Color displays, phones with embedded cameras, and the general diffusion of digital cameras along with larger phone screens will gradually enable access to richer information.

Problems with the Information-Loading Model
A more pressing problem involves the concept of the information-loading model and the way it is being implemented on these sites. Firms that are the leading providers of these services in the printed world run many of these sites and don't want to cannibalize their magazine sales. This problem exists not only in Japan but also in most of the world. These firms set rather high fees for other firms to put jobs, cars, or rentals on their mobile and fixed-line Internet sites. One result of these expensive loading charges in Japan is that the number of data points in many these sites was still very low as of late 2000 and early 2001, as compared to the potential number of data points (see Chapter 10 for more details).

Clearly, most of these firms need to adopt new and more innovative business models in order to increase the number of data points in their services. Without a larger number of points, they won't attract i-mode users and without users they won't attract more data points. In other words, these sites need to create positive feedback between the number of data points and the number of users. New business models, which will emerge as part of the overall positive feedback between content, users, phones, and portal sites, will also create this positive feedback between the number of data points and users.

New business models include lower loading charges, performance-based systems, disintermediation, discount coupons, and dynamic pricing. Clearly, Internet sites can set lower loading charges because the Internet is less expensive than the printed medium. Further, these sites can have firms and individuals input their own data. Not only will lower loading charges help sites expand the number of data points in both their fixed-line and mobile Internet sites, but offering these services over mobile phones can help them

The Mobile Internet

further expand these databases by bringing in new firms and users. Many small companies such as restaurants and bars and young users don't have PCs, and thus the mobile services would enable both of these groups to participate in the on-line service.

Performance-based systems have already become widely used in the US fixed-line Internet and it is expected that they will eventually become widely used in the mobile Internet. Many of the successful providers of rental, employment, car, and hotel sites in the US use performance-based systems in which firms pay only when some form of transaction has been completed. This allows them to avoid the issue of loading charges and, of course, they have their customers do most of the information loading on their own PCs. Disintermediation is also an appropriate business model for several of these businesses, including the used car and rental businesses. Currently, none of the i-mode car and apartment rental sites allow individuals to sell their cars or rent their apartments to other individuals. This is in spite of the fact that this form of business model, and its application on the mobile Internet, could open up an entire new market of individuals (many of whom don't own a PC) buying and selling used cars and renting apartments over the mobile Internet. The reason that these firms are not doing this is that they don't want to anger their existing customers — ie, the dealers and real estate companies who pay them to have information about their cars and apartments loaded in their magazines and Internet sites.

A lack of disintermediation, high loading charges, and in general a lack of new business models is not limited to the mobile Internet in Japan; it is a problem with the overall Japanese Internet and the Internets in many countries. It is another reason why Japan and many other countries have a lower fixed-line Internet usage than the US.

The Role of Content Screening

This lack of new and innovative business models on the mobile Internet can be exacerbated by a service provider's strict inspection of content. While a strict inspection of content is needed to offer a simple portal and thus create positive feedback in the system, it can eventually become a drag on the positive feedback in the system. It appears that this is already occurring in the Japanese mobile Internet. As will probably occur in the rest of the world, NTT DoCoMo's inspection highly favors incumbents, and we know that incumbents are often concerned more with not cannibalizing their existing sales than with creating new businesses.[14] This is particularly true with the Internet, where research on the fixed-line Internet tells us that Internet sites need to focus on new customers, or customers who currently don't pay to

Mobile versus Fixed-Line Business Models

have information about their businesses placed in magazines. And it is new entrants who will focus on new customers and create new business models. (The next section looks at some of the new entrants who are implementing new and innovative business models that take advantage of the high reach found in mobile phones.)

Further, NTT DoCoMo does not allow its official content sites to create linkages with unofficial sites. Thus, for its official rental, employment, car, hotel, and restaurant sites to create linkages with the home pages of a specific real estate company, a firm that is advertising a job, a car dealer, a hotel, or a restaurant, the official sites would have to have these linked home pages approved by NTT DoCoMo. NTT DoCoMo does not have the time, or probably the interest, to inspect all of these linkages and home pages. This rule is a strong barrier to innovation in these industries, and is of course one reason why these sites input most of the information themselves.

Western service and content providers will struggle with the same issues. Western service providers are already being criticized for restrictive practices, which are often more restrictive than NTT DoCoMo's practices, and these criticisms will increase once these service providers create positive feedback in their systems. On the other hand, content providers in countries with well-developed fixed-line Internets such as the US will probably be quicker to introduce more innovative business models than Japan or the rest of the world. As with mobile shopping, once countries such as the US create the positive feedback needed to start growth in their mobile Internets, they may experience an even faster growth in these areas than Japan, since they have already begun creating more innovative business models in the fixed-line Internets. Young people in the rest of the world may start looking for apartments and used cars on their mobile phones more than young people do in Japan.

4.6 Discount Coupons, Dynamic Pricing, and Auctions

Discount coupons, dynamic pricing, and auctions are three aspects of new business models that take advantage of the high reach of mobile phones. Discount coupons can be cheaper and more effectively distributed over the mobile Internet than with the traditional paper versions. As most readers will be aware, the purpose of discount coupons is to attract price-sensitive shoppers; thus, they are a form of personalized pricing. Price-sensitive shoppers take the trouble to look for discount coupons, while most of the rest of us pay the higher prices. In the mobile Internet, shoppers can search

The Mobile Internet

for the coupons on their phones and then merely show the mobile phone screen to the specific place of business.

One of the leading providers of discount coupons in the Japanese mobile Internet is Guru Navi. About 50% of the more than 12,000 restaurants serving Guru Navi's restaurant site provide discount coupons. The coupons typically are for a special night, but not for a limited time period on that night. They may be for a special meal, drink, or new service. As of early 2001, between 50,000 and 100,000 coupons were being redeemed in these restaurants each month.

Guru Navi does not charge users for its service; it makes money using the information-loading model. However, since it was created in 1996 as an Internet business, it does not have a magazine business to protect. Thus, it sets a relatively low fee of $30 to have information loaded, $20 for a reservation service, and $10 each on a monthly basis for a notice-board service. Guru Navi inputs all of the information itself, except on the notice-board service, which it didn't expect to start until the spring of 2001. Of course, Guru Navi must take responsibility for everything loaded on to the notice-board service in order to avoid violating NTT DoCoMo's rule against linkages with unofficial sites.

Dynamic pricing and auctions can also be more easily implemented over the Internet than in traditional businesses, and probably more effectively on the mobile Internet than in the fixed-line Internet. On-line trading is the obvious example. The Internet makes it easy for price changes to be quickly and cheaply sent to everyone, and the mobile Internet makes it easier for people to acquire this information much more quickly than on the fixed-line Internet. This is another reason why on-line trading in the Japanese mobile Internet has done so well.

It is also possible to envision the concept of dynamic pricing and auctions being applied to many other products and services, particularly those that involve perishable products. The value of airline, train, and concert seats, hotel rooms, and rental cars goes to zero when the airplane or train leaves, the concert ends, or the day ends. One could envision a situation where potential flyers were looking at recent price changes or bidding for airline tickets as the departure time approaches.

Several i-mode sites had implemented, or were planning to implement, dynamic pricing on their sites as of early 2001. Pia, the leading provider of tickets in Japan, was planning to implement such a system for sports tickets

Mobile versus Fixed-Line Business Models

in the spring of 2001. Community Network, a provider of hotel reservations, started a similar service in late November 2000. The price of hotel rooms begins declining 10 days before the day in question at a rate of several dollars per day. Another site, called Marutoku, also offers same-day discounts, but it doesn't have as many hotels as Community Network. Both of these sites plan to make money through subscriber fees from consumers and commissions from hotels.

4.7 Advertising

Advertising is becoming an important source of income for many Japanese mobile content providers, just as it has played an important role in the fixed-line Internet in Japan and elsewhere. In Japan, many people expected D2C to dominate this market since it is a joint venture between NTT DoCoMo (which owns 51%) and Dentsu and it is the only firm that is allowed to provide advertisements on official i-mode sites. But it is actually the *unofficial* sites where advertising has exploded

Key Role in Unofficial Sites
Advertising has exploded in the unofficial world, since these sites don't have access to NTT DoCoMo's micro-payment system and traffic to the unofficial sites exceeds that of official sites. For the unofficial sites, other than some sites where money is not an issue (eg, individual sites), the main sources of money for many of the most popular categories are transaction fees for the communication and dating services and advertising for the providers of ringing tones, screen savers, and other entertainment.

These activities in the unofficial world suggest that advertising on the mobile Internet is much larger than the estimates made by D2C, which focuses on the official contents. In December 2000, Dentsu estimated that the advertising market in the Japanese mobile Internet would be $10 million versus $5 million in the fixed-line Internet in fiscal 2000.[15] But these estimates suggest that mobile Internet advertising only represented 1.7% of mobile commerce, while fixed-line Internet advertising represented 7.8% of fixed-line commerce in fiscal 2000.[16] It is more likely that mobile Internet advertising is closer to the 7.8% figure than the 1.7% figure.

Higher Page View Rates
One reason why advertising may play as large or an even larger role in the mobile Internet than in the fixed-line Internet is that there is a great deal of evidence that page view rates are higher on the mobile Internet than on the

The Mobile Internet

fixed-line Internet. For example, Table 4.3 shows how Tsutaya Online, the leading provider of both music information on i-mode and video rentals plus CD sales in the bricks-and-mortar world, was getting almost twice as high page view rates on i-mode than on the PC Internet in early 2001. In this case, it splits the $0.05 from page views on the mobile Internet with D2C — not a bad source of potential income for a site with more than one million page views a day in early 2001.

Table 4.3 Page View and Mail Sending Rates for Text Advertisements on Content Pages and in Mail

	PC Internet	i-mode	Agency
Content pages	$0.025	$0.05	D2C
Opt-in mail	$0.015–$0.02	$0.20–0.30	Self-management

Source: Tsutaya Online, January 2001.

A number of explanations have been suggested for the overall higher (twice as high for content pages) page view rates on i-mode versus the PC Internet. There is some evidence that there is a higher click rate on mobile than on PC Internet pages.[17] Some people argue that the smaller screens on phones cause people to notice, read, and click on an advertisement on phones more than on PCs. Other people argue that since mobile Internet users are often killing time when they are accessing the mobile Internet, they are more likely to view and click on a mobile than a fixed-line Internet advertisement.

Mail Services

Mobile phone mail services have even higher advertising rates than mobile Internet content pages. For example, Tsutaya Online acquires advertisements for its "opt-in mail" services on its own. And as shown in Table 4.3, it is getting more money for mail messages than page views on content pages even though people may not be viewing the advertisements or even opening the mail message itself. Clearly, advertisers believe that users are more likely to look at advertisements in mail messages than on content pages. Tsutaya Online claims that users like, and pay attention to, mail. For example, Tsutaya Online experienced a 14% click rate for advertisements in the e-mail that it sent between August 22 and October 31, 2000. As we shall see in the next chapter, mail is a very important part of the content strategies used by official content providers.

Mobile versus Fixed-Line Business Models

Mail services are also an important tool for unofficial sites. For example, OZ Mall, a women's portal site that is operated by Starts Publishing, depends almost entirely on advertisements in its "opt-in" mail service for its mobile Internet income. Further, many of the unofficial sites are beginning to use these mail services to acquire users. They indiscriminately spam mobile phone users using a random phone number generator. Mobile phone users who don't change their e-mail address from the de facto address, which includes their phone number, receive about two to three mail advertisements a day, mostly from communication and dating services. By clicking on the enclosed address, users can easily access the unofficial site.

This "spamming" had gotten so out of hand that, by May 2001, it was a major subject on evening news shows. NTT DoCoMo took out full-page advertisements in major newspapers asking firms to stop sending these advertisements. It also recommended that users change their e-mail addresses in order to avoid the easy spamming. Many users are particularly incensed, since they are required to pay for incoming mail. On the other hand, the senders pay little or nothing to send mail from a PC. Even if they send the mail from a mobile phone, they are not required to pay for the mail if the mail address ends up not having a legitimate user. Thus, the spammers are incurring few costs for their random generation of potential mail addresses.

Nevertheless, the use of mail by unofficial sites suggests that advertising on the mobile Internet is already beginning to resemble advertising on the fixed-line Internet, where many people argue that the purpose of advertisements is to create a distribution channel rather than a brand image, which is typically the purpose of advertisements in the traditional economy.[18] Many fixed-line Internet sites in the US and elsewhere, and the mobile dating sites in Japan, use advertisements to attract customers to their sites. The i-mode unofficial sites are doing this with both mail and traditional page view advertisements. Communication and dating services are again the major providers of these page view advertisements, since they have a source of external income to finance the advertisements. They apparently provide a large amount of the advertising revenues for the providers of other unofficial sites such as ringing tones and screen savers.[19]

The Future

The higher view and click rates both on pages and in mail suggest that advertising will play an important role in the mobile Internet, perhaps even larger than in the fixed-line Internet. Certainly the quantity and type of advertisements on the mobile Internet will evolve over time. They will increase as mobile commerce grows, as non-Internet firms start to see the

The Mobile Internet

mobile Internet as an important place to advertise, as knowledge about appropriate advertising increases, and as technology improves. As the number of advertisers increases, there will be a better match between the advertisement, the content, and the user.

Knowledge about appropriate advertising is important, since users could easily be angered by advertisements appearing on their small screens. This is a major reason why NTT DoCoMo does not allow content providers to place advertisements on pages that require paid subscriptions. We probably all wish that cable TV stations were as magnanimous as NTT DoCoMo. DoCoMo's concern about a possible backlash is also why it must approve all advertisements before they can be placed on an official site.

Technology will also play a role in the evolution of advertisements on the mobile Internet. For example, location-based and personalized advertisements will eventually become an important part of mobile advertisements. However, as argued in Chapter 3, they will not be the initial drivers of the mobile Internet anywhere in the world. They will appear as the positive feedback between services, content, users, phones, business models, and portals/search engines causes each of these, including business models, to evolve from simple to more complex levels.

Sound Bites

1. **Service providers and manufacturers need new business models.** Service providers need to introduce a comprehensive business model that encourages co-operation from content providers, phone manufacturers, and portals/search engines. Phone manufacturers need to focus on young users.

2. **Paid content is initially the main business model content providers.** Simple screens suggest simple business models; simple content paid on a fixed-term basis is the main business model used in Japan's mobile Internet and has played an important role in the creation of positive feedback between services, content, phones, and users.

3. **Business models will evolve from simple to complex.** The positive feedback between services, content, users, phones, and business models is causing business models to evolve from simple to complex in Japan. The same will happen elsewhere.

Mobile versus Fixed-Line Business Models

4. **The rest of the world can move faster than Japan with new business models.** The rest of the world is not hindered by the number of regulations that are slowing the implementation of more sophisticated business models in the Japanese mobile and fixed-line Internets.

5. **Discount coupons and dynamic pricing will be important business models.** These business models take advantage of the high reach of mobile phones.

6. **Advertising should emphasize simplicity.** Simple screens suggest simple advertisements, while location-based advertisements will appear as a result of positive feedback between services, content, users, phones, and business models.

Appendix: Alternative Micro-Payment Schemes

Table 4.4 summarizes a number of micro-payment services that are available to non-official sites in the Japanese mobile Internet market. These services use different types of payment methods, handle different amounts of money, require the content providers to pay different levels of initial and monthly fees and commissions, and implement different levels of inspection. Most of these firms advertise their services through the content providers. When users attempt to access contents that are aligned with a specific payment system, the content provider informs the user of the appropriate payment system or systems.

Payments can be made using credit card, bank transfer, pre-paid, and other micro-payment services. NEC (BiGlobe) and Nifty provide credit card services to their fixed-line Internet service subscribers. Users can purchase products with these credit cards and pay for contents in much the same way they pay for contents with NTT DoCoMo's official sites. When subscribers access paid contents, the charges are added to their BiGlobe or Nifty fixed-line Internet bill. NEC had 25,000 users as of mid-November 2000, a very small number when compared to the total number of i-mode subscribers. Further, since BiGlobe and Nifty each have less than five million subscribers and most of these subscribers are not young people, they will face difficulty in obtaining a large number of users.

Table 4.4 Alternative Micro-Payment Systems for Content Providers

Type	Service Name	Firm	Payment (Yen) Restrictions	Initial Fees (Yen)	Monthly Fees (Yen)	Commissions	Status
Credit Cards	Yen Raku	Open Loop On the Edge	> 1,000	100,000	None	5–10%	
	Big Globe	NEC	None	50,000	10,000	¥30–80	25,000 users (mid-November 2000)
	Mobile @ Nifty	Nifty	None	None	None	20%	
Bank Transfers		Most Banks	None	None	None	¥105–630	
		Japan Net Bank	None	None	None	¥10–262	More than 20 content providers and 300,000 subscribers at end of June 2001
Pre-Paid Cards	Bit Cash	Bit Cash	From 1 to 20,000	None	None	15%	7 content providers (end of November 2000)
	C Check	Digital Check	From 2,000 to one million	None	3,800	9–13%	
	Web Money	Web Money	From 10 to 20,000	200,000	None	9–13%	
Other	Felica	Bit Wallet	> 50,000	None	None	<3%	Tests being carried out as of June 2001 40,000 users and 35 content providers (end of October 2000)
	Calle	NTT Communications	From 1 to 100,000	2,800	8,000	5%	

Mobile versus Fixed-Line Business Models

Most Japanese banks offer bank transfer services on ATMs and in their on-line services. The cost of these bank transfer services ranges from $1.05 to $6.30, depending on the amount of money sent. Clearly, these charges are too high to support micro-payment services. However, Japan Net Bank, a joint venture supported by some of Japan's largest firms, including Mitsui-Sumitomo Bank, and NTT DoCoMo, may change this situation. It started services in October 2000 and more than 300,000 people had opened accounts by the end of June 2001. The new service charges range from a low of $0.10 for transfers using i-mode phones to $2.62 for transfers over $300. Japan Net Bank has already signed up the leading mobile and fixed-line content providers in the areas of auctions, music sales, stock trading, and tickets. The key question for the mobile Internet is whether Japan Net Bank's service will be any easier to use than the current bank transfer services. Japan Net Bank's service requires users to input two three- to eight-digit passwords and four digits from a 16-digit identification code.

Pre-Paid Cards

Most pre-paid cards in Japan are like telephone cards that are used in the US and Europe: users dial a number and input a password that was revealed to them when they scratched the back of the card. In the case of Bit Cash, 600 stores sell the cards — mostly record stores, PC shops, and some bookstores. Bit Cash takes a 10% commission from the content providers and shares this with the stores. There are 300 content providers who are using Bit Cash's cards, of which seven were on i-mode as of late 2000. It is expected that sheets, which can be downloaded from terminals and in the future from multimedia kiosks in convenience stores, will replace cards since they are cheaper.

Bit Wallet, which is owned by Sony, NTT DoCoMo, and others, is currently testing an IC-chip-based pre-paid card service that probably has a much higher chance of success than current pre-paid cards. Consumers can use these cards by themselves or in conjunction with mobile phones, since mobile phone service providers and manufacturers are expected to place the cards inside the phones in order to promote mobile commerce. Although many firms have tried unsuccessfully to promote IC chips in credit and other cards, this time it may work because several leading Japanese firms believe they will benefit from the use of these cards. These firms include convenience stores and train companies, both of which would like to eliminate the use of coins since the cost of handling coins represents a significant portion of their total costs. Tests have shown that the use of these cards enables convenience stores to handle twice the number of customers, and train companies to eliminate costly ticket-selling machines and related activities.

The Mobile Internet

Other Services

NTT Communications, the largest provider of long-distance fixed-line services in Japan, offers an i-mode micro-payment service to its fixed-line subscribers. Similar to NTT DoCoMo's micro-payment service, it adds content charges to the long-distance bills of its fixed-line subscribers. As of mid-October 2000, it had 40,000 users, 35 content providers, and 50–60 sites that were using the service. It is approving about 10 new sites each month. NTT Communications' large number of fixed-line subscribers (almost 60 million) makes this a potentially large service. The problem is that few young people, the main i-mode users, have a subscription with NTT since they either live with their parents or have opted not to subscribe to NTT due to its high subscription cost. Thus, it is doubtful whether this micro-payment service will ever acquire a significant proportion of i-mode users.

Keitai Net offers several interesting twists to micro-payment systems. Similar to the other services, it allows users to deduct charges from an existing account, which in this case is Japan's postal savings accounts. Like NTT Communications' fixed-line subscribers, there are a lot of postal savings accounts, but the problem is that few young people have one. The first twist is that the service enables subscribers to accumulate monies when they view advertisements. Subscribers are given a virtual account when they register with Keitai Net. Keitai Net pays the subscribers when they view advertisements that are provided by participating content providers. The subscribers can use these monies to view contents for which Keitai Net takes 15% of the contents charges as a handling charge.

The second twist is that these activities are carried out on a portal site that is managed by Keitai Net. As is described later, this is an interesting example of how portal sites are different in the mobile and fixed-line Internets. Micro-payment services appear to be a necessary part of mobile Internet portals. Keitai Net's portal offers a search engine, a site-creation service for content providers (there were 60–70 as of late 2000), and a chat group/communication service by topic (about 15 topics) in addition to the cash-back service. As of mid-October 2000, the search engine contained several thousand sites, of which entertainment and individual sites are the most popular. There were eight companies paying to have their advertisements viewed, 73,000 subscribers (12,000 new subscribers a month), 60–70 content providers, and it was receiving 200,000 accesses per day.

Role of Positive Feedback

Positive feedback plays an important role in the competition between these micro-payment schemes, just as it does in the overall creation of a successful

Mobile versus Fixed-Line Business Models

mobile Internet. The more content providers that support a specific micro-payment system, the greater the incentive for mobile Internet subscribers to use that system. Similarly, the more mobile Internet subscribers that use a specific micro-payment system, the greater the incentive for content providers to support that system. Therefore, micro-payment schemes must obtain a large number of both mobile Internet users and content providers, and to do this they must make it easy for them to participate in the schemes.

None of the current micro-payment services in Japan had generated sufficient positive feedback as of mid-2001. The commissions on credit cards are too high to purchase content, and many people, particularly young people, in Japan, the US, and Europe don't own them. Japan Net Bank's bank transfer service has very low commissions, but the ease of use is a major question. And even if the service is easy to use, it will take time before the number of subscribers in Japan reaches a critical mass. Pre-paid cards are still inconvenient to purchase, although Sony's service may make it possible to use phones as money and tickets. But Sony's service will probably have little impact on content purchases.

A wireline micro-payment service may have a greater chance of success outside of Japan. In the West, a fixed-line phone or Internet micro-payment service would be much easier for people of all ages to use, since more people in the West live alone and thus have their own fixed-line telephone service. They also use the fixed-line Internet more than their counterparts in Japan. However, even if they are major users of the fixed-line Internet, many people are not subscribers to an Internet service. They may use their parents', school's, or even their company's Internet service.

To obtain a large number of content providers, the micro-payment scheme must make it easy for the content providers to participate. Low initial costs are obviously important, but they make it necessary for the micro-payment scheme to evaluate the content provider, which, as discussed earlier, is not a simple matter. It is complicated by the popularity of entertainment and chat groups in the mobile Internet and by concerns to avoid pornography and other controversial activities. NTT Communications, Keitai Net, and Bit Cash all provide relatively severe inspections, albeit not as severe as NTT DoCoMo. On the other hand, Web Money and BiGlobe provide much lighter inspections since they charge relatively high initial fees. Thus, the winner is still unclear, although, Japan Net Bank and Sony's Bit Wallet appear to be the front runners.

The Mobile Internet

1. Typically, NTT DoCoMo has paid the lower amount, KDDI has paid the higher amount, and J-Phone has paid an intermediate amount.
2. Phone manufacturing costs have also risen in the last few years due to the large number of new technologies that are used in phones, such as color displays.
3. NEC and Matsushita also make these phones available first to NTT DoCoMo and much later to other service providers. This is discussed in more detail in J. Funk, *Competition Between and Within Standards: The Case of Mobile Communications* (London: Palgrave, 2001), Chapter 5.
4. For example, in 1997 more than half the phones sold in Japan were lighter than 100 grams, while the most popular GSM phones were between 150 and 250 grams. Even in 2001, only the most expensive GSM phones are less than 100 grams, while the lightest i-mode phones, which include a much larger screen than the GSM phones, are less than 75 grams.
5. All of the service providers make about $80 per subscriber per month in voice services. The income from mobile Internet services varies by service provider, with NTT DoCoMo making about $20 — and the other two service providers about $10 — per month per subscriber. Thus, it only takes NTT DoCoMo three months to begin making money on a mobile Internet subscriber, while it takes as long as four-and-a-half months for KDDI to make money.
6. "Gekiyasu tanmatsu ga shijou kara kieru (The very cheap handsets will disappear from the market)," *Toyo Keizai*, March 31, 2001, p. 48.
7. "Gyakufushita no kigyou shuekei jizokuryoku wo tenken (3) KDDI — gakusei mukei keitai waribiki ga kouka = teisei ari (Looking at KDDI's income-generating capability — the effect of the student discounts)," *Nikkei Shinbun*, June 9, 2001, p. 15.
8. Some people argue that the activation commissions in Japan are declining due to the lower number of new users. See "Gekiyasu tanmatsu ga shijou kara kieru (The very cheap handsets will disappear from the market)," *Toyo Keizai*, March 31, 2000, p. 48.
9. This is described in more detail in J. Funk, *Competition Between and Within Standards: the case of mobile phones* (London: Palgrave, 2001).
10. See "Who needs 3G anyway?," *Business Week International*, March 26, 2001, pp. 26–27.
11. The commerce included $50 million in travel products and $25 million in CDs and books. "Dai2bu erite-ru kakumei tokushu — keitai netto hansoku ni iryoku, 2chouen shijou he (The second e-commerce revolution — the power of the mobile Internet)," *Nikkei Distribution*, March 6, 2001, p. 5.

Mobile versus Fixed-Line Business Models

12. The Japanese Government announced in early March 2001 that it would require NTT DoCoMo to open its micro-payment system to all content providers, including those that were not on NTT DoCoMo's official menu.
13. Mobile commerce, and e-commerce in general, would be much higher in Japan if the Japanese Government pursued deregulation more vigorously. This is discussed in more detail in Chapter 10.
14. See, for example, J. Utterback, *Mastering the Dynamics of Innovation* (Boston: Harvard Business Press, 1996).
15. "Keitai muke kokoku haishin honkakuka — KDDI, 5sha de shinkaisha setsuritsu, daburukurikku, raishun kaishi (The real start of ads for mobile phones — KDDI and five firms including double click establish a new firm next spring)," *Nikkei Distribution*, December 12, 2000, p. 5; "Netto kokoku gyokai, seiryoku 2 kokuka, wakuhanbai-haishin no bungyo mo — kotaiiki nirami chiraku hendo mo (Tectonic changes in the net advertising industry, which is being polarized into two camps)," *Nikkei Iindustrial*, p. 2.
16. These calculations are based on numbers found in the articles cited in the previous endnote and in the estimate for the ratio of the mobile to fixed-line commerce markets in Table 4.1.
17. I have heard a variety of different numbers and seen an equal variety in the Japanese press. Some of these estimated click rates are as high as 6% (eg, see "Wireless ads on mobile phones garner high response rates in Japan," *Asia Biz Tech.com*, March 5, 2001). But greater than 2% on the mobile versus less than 0.5% on the PC Internet appear to be the commonly cited numbers. Of course, many people argue that the higher numbers are due to the initial novelty of seeing advertisements on mobile phone screens.
18. For example, see Mary Modahl, *Now or Never: How Companies Must Change Today to Win the Battle for Internet Consumers* (New York: HarperBusiness, 2000), Chapters 6–8.
19. They provide about the same number of advertisements as the automatic money lending services, which exist widely in Japan due to the relative lack of credit cards.

Chapter Five:
Mobile Versus Fixed-Line Information Strategies for Content Providers

Content providers have used different information strategies in the mobile and fixed-line Internet, and these strategies have played an important role in creating positive feedback in the Japanese mobile Internet. While in the fixed-line Internet information strategies have primarily focused on richness,[1] reach is the critical variable in the mobile Internet. Content providers need to focus on reach before richness in order to exploit the large *potential reach* of mobile phones. (The figures discussed in Chapter 3 represent potential and not actual reach.) This potential reach will only be realized when content providers implement the appropriate information strategies.

5.1 Reach is Critical in the Mobile Internet

The successful content providers in the Japanese mobile Internet have realized the full potential of mobile phones by first simplifying their services for the mobile Internet. This has resulted in a discontinuity between the fixed-line and mobile Internet services. Second, they have expanded the breadth of the content and services. The breadth of the content will determine the number of people who will have an interest in the content. For example, the number of different stocks and bonds, concerts, news stories, ringing tones, and horoscopes that are available on these sites will determine the number of people who will have an interest in accessing the sites.

The breadth of the services will determine the ease with which people can access the content, and thus their reach. Two key services for expanding the reach of content are mail and site customization services. Most Japanese content providers give users the opportunity to select and receive mail about various topics. In fact, the most popular mail service was so popular it had

The Mobile Internet

to be discontinued. Recruit, the leading provider of information on jobs for soon-to-be-graduating college students, offered a mail service on upcoming company presentations about new jobs, as well as the means to register for these presentations. Unfortunately, it is difficult to control when the mail reaches a specific user, and thus many users complained that their friends were receiving the mail before they were! In the PC world, few people notice whether their friends or colleagues receive mail a few minutes before they do. But in the mobile world, mail can become the difference between finding and not finding a job.

Content providers may also enable their users to customize their site such that when users access the site, information about their chosen topic is displayed on the site. A variation of this service is to allow users to save recent search conditions so that they don't have to constantly re-enter the desired characteristics of an apartment, used car, job, or other item they are searching for. Both the customization and mail services make it easier for users to find specific information with a minimal use of the small keyboards and screens found on mobile phones.[2] For the content provider, the advantage of customization services is that they don't have to send mail, which costs them and their users money. On the other hand, mail makes the information more accessible to the user, since it makes it unnecessary for them to remember and actually access the site.

A final key point about reach is that content providers must expand their content in a way that makes them interesting to the major users of the mobile Internet. This is because the potential reach of a specific content provider's service is defined in terms of the major users of the associated device(s). The concepts of reach and richness and the experience in Japan suggest that initially the major users of the mobile Internet will be young people. Thus, content providers must initially design their content so that they appeal to young people. Of course, the users of the mobile Internet in Japan are evolving from young people to people of all ages, and they will evolve differently in different countries. Thus, content providers must constantly consider who is actually using the mobile Internet when they devise their content, in order to realize the maximum reach of mobile phones.

Once content providers have realized the potential reach of the mobile phones in their mobile services, they begin adding more richness to their content and services. Increased richness includes more information about each data point, be it each stock, bond, concert, train station, apartment rental, or news story. But it is important not to burden users with too much information about each data point, due to the small phone screens, relatively high

Mobile vs Fixed-Line Information Strategies for Content Providers

transmission charges, and short time periods in which the mobile Internet is accessed. Thus, the challenge is to add this richness in a way that adds value and doesn't burden users. This will require content providers to utilize pictures, graphs, and other techniques to present information in a concise and effective manner. Color screens and content, along with Java, new input methods, and high-speed data services will play a role in providing this rich information.

This chapter looks at these issues in more detail using examples from on-line stock trading, concert tickets, train navigation, news, and entertainment.

5.2 On-Line Stock Trading

On-line trading is very successful both in the US and Japan. More than 20% of trades in Japan, and probably more than 40% of trades in the US, are conducted on-line. Although on-line trading did not start until the early to mid-1990s, the changes in the US that actually led to on-line trading were instituted in the mid-1970s. This was when the US Securities and Exchange Commission (SEC) deregulated trading commissions. Japan did this only in October 1999.

The SEC's deregulation of commissions in 1975 opened up new opportunities in the trade-off between reach and richness. Previously, brokerages had competed through strong relationships with fairly wealthy clients. They provided these clients with a broad range of integrated services that created high switching costs for the clients. However, as shown in Figure 5.1, the deregulation of commissions provided brokerages with the opportunity to position themselves at a different place in the trade-off between reach and richness. The firm that moved the most aggressively was Charles Schwab; it set low commissions and offered telephone orders, and later touch-tone-dial-in services (see arrow labeled #1 in Figure 5.1). These services enabled it to expand its reach and thus allowed a much larger group of people to participate in the US stock market. By 1997, Charles Schwab's share of New York Stock Exchange commissions had increased to 15%.[3]

On-line trading provided the second set of opportunities in the trade-off between reach and richness. Initially, these providers of on-line trading competed on the basis of lower costs, which were achieved through the lack of expensive call centers. However, the relatively large PC screens and rich information that Charles Schwab and, of course, other brokers possessed enabled them to begin offering richer information. Thus, to some extent,

Figure 5.1 Full- and Limited-Service Brokerages

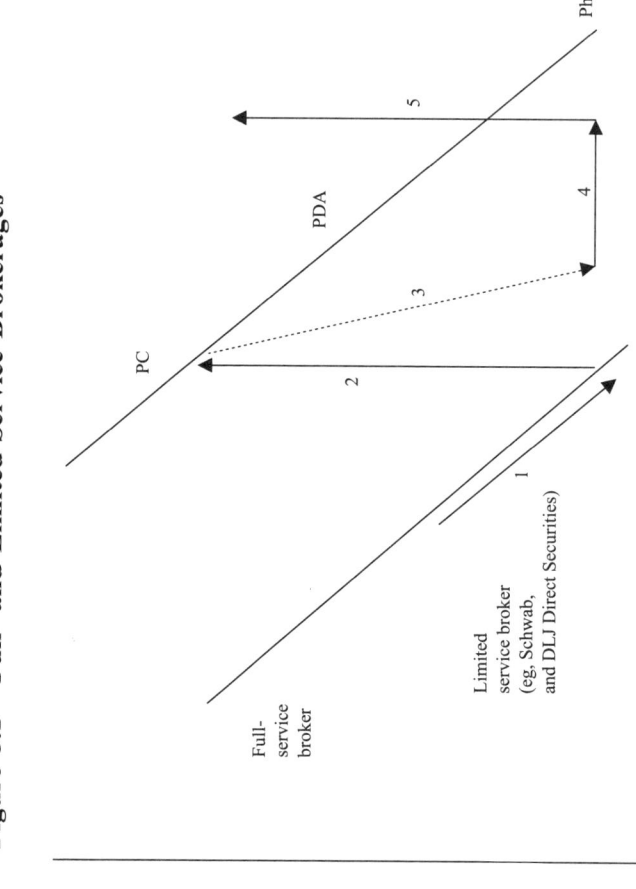

1: Provide telephone brokerage services
2: Provide brokerage services on PCs
3: Simplify the PC services for mobile phones
4: Add mail and pre-registration services
5: Add richness with existing and new technology

Mobile vs Fixed-Line Information Strategies for Content Providers

competition changed from cut-throat price competition in the mid-1990s to competition to offer portfolio tracking, records management, cash management, and other services in the late 1990s (see arrow labeled #2 in Figure 5.1).

The Mobile Internet

Mobile trading provides the third set of opportunities in the trade-off between reach and richness. In spite of Japan's slow pace at deregulating trading commissions, mobile trading emerged first in Japan due to its more successful mobile Internet. Since trading commissions were not deregulated in Japan until October 1999, most brokers did not offer inexpensive telephone orders or touch-tone dial-in services, and even PC on-line trading had not taken off when NTT DoCoMo started its i-mode services in February 1999. Thus, the changes associated with the arrow labeled #1 in Figure 5.1 hardly occurred in Japan, and the changes associated with the arrow labeled #2 in the figure had barely started when the third opportunity presented itself.

New entrants such as DLJ Direct Securities and traditional brokers such as Daiwa, Nikko, and Nomura Securities began offering i-mode services in 1999. While the traditional brokers had already introduced on-line PC services, DLJ Direct Securities began offering PC services at approximately the same time as it began offering i-mode services. For all of the brokerages, the mobile services are a simplified version of the PC services, which is represented in Figure 5.1 as a discontinuous change from the fixed-line services. While these brokerages offer many of the functions on their PC services that are available in the US, initially the i-mode services were primarily limited to quotes and buying and selling functions. These buying and selling functions were offered first for individual stocks, but most of the firms have gradually expanded their product breadth to include mutual funds, money management funds, and foreign exchanges.

One of the leaders in Japan's on-line trading market is DLJ Direct Securities. Fifty percent of DLJ's i-mode users also use its PC services, of which the account numbers and passwords are the same. The dual users tend to do analysis on the PC and make the actual transaction on the phone. They tend to watch the price movements while the market is open and then make a decision to buy or sell. Of course, mobile trading requires users to access a larger number of pages than on-line trading with the PC. In the case of DLJ's services, the PC requires three pages to buy or sell stocks while an i-mode phone requires eight pages to buy and seven pages to sell a stock. The large number of pages required to make these transactions on a mobile

The Mobile Internet

phone tends to restrict the reach of mobile trading and thus prevents DLJ Direct Securities from realizing the potential reach of the mobile phone.

Mail and Site Customization Services

The leading providers of mobile trading have introduced mail and site customization services to increase the reach of their services (see arrow labeled #4 on Figure 5.1). For example, Daiwa Securities provides a service where users can register to receive mail when the Nikkei average or a specific stock rises above or falls below a certain level. It is also possible to register to receive mail when the value of the Nikkei or a specific stock experiences a particular percentage change. Although this service is also available with Daiwa's PC on-line service, it has much more significance with mobile phones since it enables people to stay aware of key events even while they are not in front of their PC. As of early 2001, Daiwa had between 20,000 and 30,000 users of this service, or almost half the number of its total mobile subscribers.

Daiwa and others also provide a site customization service. For example, Daiwa users can register up to 70 stocks so that when a user accesses Daiwa's home page, the prices of these stocks appear. This service enables users to click on a stock and make a purchase in four pages as opposed to the usual eight pages. A big improvement was putting the stock price and the place to input the number of shares to purchase on the same page. Previously, users had spent a great deal of time moving between the page where they input quantities and the page where they confirmed the stock price.

The relative success of mobile trading is in spite of the large number of young mobile Internet users in Japan. As discussed in Chapter 2, almost half of the i-mode users of DLJ Direct Securities are more than 40 years old. However, DLJ Direct would like also to reach young people, the main users of the mobile Internet in Japan. Therefore, it offers a trading game that simulates the stock market. By late February 2001, there were 30,000 users of the game, with an average age of 22. In the future, it hopes to charge people to play the game and then to convert them to subscribers of its real business of providing on-line trading.

Most firms that offer mobile trading are now trying to move along the path designated by arrow labeled #5 in Figure 5.1 in order to increase the richness of their services. The problem is that the small screens and other factors make it relatively difficult to add richness. Key technologies include Java and high-speed data services. Java enables programs to be downloaded once

Mobile vs Fixed-Line Information Strategies for Content Providers

and then used multiple times. In early 2001 some firms introduced Java-based programs that can display graphs and other pictorial representations of data, but the memory restrictions associated with downloading a so-called i-applet along with handset differences have prevented these contents from being widely used. Some firms believe that these i-applets will become more widely used once W-CDMA services are started in October 2001. Real-time streaming quotes and video streaming are two applications that are widely discussed.

5.3 Concert Tickets

Concert tickets are the most successful application of shopping in the mobile Internet in Japan. Some participants estimate that more than 10% of the tickets for concerts aimed at young people are reserved over mobile phones in Japan. For example, almost 50% of the ticket reservations taken by Lawson, the leading provider of these mobile services, are taken from mobile phones.

Like in many countries, in Japan concert tickets are typically reserved and purchased over the phone, not in person. In the US, Ticketmaster has been the leading provider of tickets for many years, while Pia has been the leader in Japan since it began publishing magazines that contained information on concerts and other parts of the entertainment industry in the mid-1970s. This enabled Pia to dramatically expand the reach of its services, as shown by the arrow labeled #2 in Figure 5.2. In 1980, it became the first firm to include seat information in computers, which eliminated the inventory management problem associated with physical tickets.

Unlike Ticketmaster, Pia and other Japanese firms were relatively slow to begin providing web-based services. Pia was concerned about losing magazine sales, which, as of early 2001, still represented a larger percentage of income to Pia than ticket sales. It started its web-based services in 1997 when overcrowded phone lines raised concerns about lost sales. Lawson was somewhat faster than Pia, particularly in offering services on the mobile Internet. Lawson began taking reservations over the telephone in 1996 in co-operation with several concert promoters who saw Lawson's convenience stores as a useful place for consumers to pick up and pay for tickets. As discussed in Chapter 7, Lawson introduced a number of technologies into its convenience stores that have supported the integration of its mobile and fixed-line activities.

Figure 5.2 Concert Tickets in Japan

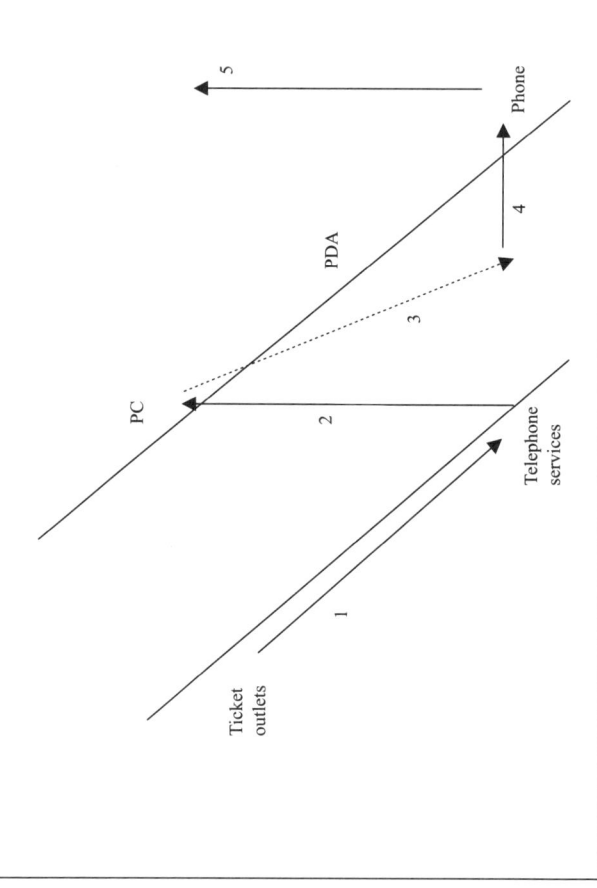

1: Provide telephone ticket-ordering services
2: Increase reach and richness through PC-based websites
3: Increase reach of PC-based websites with mobile-phone services
4: Add mail and registration services
5: Increase richness with existing and new technology

Mobile vs Fixed-Line Information Strategies for Content Providers

In February 1999, Lawson and Pia began offering i-mode concert ticket services, which are a simplified version of their PC services (shown as discontinuous change from the fixed-line content in the arrow labeled #3 in Figure 5.2). Lawson was much quicker to expand the breadth of its products, and this is why it is now the leading supplier of mobile ticket services. At the start of i-mode services it offered reservation services on over 8,000 different kinds of events, including concerts, plays, and sports, and since then has expanded this number many times. Pia did not expand the number of its products beyond the initial 400 types until December 1999 when it made all of its tickets available on i-mode (a total of 20,000).

Mail and Registration Services

Like the providers of on-line mobile trading services, Pia and Lawson provide mail and registration services to help them expand the reach of their services, since searching through 20,000 different events can be very difficult and time-consuming. For example, Pia offers 800 different mail services, which vary by artist and sports team. It sends mail to users (only to those who register for the mail) just before tickets go on sale for the specific artist or sports team's performance. As of early 2001, on-line ticket sales obtained via this mail equaled those conducted through a search on Pia's mobile site. These mail services are free to Club Pia members, and membership costs $2 a month. As of early 2001, there were around 100,000 members of whom 70% were PC-based users and 30% were mobile-based users. Membership also simplifies the purchasing process for Pia users. Since their name, address, and credit card number are already registered, Club Pia members only have to input their Club Pia number when they purchase a ticket. This number and the telephone number are used to confirm the member's identity.

Lawson provides a site customization service called "my box" to help users navigate through the large number of tickets that it offers. Users choose artists, and then information about these artists is put into their own "my box." When users access the Lawson site, "my box" appears at the top of the page and flashes when new information is in the box. Both the customization and the mail services make it easier for users to receive information about the specific concerts in which they have an interest. They are different in that users must go to the site and click on "my box," while the mail comes to them.

Both Lawson and Pia are now trying to move along the path designated by arrow #5 in Figure 5.2 in order to increase the richness of their services. As with the firms that are offering mobile trading services, the problem is that

The Mobile Internet

the small screens and other factors make it relatively difficult to add richness. Lawson and Pia would like to offer more detailed information on artists, their music and related products, and concert seating. In particular, information on concert seating arrangements is considered a very valuable part of their PC-based services. Although both Lawson and Pia would like to offer this information in their mobile services, current technology does not allow it. Better color resolution screens, Java, and higher-speed data services will eventually enable Lawson and Pia to provide information on seating arrangements.

Phones as Tickets and Money

An even more interesting twist to buying concert and other tickets on mobile phones is using the mobile phones as tickets. As discussed in the appendix on alternative payment systems at the end of Chapter 4, Bit Wallet has developed and is currently testing a pre-paid card that contains integrated circuits. Mobile phone service providers and manufacturers are expected to place these or similar IC-based pre-paid cards inside the phones in the same way that SIM (Subscriber Identity Module) cards are used in GSM phones. [4] Other ideas include the use of bar codes in phones for tickets. In both cases, users could receive mail containing the relevant concert information after purchasing a ticket on their mobile phone. This information could be saved in the IC card or as a bar code that designates the concert and seat. Users would then have their IC cards or the bar codes on their phone display scanned automatically when they have entered the concert arena, thus eliminating the need for manual ticket checks.

Other firms are also trying to user mobile phones as tickets and money. The Japanese Railways, commonly known as "JR," expects to have a system in place on some rail lines by 2001 that accepts tickets that are inside mobile phones. It is expected that this system will be based on Sony's technology, as will systems for making small payments with phones at places such as convenience stores. Further, it is already possible to use phones to pay for items in vending machines in Finland, although NTT DoCoMo will probably be the first firm to actually do this on a large scale.

5.4 Navigation Services

Navigation services will clearly be a major application on the mobile Internet. As discussed in earlier chapters, outside of Japan, navigation and location-based services are receiving a great deal of attention by technology and service providers who believe these services will be the most important

Mobile vs Fixed-Line Information Strategies for Content Providers

application on the mobile Internet. The problem is that users are not displaying the same level of interest. The concepts of reach and richness and their implications for information strategies explain many of the current problems with these complex navigation and location-based systems that are being developed outside of Japan.

Traditionally, firms and consumers have relied on a large number of information sources and services to navigate locally, nationally, and internationally. These information sources include many forms of maps, hotel directories, and various schedules for trains, buses, boats, and airplanes. Most of the analytical tools have been contained in expensive proprietary computer systems and thus could only be used by travel agents and for industrial applications (see Figure 5.3).

The rise of the Internet has dramatically changed this situation by making available a plethora of tools and information sources. Many people now bypass or work in tandem with travel agents to analyze and reserve hotels, airline seats, and other forms of travel. The rise of the Internet is also causing many firms to replace their proprietary computer systems with Internet applications, due to the lower cost of the Internet. While in the West, these applications primarily focus on hotels and airlines, both domestically and internationally, in Japan it is car and train navigation systems for domestic travel that have been the most popular.

Japan's system of narrow and crowded roads that are constantly under construction has caused the Japanese people to demand — and Japan's electronics sector to produce — extremely high-quality, albeit expensive (between $1,000 and $3,000), car navigation systems that provide display- and voice-based directions. As of February 2000, there were more than five million car navigation systems installed in Japan, or about 7.5% of total cars. And partly since car navigation systems are becoming standard items in many new Japanese cars, this number is growing at more than 15% a year.

Japan's inexpensive car navigation systems rely on compact discs (CDs), while the newer and more expensive systems access data from DVDs. With data access rates as high as 40 million bits per second, the DVD-based systems can access a lot of detailed data. Thus, competition in Japan's car navigation market currently focuses on adding more richness in the maps along with improved display quality and higher search speeds. Manufacturers continue to add details of buildings, lanes, underpasses, small bridges,

Figure 5.3 Maps and Navigation Services

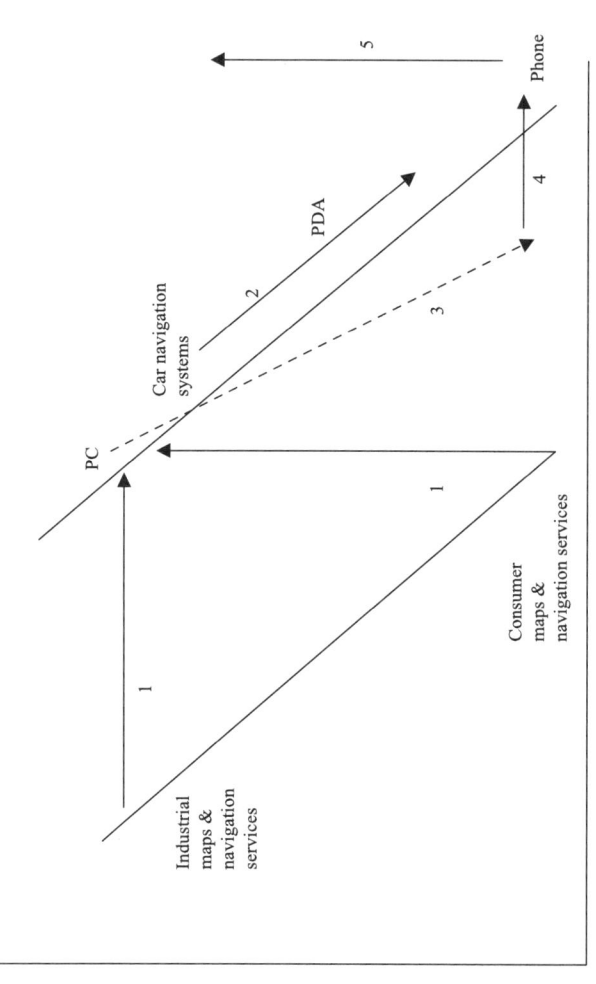

1: Provide maps and navigation services on the PC and car navigation systems
2: Simplify the car navigation services for PDAs and eventually for phones
3: Simplify the PC train and map services for phones
4: Add train station and other registration capability
5: Use new technology to offer richer map and navigation services on mobile phones.

Mobile vs Fixed-Line Information Strategies for Content Providers

parking garages, and entrances to stores to these already detailed maps. The mobile Internet opens up new possibilities in the reach and richness domain and thus will change Japan's navigation market, including the car navigation market. Firms are attempting to simplify the car navigation services for both PDAs and mobile phones. For example, NTT DoCoMo has offered a PDA-based mobile service that provides GPS (global positioning system) capabilities and map information since January 2000.[5]

The user's position is shown on a map on the PDA display along with the locations of roads, buildings, train stations, restaurants, and stores, and directions to any of them.[6] Several firms also offer map-based services for mobile phones. Users can access simple maps on their mobile phones through a hierarchical menu of locations and send these maps to other people via e-mail. They can also search for restaurants, stores, parking lots, and other places, and download maps that display their locations.

Managing the Reach and Richness Domain: Toshiba's Train Service

However, a much more successful application on the Japanese mobile Internet involves train navigation and is provided by Toshiba. Toshiba's mobile Internet service is a simplified version of a PC-based service that has been very popular in Japan for many years. Users input the departure and destination train stations, and the software calculates the optimal (calculated either in terms of time or money) set of trains to take and provides their departure and arrival times. The site also provides data on the last trains, and this feature is particularly popular around midnight when everyone is trying to figure out whether they have time for another beer.

Toshiba's train service is more popular than the simplified car navigation systems because it manages the reach and richness domain better than they do. As discussed in Chapter 3, mobile phones are suited for services that have high reach and low richness. How to simplify PC and car navigation services for the mobile phone is a critical question in all applications. But it is a more complex question in the navigation area, since there are more candidates for the most appropriate "simple" information than in other applications. For example, does the most appropriate simple information included roads, buildings, bus stops, or train stations?

It takes less information to describe an area such as Tokyo in terms of train stations than either roads or buildings. This makes Toshiba's system perfect for the mobile phone. The simplified car navigation and map services were too complex to be "the" initially successful applications in Japan's mobile Internet. There are few users of PDAs, the maps don't have enough detail

The Mobile Internet

for pedestrians, the PDA and phone displays lack sufficient resolution to display a useful map, and there is insufficient memory and processing power for calculating user locations or optimal routes.

There are even more problems with providing these services on mobile phones where the small screens make the maps small and key information is often "cut off" at the edges of the display. For example, addresses, street and building names, and other text information often includes many characters that often start or end on a part of the map that the user is not currently viewing. And a partial address or name can be easily mistaken for a completely different address or place name. For this reason, providers of these map services in Japan have eliminated most addresses and names from their maps, thus reducing the value of the map services.

Of course, for countries where trains are not widely used, content providers will have to come up with a different set of appropriate "simple" information. While trains are widely used in Europe and Asia, they are not widely used in the US. This may make walking maps, which are made for very specific downtown areas such as Manhattan, more appropriate applications for mobile phones in the US than train navigation services. But the US content providers will have to be careful to focus on the appropriate simple information (eg, key landmarks) from which to add richness to their services.

Toshiba's Move to Reach and Later to Richness

Like the firms that offer mobile trading and concert tickets, Toshiba expanded the breadth of its products and services before it began adding richness (see arrows labeled #4 and #5 on Figure 5.3). It expanded on a geographical basis from Tokyo to the other regions and included all of the train lines in its service for each region when the service was started in that region. It now provides a service where users can register their most widely used train stations in order to more quickly find route information, schedules, and final train information for these stations. Further, besides being a useful service for users, Toshiba is also planning to use this registered information and information about users' travel habits to send advertisements to them as it adds richness to its site.

Toshiba is now adding richness to its site in a number of different ways. It added a Java-based alarm service in January 2001 which alerts users that they are about to reach their destination station. Japan's well-run trains make this possible, since Toshiba's alarm service is based on time. More interestingly, Toshiba is trying to use its success as a provider of train

Mobile vs Fixed-Line Information Strategies for Content Providers

navigation services to provide maps and information on bars, restaurants, stores, and other places that are *near* train stations. As argued earlier, firms should realize the potential reach of mobile phones before they begin adding rich information. In the navigation area, realizing this potential reach required the use of appropriate simple information, which Toshiba has done with train stations.

Toshiba's successful train service has already made it very easy and logical for Toshiba to gradually add information about the areas surrounding train stations. Its users are primarily concerned with these areas, since they are regular train users. This has made it easier for Toshiba to create positive feedback between users and data points than for other firms, some of which were discussed in Chapter 4. With 400,000 paying subscribers ($3 a month) at the end of March 2001 and 30,000 new subscribers each month, Toshiba has used this market power to attract bars, restaurants, stores, and other places that are near train stations, to its service. This information helps its users navigate both the trains and places around the train stations, thus making its service even more popular. Eventually, if it can combine a large database of places with some simple GPS capabilities such as those described previously, it can be the successful provider of rich content and complex navigation services in spite of the fact that it initially began with simplicity.

As we shall see in later chapters, multi-channel convergence and new technologies will provide many new opportunities in the reach and richness domain of navigation services. Chapter 7 describes how multi-channel convergence enables firms to manage the trade-off between reach and richness in slightly different ways. For example, phones can be used to provide positioning information, while PCs can be used to display and analyze the information. Internet-compatible car navigation systems will enable users to access much richer content than mobile phones and these systems have few disadvantages with respect to reach for car users. Chapter 8 describes how new technologies will change the trade-off between reach and richness for both phones and PDAs, thus enabling them to better provide the navigation and map services which they currently have trouble providing.

5.5 News

News is a major application on the fixed-line and mobile Internet. As shown in Figure 5.4, the fixed-line Internet has enabled specialty newspapers, magazines, and other information sources to add reach, and general newspapers, magazines, and other information to add richness. Before the

Figure 5.4 News and Information Services

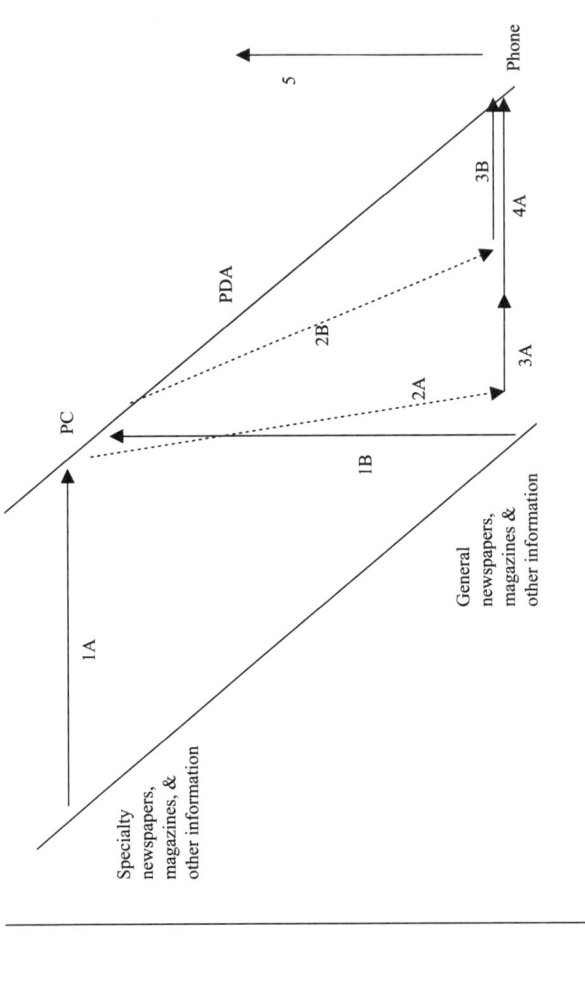

1: Provide specialty and general-purpose news on PCs
2: Provide a simplified version of the PC services on mobile phones
3: Expand reach with mail services
4: Specialty news services modify the mobile version to match needs of main mobile Internet users
5: Richer content with existing or new technology

Mobile vs Fixed-Line Information Strategies for Content Providers

Internet, it was difficult to find many specialty newspapers, magazines, and other information sources, because few libraries had them and few people knew about them. Now, many of these specialty newspapers, magazines, and other information sources are not only easy to find, but can now more easily sell their extensive databases of information. For general newspapers, magazines, and other information sources, the Internet enables them to offer a much richer set of services, including linkages to the specialty information sources.

The mobile Internet opens up new possibilities in the trade-off between reach and richness. As discussed earlier, the most popular news sites have simple and general information such as weather and entertainment that are of interest to many people, including young people.

Mail Services

Like many of the other content providers discussed in this chapter, mail is an important part of these news services since it helps them expand the reach of their services (see arrow labeled #3 in Figure 5.4). For example, WNI (Weather News International) sends mail to paying subscribers when the chance of rain exceeds a certain percentage. Tsutaya Online, one of the leading providers of video and music in the bricks-and-mortar world, offered its subscribers 30 kinds of music-related mail along with general information on movies, books, and games as of early January 2001. Nikkei offers a company-specific mail service where paid subscribers receive mail containing new articles about companies they register for. Impress, the leading provider of information on information technology in the fixed-line world, sends mail about new IT developments to its mobile phone subscribers, sometimes as often as once an hour. PA, the leading provider of employment services in the IT field, sends mail containing job-related news. Each of these mail services increases the reach of the services, since the mail services make it easier for the users to acquire the information.

There is, of course, a large discrepancy in the number of subscribers to these mail services and thus in their reach (see Figure 5.4). While WNI and Tsutaya Online have more than 600,000 subscribers to their services, many of the other firms have fewer than 10,000 subscribers since their services are not aimed at the main i-mode users. However, the latter firms are not assuming they will always be niche providers in the mobile Internet, nor are they waiting for Japan's mobile Internet users to evolve from people in their early twenties to those in their forties.

The Mobile Internet

Reaching the Youth Market
Many of these firms are modifying their services to match the main users of Japan's mobile Internet. For example, Impress offers a quiz game concerning information technology. It believes that most young people are interested in IT, although the information must be modified to match their needs. The quiz game is the first step in Impress's efforts to develop free, and subsequently paid, services for these young people. It also expects that many of these young users will eventually become users of its main IT news services.

PA is focusing on the educational and licensing side of its employment service for the mobile Internet. Information on IT education, and licensing tests and programs are not its main fixed-line Internet information services. However, young people — in particular, students — are more interested in information about IT education and licensing tests than about IT jobs. PA makes money through referrals to companies that provide these tests and educational programs, and, like Impress, expects that many of these young users will eventually become users of its employment services.

Mail, Young People, and Market Research
The most interesting example, however, of a news content provider trying to broaden its appeal is a joint venture between Asahi News and Nikkei News. The two started a quiz game that is designed to attract subscribers in the short run and market research monies in the long run. Users answer five questions about today's news to accumulate points, which they can use to win prizes. The users can choose their questions from political and economic news, entertainment, trends, sports, or special issues. As you can guess, young people tend to go for the entertainment questions, while older people are more likely to choose questions about politics. The two companies acquired more than 10,000 paying subscribers within a little more than one month of starting the real service and two months of starting the experimental service.

In the long run, they will use the answers to the questions to test the effect of television and other advertisements. For example, the category called "trends" includes questions about new products and commercials. By including questions about recently released products or television commercials, they can quickly determine people's reactions to new products and commercials. They hope that firms will pay to have questions about their products and commercials included in this and other categories of the quiz game.

Mobile vs Fixed-Line Information Strategies for Content Providers

This game is part of a larger trend in Japan to use the mobile phone and mail to do market research. Already many market research firms have accumulated large groups of people who are willing to quickly answer questions about a specific product, commercial, or other topic within hours of receiving mail. These people participate to win prizes and are usually reimbursed for their mail charges. The firms typically experience response rates of more than 30% in the first few hours and thus they are able to gather meaningful responses in one day. Content providers with many subscribers, such as Asahi News and Nikkei News, realize that their subscribers represent potential participants in these surveys and thus new sources of income.

The Challenges for Rich Information

The leading provider of rich news information in Japan is WNI. It has used its success in providing weather information to expand into other information services. In combination with more than 50 partners, it also provides information on the makeup, clothing, drinks, food, and other products that are most appropriate for the current weather conditions. Further, it has used its weather information services for specific golf clubs, fishing locations, ski resorts, amusement parks, national and regional parks, and other places to provide information on products that can be used in these activities. In some cases, WNI receives advertising fees from the manufacturers of these products; in others it merely sees the information as an added benefit for its users. Offering richer information — ie, non-text information — is the next challenge for news content providers. Like the providers of concert tickets, mobile trading, and navigation services, it is difficult to provide rich information to the small screens found on mobile phones. Color figures, graphs, and pictures are the obvious direction, but few if any of the news providers have started offering these types of services. Concerns about data charges and handset differences have slowed the application of Java; this will probably change as content providers develop more experience with Java and higher-speed data services become available.

Linkages between pages are also critical. In the fixed-line Internet, linkages enable people to easily move between articles, between articles and firm home pages, between different firms, and between different news sources, thus enabling them to obtain a vast amount of rich information. Linkages can also play a similar, albeit smaller, role in the mobile Internet. This is not just true in the news area but also in the other examples described in this chapter, including concert tickets, on-line trading, and navigation. Questions remain, however, as to whether users really want to access rich information

The Mobile Internet

such as detailed news articles on their mobile phones. Unfortunately, NTT DoCoMo's rules that restrict linkages between different sites prevent us from knowing whether users are interested in using links to access richer information. This is another example of where the rest of the world can move much faster than Japan if it ever creates the necessary positive feedback between content, users, and phones.

5.6 Entertainment

Simple entertainment contents started the positive feedback in the Japanese mobile Internet, and this book argues that it will probably do the same in other countries. The reason is that this simple content matches the high reach and low richness of mobile phones, and, like the other applications described in this chapter, the entertainment content providers focused on reach before richness. Because the entertainment content has the highest traffic in the Japanese mobile Internet, they were the first content providers to achieve the potential reach of the mobile Internet and can thus begin adding richness.

Providers of the most successful entertainment content, such as ringing tones, screen savers (ie, character downloading), and horoscopes, quickly expanded the breadth of their products in order to expand the reach of their contents. They increased the number of songs, characters, and types of horoscopes, which increased the number of people who would be interested in the service. Positive feedback between song and character providers and users, along with economies of scale, now provide the early entrants with a strong competitive advantage. For example, Giga Networks is one of the leading providers of ringing tones, since it was the first firm to start these services and to offer a large number of songs. Through the positive feedback between the number of songs and users, the early lead in the number of songs caused the number of its users to increase, leading to more song providers to work with Giga Networks. The other providers of ringing tone services have been forced to create original songs or to offer much lower prices than Giga Networks and other market leaders in order to make up for their disadvantage in the number of songs.

Similar effects can be found in screen savers (character downloading), horoscopes, and games. Bandai has become the leading provider of character downloading services through its early start, accumulation of character licenses, and creation of positive feedback between the number of character licenses and the number of users. But here, the number of character licenses is even more limited than the number of songs; new characters don't appear

Mobile vs Fixed-Line Information Strategies for Content Providers

as often as new songs do. This makes Bandai's early advantage even more important than that for Giga Networks. Like the competition between providers of ringing tones, Bandai's competitors have been forced to create original material, in this case original characters, in order to compete, which is clearly a very difficult challenge.

Index became the leading provider of horoscopes through its early start and complete offering of horoscopes concerned with love. Here, Index's success is related more to economies of scale than positive feedback, since Index has created its own horoscopes. Love is the most popular topic with young i-mode users, in particular young female users. Index was the first firm to offer a full line of love-related horoscopes, including horoscopes that are based on birth dates, blood types, Tarot cards, and other methods.

Interestingly, mail is an important part of some of these services. Many of the screen saver providers such as Bandai send new characters to their users every day so that they don't have to actually visit the site to change their screens. Many of the screen saver, ringing tone, and horoscope providers offer services in which it is possible for users to add these characters, ringing tones, and horoscopes to their mail. Further, many of them also enable their users to communicate with each other through blind e-mail; NTT DoCoMo requires this blindness for the same reasons it does not allow communication/ dating services on its official menu.

These mail services, the broad product offerings by the leading providers of entertainment services, and the fundamental simplicity of most entertainment have caused these content providers to begin focusing on richness. As described in Chapter 3, the definition of richness depends on the particular contents. While for many contents, richness can be defined in terms of the volume of information to be read or input, in entertainment it can probably be better defined in terms of the need for colors and the number of colors needed, the necessary speeds of moving images, and the necessary display resolution for the pictures and graphs.

Entertainment content providers began offering color content in early 2000, and, in early 2001, color content that took advantage of higher-resolution color phones and Java-based contents. For example, screen savers, horoscopes, and games have been available in color since early 2000. Further, these and other sites use Java to provide moving images in the screen savers, horoscopes, and other entertainment contents. For example, Index's horoscope site shows Tarot cards being dealt when a user requests a Tarot-based horoscope. Simple games can be downloaded and played without connecting to the network.

The Mobile Internet

The entertainment content providers are also developing content for the high-speed data services that NTT DoCoMo planned (as of July 2001) to start in October 2001. This is discussed further in Chapter 8.

Sound Bites

1. **Reach is the critical variable in the mobile Internet.** Content providers must realize the potential reach of mobile phones before they begin adding richness.

2. **Simplify content for the mobile Internet.** This is an important part of realizing the potential reach of mobile phones, and one result will be a discontinuity between the fixed-line and mobile contents.

3. **Expand the breadth of content and services.** The number of different stocks and bonds, concerts, news stories, ringing tones, and horoscopes that are available on a site will determine the number of people who will have an interest in accessing the site and thus the reach of the site.

4. **Expand the breadth of contents in a way that makes them interesting to the major users of the mobile Internet.** The potential reach of a device is defined in terms of the major users of that device. The concepts of reach and richness and the experience in Japan suggest that initially the major users of the mobile Internet will be young people.

5. **Provide users with mail and site customization services.** Provide users with the opportunity both to receive mail about specific topics and to customize sites so that when they access the site, the information they are interested in is easily accessed from the top page.

6. **Don't burden users with excessively rich information.** Only add richness after you have achieved reach, and add it in a way that does not burden users with too much information.

Mobile vs Fixed-Line Information Strategies for Content Providers

Notes:

1. For example, see Philip Evans and Thomas Wurster, *Blown to Bits* (Boston: Harvard Business Press, 2000), Chapter 5.
2. These two kinds of services are an example of how content providers in many types of media charge different users different prices for the same information simply by reconfiguring the information. See C. Shapiro and H. Varian, *Information Rules: A Strategic Guide to the Network Economy* (Boston: Harvard Business School Press, 1999).
3. Philip Evans and Thomas Wurster, *Blown to Bits* (Boston: Harvard Business Press, 2000), p. 74.
4. All GSM phones use SIM cards, which contain personal information about the user. These SIM cards can be inserted into another phone, thus enabling someone to use that phone and have the phone calls charged to their personal phone number.
5. The service uses network-based GPS and it is based on technology from US-based Snap Track.
6. There are also several services that provide information on the location of many types of devices.

Chapter Six:
Mobile versus Fixed-Line Portal Sites and Search Engines

Information navigators assist people in finding information and traveling in cyberspace, just as physical navigators such as maps and other tools assist them in traveling in the physical world. Information navigators enable users to move from the south-east part of the reach and richness domain (low-rich/high-reach information) to the north-west part of the domain (high-rich/low-reach information). Traditional information navigators include phone books, newspapers and magazines (including their advertisements), salespeople, and consultants. Generally only the navigators that lie in the south-east part of the reach and richness domain, such as phone books, can be considered affiliated with the buyer. As we move north-west along the reach and richness curve, most of the navigators are associated with the seller (salespeople or advertisements in magazines) or they are very expensive, such as consultants or purchasing departments. Large companies can afford consultants and purchasing departments, but the general public is usually forced to rely on salespeople who, of course, are often affiliated with the seller. This has traditionally made it difficult for consumers to obtain unbiased rich information.

The Internet reduces the cost of navigation and thus threatens traditional navigators. The low cost and high interconnectivity of the Internet make it possible for new navigators to affiliate themselves with consumers and offer them inexpensive services. These navigators can be portals, search engines, or even sites themselves. Portals categorize, organize, and screen information, while search engines typically include a broader set of sites in their database. Some of these portals, such as Yahoo!, provide navigation services at the most general level, while many individual sites act as a portal or a search engine for a specific category such as books (eg, Amazon.com). Because

Figure 6.1 The Role of Navigators in the Fixed-Line and Mobile Internet

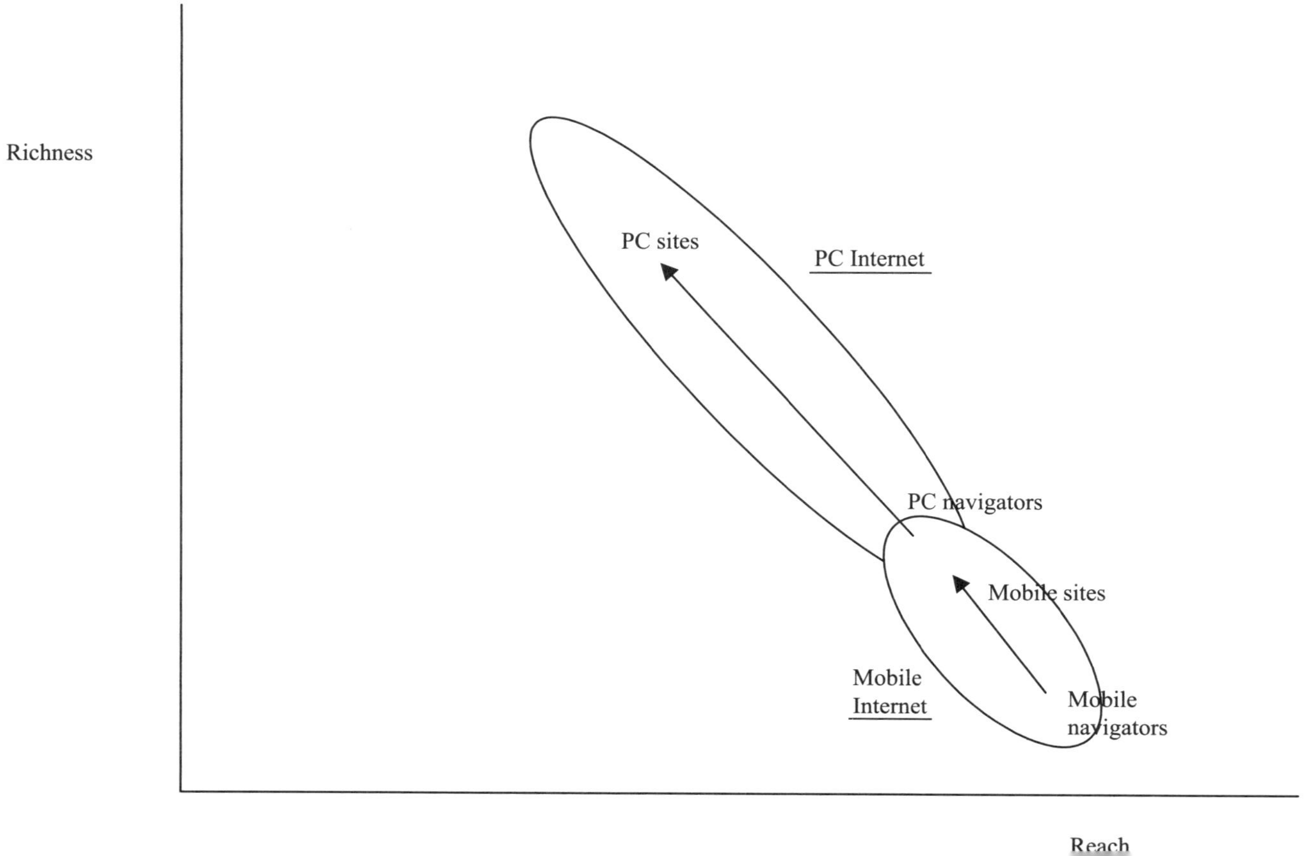

Richness

PC sites

PC Internet

PC navigators

Mobile sites

Mobile navigators

Mobile Internet

Reach

Mobile versus Fixed-Line Portal Sites and Search Engines

these new navigators are much cheaper than the traditional alternatives and often affiliate themselves more with the buyer than the seller, they threaten the traditional navigators such as salespeople and consultants.

This chapter uses the concepts of reach and richness to describe the roles of portals and search engines in the mobile Internet and to explain how they must use strategies that are different from those used in the fixed-line Internet. Mobile portals and search engines need to provide more screening of content than in the fixed-line Internet, due to the smaller screens, relatively high transmission charges, and short viewing times of the mobile Internet. They must emphasize the simplification of information access more so than on the fixed-line Internet. The existence of multiple mark-up languages, the need for micro-payment and user tracking services, and the variety of mobile devices (such as phones and PDAs) and screen sizes also provide different challenges for portals and search engines on the mobile Internet.

6.1 Basic Differences between Fixed-Line and Mobile Portals and Search Engines

Portals and search engines help people move from the south-east to the north-west part of the reach and richness domain. But the limits of mobile phones constrain the extent to which users can access rich information on the mobile Internet. This means that mobile navigators can only take users so far in the north-west direction. Further, the limits of mobile phones constrain the actual navigation functions. It is difficult to present the user with a great deal of choices on the small screen of a mobile phone. Thus, the mobile Internet portals and search engines must be simpler, and must position themselves more toward the south-east corner of the reach and richness domain, than the fixed-line Internet portals and search engines.

Figure 6.1 summarizes this situation. PC portals and search engines help people to move within a large part of the reach and richness domain, while mobile portals and search engines help them to move just within the south-east area of the domain. Further, since portals categorize, screen, and organize information and thus make it easier for people to find general information than do search engines, they have higher reach but lower richness than search engines. Although search engines generally provide less categorizing, screening, and organizing of information than do portals, they typically include a larger number of sites in their database and thus they can access this greater number of sites and provide richer information.

The Mobile Internet

Figure 6.2 summarizes this comparison between portals and search engines in a slightly exaggerated fashion. The PC and mobile worlds have been separated in order to show more details about each type of portal and search engine. For example, in the PC world, Yahoo! organizes many millions of sites into 14 basic categories and hundreds of sub-categories. This provides users with a simple way to search hierarchically for information. Further, many of the actual sites in Yahoo!'s database provide links to even more detailed information.

Yahoo! became the leading portal due to its early start and the creation of positive feedback between users and information providers. As the number of Internet users grew, the number of Yahoo! users grew, since Yahoo! was the only game in town. And as the number of users increased, the number of firms that wanted to be included on Yahoo!'s portal site also increased; thus positive feedback between users and firms had been created.

The limitation of Yahoo!'s service is that it cannot include as many sites in its service as a search engine service can, because Yahoo! provides a much more extensive screening process than the search engine services. Thus, there is a trade-off between the degree of screening and the number of sites in the database. Categorizing, screening, and organizing sites makes it easier for users to find general information, but no portal site can keep up with the large number of new sites created each day.

For example, as of early April 2001, Yahoo! had 18 sub-categories within the overall category called "e-commerce," which was one of 35 categories within the overall category called "business and economy." But within "e-commerce" there was no category called "mobile Internet." Further, when I did a search of Yahoo!'s e-commerce category in April 2000, I found only one article about the mobile Internet in its database. On the other hand, special-purpose search engine services such as Lycos, Excite, and MSN provided a much longer list of results when I entered the term "mobile Internet."

There are also many specialized portals and search engines in the fixed-line Internet. Amazon.com provides a search service for books and CDs, while other sites provide search services for jobs, hotels, and restaurants. As discussed in Chapter 4, positive feedback between users and firms plays a critical role in the competition between specialized portals and search engines.

Figure 6.2 The Role of Portals and Search Engines in the Fixed-Line and Mobile Internet

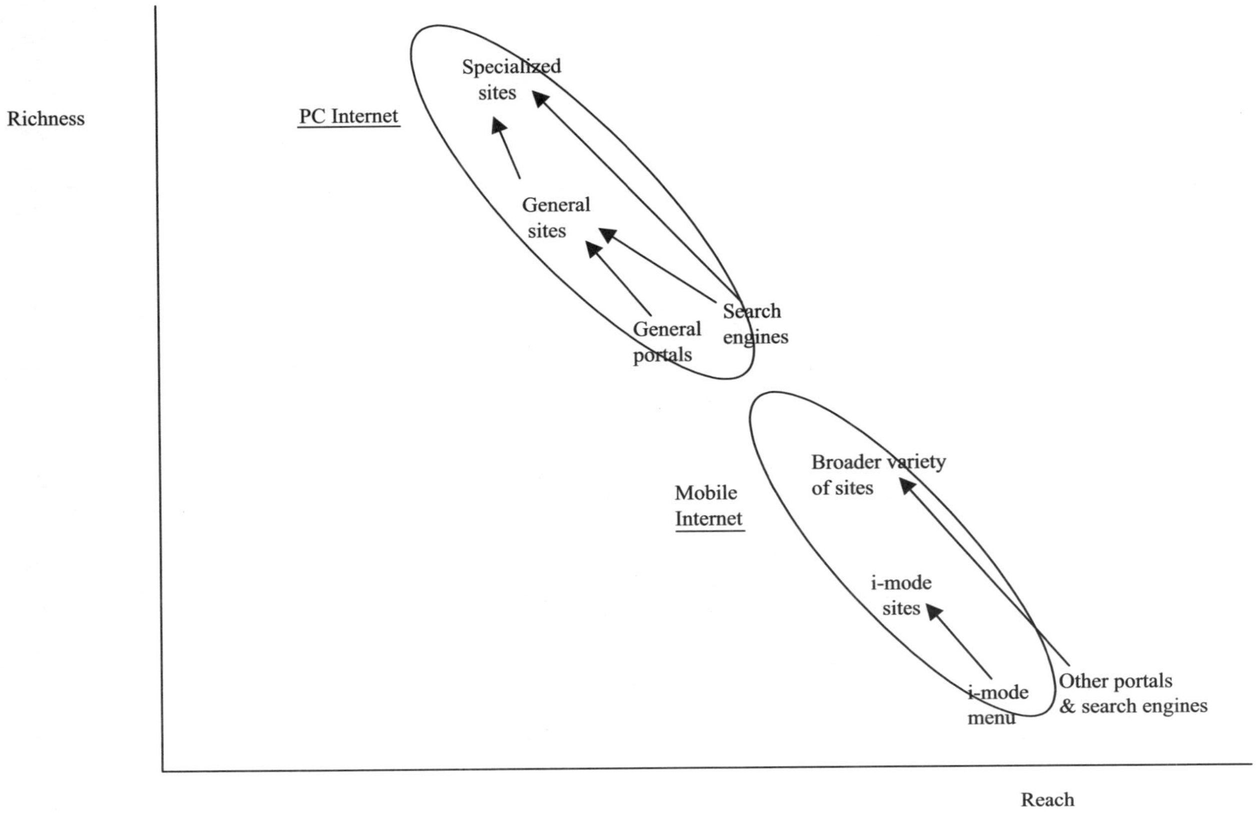

Richness

PC Internet
- Specialized sites
- General sites
- General portals
- Search engines

Mobile Internet
- Broader variety of sites
- i-mode sites
- i-mode menu
- Other portals & search engines

Reach

The Mobile Internet

6.2 Japanese Mobile Portals and Search Engines

NTT DoCoMo's i-mode service includes a portal service which can be characterized as a semi-walled garden approach. When users push the "i" button on their phone, they are presented with a menu of options that includes selections such as "Internet," "bookmark," and "i-mode menu." Since users can access regular home pages through selecting the "bookmark" or "Internet" options, the i-mode service is not a walled garden like those fixed-line portals that pre-date the emergence of the Internet, or like many mobile portals being offered in the US and Europe where users can only access the official contents that the service providers have prepared.

i-mode's "bookmark" option functions in the same way as the "bookmark" selection on the PC; it enables users to register home pages and thus create their own menus. Similarly, the "Internet" selection allows i-mode users to access any home page that is written in c-HTML simply by inputting the URL in much the same way as they access HTML pages (ie., the World Wide Web) on their PC. HTML is the language in which PC home pages are written, and c-HTML is a compact form of HTML that largely restricts the information to text-based information.[1]

The "i-mode menu" is a portal site that provides easy access to NTT DoCoMo's official sites. Like Yahoo!, NTT DoCoMo categorizes, screens, and organizes sites for its users. There were 11 main categories, over 50 sub-categories, and about 4,000 individual sites (offered by 1,480 firms) as of early 2001 on NTT DoCoMo's official menu. These sites have always been free to provide the same information on the fixed-line Internet and other mobile Internet services such as those offered by NTT DoCoMo's competitors.

There are several differences between Yahoo! and NTT DoCoMo's i-mode menu. The key differences include NTT DoCoMo's micro-payment service and its restrictions on linkages to other sites, advertisements, and portals. NTT DoCoMo does not allow linkages between unofficial and official sites, and it must approve linkages between official sites, including the creation of portals by official content providers. These differences are why some people characterize NTT DoCoMo's i-mode service as a semi-walled garden as opposed to a truly open service. The key problem is that NTT DoCoMo's restrictions on linkages between sites prevent the sites on its official menu from directing people to richer information, as Yahoo!'s sites do (see Figure 6.2). This restriction will slow the introduction of richer contents in the Japanese mobile Internet.

Mobile versus Fixed-Line Portal Sites and Search Engines

These restrictions, and the difficulty of NTT DoCoMo keeping up with the large number of applications from content providers, are why there has been tremendous growth in the number of unofficial sites on i-mode. As discussed in Chapter 2, there are more than 10 times the number of unofficial sites as official sites, and if we count pages, the ratio becomes even larger. Digital Street's Oh! New? is by far the largest search engine; in fact, its total number of catalogued sites is considered the "official" number of unofficial sites by NTT DoCoMo and the Japanese press.

The competition between these and other portals and search engines in the Japanese mobile Internet tells us a great deal about the differences between fixed-line and mobile portals and search engines. As with the competition between content providers described in Chapter 5, reach is also the critical variable in the competition between portals and search engines. Portals must first expand the breadth of their services and sites. The breadth of their services will determine the ease with which people can access the sites and, thus, the reach of the portal. The breadth of the sites will determine the number of people who will have an interest in the portal. Once portals have realized the potential reach of mobile phones in their mobile services and sites, they need to turn to richness. We will deal first with services.

6.3 Expanded Reach through New Services

One key service is the screening of content. Mobile portals and search engines need to provide more screening of content than in the fixed-line Internet, due to the smaller screens, relatively high transmission charges, and short viewing times of the mobile Internet. This is one reason why NTT DoCoMo's official content has become so popular. At the other extreme, Digital Street carried out almost no screening in late 2000 and this was readily apparent when one used Oh! New? and received URLs for a large number of sites that had been created by individuals and contained almost no information. This, combined with the fact that users are paying to download this information and may have only a few moments to look at it before they must get off their train or bus, meant there were reportedly many unsatisfied users.

The extreme differences between Oh! New? and the i-mode portal in terms of screening suggests there are probably some intermediate approaches to screening content and providing search routines. These include user evaluations, simpler search routines, multi-channel convergence, and site customization services.

The Mobile Internet

User Evaluations

An inexpensive way to screen content is to provide user evaluations of contents. Digital Street began doing this in early 2001,[2] but more interesting examples can be found in the many magazines that provide information on i-mode unofficial sites. These magazines carry out a screening process in that they provide information on and evaluations of many sites. For example, magazines such as *Nikkei Mobile*, *Dime*, and *Trendy* provide regular evaluations of a large number of phones, PDAs, laptop computers, and mobile Internet content, including unofficial contents.

Simpler Search Routines

Two companies in collaboration with two magazines take the user evaluations one step further and provide an additional and critical mobile portal service of simplifying the method of accessing sites. Although simplifying the inputting of information is also important on the PC Internet, it is even more important in the mobile Internet. For example, Softbank and Giga Flops assign four- to six-digit codes to sites for a small fee and provide a portal site where users can access these individual sites by inputting the codes as opposed to the URLs. Since the URLs for many of these unofficial sites can be as long as 30 digits, the four- to six-digit codes make it much easier for users to access the sites and then bookmark them for future reference.

Softbank does this in collaboration with its magazine *Mobile i*, and Giga Flops does it with Mainichi Communication, which publishes *i-mode Fan*. Both magazines publish the codes next to descriptions of the sites, which, using data from their portal site, they rank in terms of traffic. For example, *Mobile i* ranks all of its sites along with sites in the categories of ringing tones, screen savers, and dating services, while *i-mode Fan* ranks sites in these categories plus sites in the categories of shopping, games, travel, cosmetics and health, gaming and adult, and search and utility. As discussed in Chapter 7, this is one more example of multi-channel convergence where magazines, which currently can provide richer information than phones, complement the high reach of phones.

Fixed-Line Convergence

Yahoo! Japan provides another example of multi-channel convergence and simplifying site access. Here the multi-channel convergence is between the fixed-line and the mobile Internets. Yahoo! Japan is the leading fixed-line Internet portal in Japan (as Yahoo! is in the US), receiving the largest number of page views of all sites in Japan. Although Yahoo! Japan was very slow to enter the mobile Internet, it used its strength in the fixed-line Internet to

Mobile versus Fixed-Line Portal Sites and Search Engines

create a mobile Internet portal in mid-2000; by January 2001, this service was getting more than one million page views a day.

Yahoo! Japan has done this by translating and simplifying about 100 PC sites, which are written in HTML, into mobile sites for i-mode (written in c-HTML) and J-Phone's Sky Service (written in MML).[3] The information on the PC sites is from other companies but it carries the Yahoo! brand name, which means the sites have been screened for quality and interest. The translation is done to some extent automatically using technology that converts documents from one mark-up language to another.

Site Customization Services

Yahoo! Japan also enables its registered users to customize many of these translated PC sites in the same way that the content providers described in Chapter 5 do for their subscribers. Yahoo! Japan provides this service for free to subscribers, who provide it with a variety of personal information. After a user customizes and then accesses a specific Yahoo! site, information about the user's chosen topics is displayed on the site. For example, users can choose specific region(s), company name(s), and product(s), so that when they access the Yahoo! weather, financial, or auction site, the weather for that specific region, the stock price of that specific company, or information about an auction for that specific product is immediately displayed. This reduces the number of inputs that users must perform in order to acquire specific information.

6.4 Expanded Reach through Greater Breadth of Sites

Portal sites clearly need to increase the number and breadth of sites on their portal, since this will determine the number of people who will have an interest in the portal. The portals that obtain an early lead in sites, and thus first create positive feedback between users and sites, often end up the winner. This is how Yahoo! became the leading portal in the fixed-line Internet, and it may have made Oh! New? the winner in the mobile Internet. It is also why leading content providers such as Bandai, Giga Networks, and Toshiba appear to have created a strong advantage in their various content areas.

However, there are several key differences between the fixed-line and mobile Internet which suggest that the competition is not yet over in Japan and is certainly not over elsewhere. The last section discussed the greater importance of screening and simplified inputs in the mobile Internet than in the fixed-line Internet. This section discusses several other differences that

The Mobile Internet

are important for increasing the number of sites on a portal. These include the need to overcome the existence of multiple mark-up languages and the need for micro-payment and user tracking services. Offering these services will provide content providers with more incentives to become part of a specific portal site.

Increase Number of Sites by Adjusting Content to the Handset's Mark-Up Language
Three different mark-up languages are used in Japan, and there will probably be multiple mark-up languages used elsewhere in the world due to the evolution, and gradual convergence, of WAP and c-HTML. In the short term, this convergence will probably increase the number of mark-up languages used, since different content providers and phone manufacturers will move to the new versions of the mark-up languages at different speeds, thus causing a variety of hybrids to appear. Further, the operation of Java programs is very handset-dependent, and thus content providers are forced to develop Java-based content for each type of handset.

In a market in which there is more than one mark-up language and other handset differences, search engines and portals can provide more content — and thus more value — to users by offering the capability to adjust the content to match the specific mark-up language that is used in the phone. This type of search engine or portal would be particularly valuable to subscribers of the service providers who have the least content, and thus probably the fewest subscribers. For example, such a search engine or portal would allow KDDI and J-Phone subscribers to access i-mode content and thus enable these two service providers to overcome their weakness in content as compared to NTT DoCoMo. As described above, Yahoo! Japan is already providing such a service. It adjusts the content to match the mark-up languages used by NTT DoCoMo and J-Phone in their i-mode Sky Web services. Other firms have also announced the start of such portals, although their level of success is still unclear.[4]

Increase Number of Sites by Offering Micro-Payment Services
Second, there are many unofficial sites in Japan that don't have access to the micro-payment services that are available from NTT DoCoMo and the other Japanese service providers. Therefore, many firms are creating alternative micro-payment schemes that use bank transfers, or credit or pre-paid cards, or rely on fixed-line phone or Internet bills. As discussed in the appendix to Chapter 4, none of these micro-payment schemes appears to be generating a very large following. The commissions are quite high for micro-

Mobile versus Fixed-Line Portal Sites and Search Engines

payments with most bank transfers and credit cards, and most of the schemes are difficult to use. Many of the main users of the Japanese mobile Internet don't have credit cards or fixed-line phone or Internet subscriptions. Further, the pre-paid cards are difficult to obtain. Thus, the competition between micro-payment schemes is still wide open and a portal site that also offered a successful micro-payment scheme might be able to attract more content providers than one that did not offer such a service.

As discussed in the appendix to Chapter 4, Keitai Net offers such a micro-payment service, although its success is still uncertain. Users can receive money when they successfully answer questions about advertisements. The money can be used to purchase contents, or it can be downloaded into a postal savings account. Since Keitai Net also offers a search engine, a content production service, and a chat group/communication service, it now offers the widest variety of capabilities of any portal site. However, it had less content and page views than Oh! New? as of early 2001, due primarily to its late start, but also perhaps to the limitations with the micro-payment system. Like the largest search engine provider, Digital Street, Keitai Net would probably increase its chances of success if it also provided a credit card, bank transfer, and/or pre-paid card micro-payment service in its portal.

The third difference between mobile and fixed-line portals and search engines concerns the collection of data on user actions on the Internet and the use of this information for advertising. It is currently not possible for content providers to follow user movements in the Japanese or other mobile Internet markets in the way that it is possible for content providers to do this in the fixed-line Internet. From a privacy standpoint this might be considered an advantage of the mobile Internet, which is of course why many people disable the cookies function in their browser, thus preventing content providers from following their movements.

However, from the standpoint of portals and search engines, the current inability of content providers to follow user movements in the mobile Internet provides them with another opportunity. Portal sites can provide more value to content providers if they offer them the capability to follow user movements within the contents that are in the portal site. This would enable content providers to increase their advertising income and, clearly, their interest in participating in such a portal.

The Mobile Internet

6.5 Expanding Richness

It is expected that competition between portals and search engines will change from reach to richness as the positive feedback in the Japanese mobile Internet causes an evolution of services, phones, content, business models, and portals and search engines. Currently none of the portals and search engines in Japan is providing the kinds of services associated with increased richness that are described here. But just as content providers began turning their attention to richness once they had achieved the potential reach of phones, we can expect to see portal sites and search engines do the same thing once they have realized the potential reach of mobile phones through their expansion of services and sites.

The small size of phone displays and input devices (eg, keyboards) limits the ability of phones to access rich information. And although displays on Japanese mobile Internet phones are much larger than those found outside of Japan, and became larger in 2000 through the success of large-screen phones such as NEC's phones, even larger displays and more innovative input devices will become available in the future. As discussed in Chapter 8, advances in integrated circuits and discrete components continue to reduce the size of the communication functions in phones. This continued miniaturization of the communication functions enables phone manufacturers to increase the size of displays and input devices without increasing the overall size and weight of the phone. Further, as Japanese phone manufacturers have recognized the criticality of displays and input devices, high-performance displays and input devices have emerged and will continue to emerge.

Even now, phone manufacturers could increase the size of displays by making some sacrifices in weight and size. For example, the display size for the NEC phone that was first sold in March 1999 has become the standard display size for phones in Japan. While others have increased the size of their displays to match the size of NEC's phone display, NEC has not increased the size of its displays. Instead, it has retained the same display size and merely reduced the weight in phones that it released in early 2000 and early 2001.

One reason that NEC has done this is that content providers don't adjust their content for the width of phone screens. There are a standard number of characters on one line, and the phones automatically adjust the size of these characters so that one line of characters can fit the width of the phone screen.

Mobile versus Fixed-Line Portal Sites and Search Engines

Thus, phones with wider screens don't necessarily provide the user with a better experience, since currently they either make the characters larger or they leave a blank space at the end of the line.

Adjust Content to Match PDA Screen Sizes

Screen size becomes an even more interesting problem when we consider alternative devices for accessing the mobile Internet, such as PDAs and car navigation systems. Currently, few people access i-mode contents through their PDA or car navigation system, although it is possible to do so by connecting the devices to i-mode phones with the appropriate cables and, in the future, with Bluetooth. One reason few people do this is because, as of July 2001, most i-mode content was not configured for PDA and car navigation screens. Thus, users of these devices don't receive the full benefits from viewing i-mode contents. While one solution is to have content providers independently create special pages for these devices, portals can also provide a useful service in the same way that they can help mobile phone users deal with the different types of mark-up languages that exist in the mobile phone world. Portals can adjust content to fit the size of the PDA or car navigation screen.

Palm Computing has created in the US, and is currently creating in Japan, its own portal site that offers a web clipping service. This service enables users to view PC-based web pages on their Palm Pilots. Although Palm Computing's portals don't automatically adjust mobile or fixed-line Internet content to match the size of its screen, it does provide content providers with a set of tools for adapting their PC-based content for the display size of the Palm Pilot. This is already a successful service in the US, where Palm has acquired several hundred thousand subscribers, and it will also probably be successful in Japan. However, a portal site that automatically adjusted PC-based or mobile phone-based (ie, WAP or i-mode) content for Palm Pilots (or vice versa) would provide additional value for Palm Pilot users.

Adjust Content to Match Car Navigation Screen Sizes
Similar arguments can be made with car navigation systems. Car navigation systems can provide almost the same level of rich information as PCs, and for people who commute by car, they can provide almost the same reach as phones. Thus, car navigation systems could dramatically change the trade-off between reach and richness for car navigation users, of which there are more than five million in Japan.

The Mobile Internet

One of the problems is the need for content that is configured for the car navigation screen. NTT DoCoMo is currently working with several firms to do this for its official i-mode content. But there is a lot of unofficial content that has been created for i-mode and, more importantly, there is a lot of fixed-line content that would be useful for these commuters by car. Portals that can help content providers create this content, or that can automatically adjust the PC or mobile content for car navigation systems, will be more likely to become the winning portals in this area than portals that do otherwise.

Sound Bites

1. **Navigators such as search engines and portals help people to find information.** Navigators help people move from the south-east part of the reach and richness domain to the north-west part of the domain.

2. **Mobile search engines and portals only operate in the south-west corner of the reach and richness domain.** The small screens and keyboards on phones limit their search engines and portals to a small part of the reach and richness domain.

3. **Screening of sites and simplified site access, including customization capabilities, are critical services.** The small screens and keyboards make these services more important on mobile than fixed-line portals and search engines.

4. **Mobile portals and search engines must deal with multiple mark-up languages and screen sizes.** Mobile portals and search engines can provide more content, and thus more value, to users by adjusting content to the device's mark-up language and screen size.

5. **Portals and search engines are positioned to provide micro-payment services and track user movements.** These capabilities are more important for mobile than fixed-line portals and search engines.

Mobile versus Fixed-Line Portal Sites and Search Engines

Notes:

1. In reality, the i-mode phone can access any page that is written in HTML. However, the i-mode browser strips out any non-text information and often presents the text information in a completely disorganized fashion.
2. Digital Street had added a portal service where sites were organized by the type of site, and included recommended sites, by early 2001.
3. Yahoo! Japan also provides a search service for a larger number of sites (>2,000 as of early 2000) that it screens for quality.
4. For example, Access, Excite, and Flex Farm, the latter in combination with Giga Flops, announced the start of such services in 2000.

Chapter Seven:
Multi-Channel Convergence

The mobile Internet is not a simple substitute for the fixed-line Internet, nor is it a simple substitute for TVs, the traditional print media, or even bricks-and-mortar businesses. Yes, there will be competition between these media, and some media will decline in importance. But the real issue is how to effectively combine these different media. This chapter will look at how Japanese firms are combining, and the rest of the world *could* combine, their mobile Internet services with other media in order to utilize the relative advantages of each.

Japanese firms are combining these media for two reasons. First, the high reach, interactivity, and personalization of mobile phones complements the greater richness of other interactive media, such as PCs, car navigation systems, and PDAs, as well as the richness of non-interactive and relatively non-personal devices such as magazines and TVs.

Second, bricks and mortar are a necessary part of many fixed-line and mobile Internet services that involve physical products. Many products can, of course, be special delivered by UPS, Federal Express, or other means, but the delivery fees can sometimes be expensive, particularly in relation to the price of the actual product. Further, there are many cases where people would like to see the physical product before they make a purchase, or they are not at home often enough to receive deliveries there, or they would like someone to handle returns for them. Bricks and mortar provide a way for people to receive, pay for, and, if necessary, return products that they have ordered on the mobile or fixed-line Internets. This is one reason why many bricks-and-mortar companies are playing an important role in the fixed-line Internet.[1]

Figure 7.1 How the Mobile Internet is Changing Product Purchases

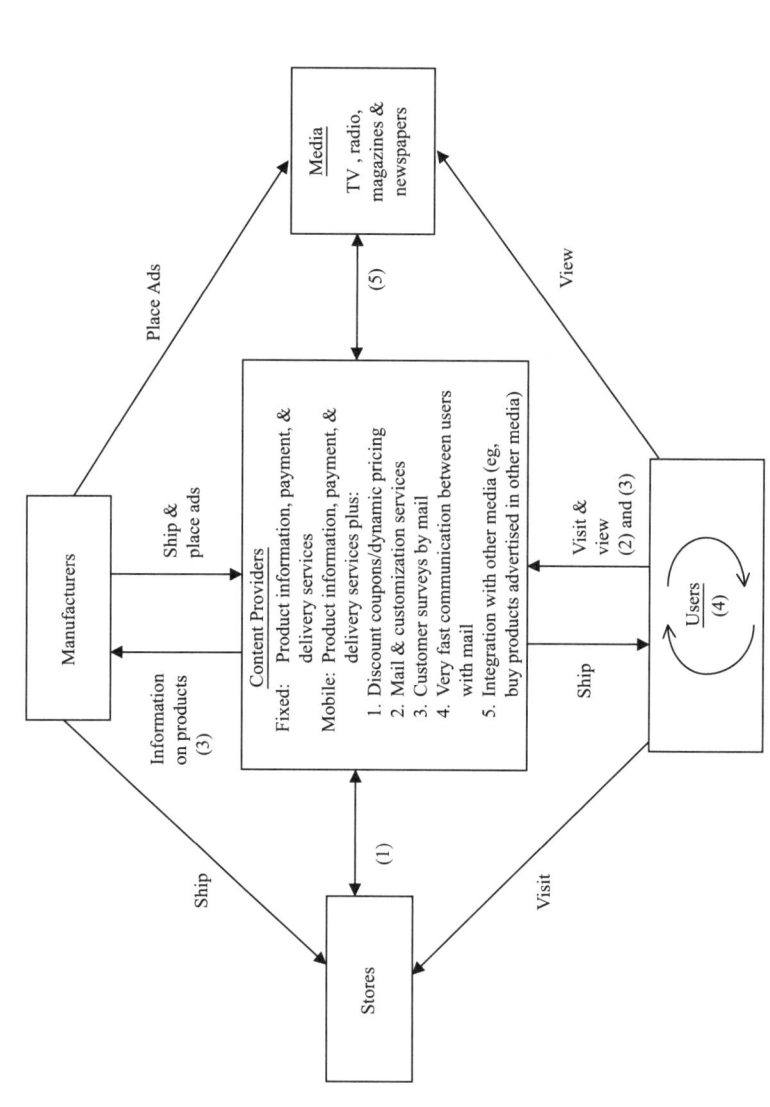

Multi-Channel Convergence

However, mobile phones add some interesting twists to the combination of on-line systems and bricks and mortar — or what will be called here "clicks and mortar." These new twists have been mentioned in earlier chapters but are summarized in Figure 7.1 for one application on the mobile Internet, mobile shopping. As shown in the figure, the discount coupons and dynamic pricing mentioned in Chapter 4, the mail, customization, and survey services described in Chapter 5, and the integration with other media discussed in this chapter will change product purchases by tightening the linkages between content providers, users, stores, the media, and manufacturers. Manufacturers and stores can send discount coupons to phones. Content providers can send mail (including surveys) and provide customization services to users. Mobile mail also tightens the linkages between users, since they can forward mail quickly to friends, colleagues, and family members.

This chapter discusses how some firms are using these techniques to provide customers with new value. But as will become clear, no single firm is using all of these techniques. Thus, we can expect further innovations in the Japanese mobile Internet and elsewhere as firms learn to use all of its new capabilities.

7.1 Fixed-Mobile Convergence

Many people argue that the high growth in the Japanese mobile Internet is due to the low fixed-line Internet usage in Japan. Certainly, Japan's fixed-line Internet usage is lower than in the US but not as low as in many European countries. More importantly, as argued several times in this book, the mobile and fixed-line Internets are complements and not substitutes. Japanese government figures bear this out. At the end of 2000, the government estimated that 37% of Japanese were Internet users, of which 50% were purely PC users, 17% were purely mobile users, and 32% used both platforms.[2] Thus, almost twice the number of people were using both platforms as opposed to just the mobile phone to access the Internet. This high percentage of joint users suggests there is positive feedback occurring between the PC and mobile Internets in Japan. Further, given this high percentage of joint users and the fact that the number of mobile Internet users is growing at about two million per month, it is likely that this positive feedback will continue and that joint users will grow the fastest, followed by the pure mobile users.

The large number of joint users is why almost all Japanese content providers are pursuing fixed-mobile convergence by integrating their fixed-line and

The Mobile Internet

mobile content. Many of them have been providing fixed-line content since 1996 or 1997, and then added mobile content in 1999 or 2000, using the same database and information systems. Their information systems recognize whether the accessing device is a PC or a mobile phone and automatically adjust the content accordingly. As discussed in Chapter 5, they also provide their users with a single integrated account, where users can customize their mobile sites and register for mobile phone mail using either their mobile phone or their PC.

For example, Daiwa and DLJ Direct Securities allow their subscribers to create a single account, which can be accessed from either their PC or their mobile phone. Daiwa subscribers can use the mobile phone or the PC to choose the stocks to be displayed on their mobile phones. These subscribers often use their PCs for analysis and their phones for placing orders.

Toshiba's subscribers can use the PC to select the stations to be displayed on their mobile phones. These subscribers often use the PC site for planning, while the phone is used for real-time information. In the future, Toshiba will enable its subscribers to access information, which they have discovered on the PC site, on the mobile phone site.

Other examples in Chapter 5 of content providers who enable their users to customize their mobile sites and register for mobile phone mail using both their PCs and mobile phones include concert ticket, news, and job information providers. Of course, these types of services can be envisioned for almost all types of content, from cars and hotels, to travel and shopping. As these content providers consider these services, they will need to grapple with the question of how to break up the mobile phone and PC functions and the degree of complexity they offer in each service.

Entertainment providers have a different set of issues to consider when they try to integrate their mobile phone, PC, and even game console (eg, Playstation) services. Many game players would like to continue playing the same or a similar game on their mobile phone when they leave the home. Others might want to transfer the characters between their phones, PCs, and game consoles. Bandai plans to begin offering such a service sometime in 2001. According to Bandai, key issues include user authentication, links between different pages, and a payment mechanism on PCs.

Multi-Channel Convergence

7.2 Phones and Other Mobile Devices

Phones can also be combined with other mobile devices such as PDAs and car navigation systems. Many of the critical issues here are the same as for fixed-mobile convergence. This includes the ability to create a single account for the multiple devices, to exchange information between the devices, and to use the PC to customize sites for the PDAs and car navigation systems. Further, as discussed at the end of Chapter 6, content providers and portals need to adjust their content for the multiple media. Although most Japanese content providers are already doing this for the fixed-line and mobile Internet, they will also need to do it for PDAs and car navigation systems.

One of the challenging aspects of integrating mobile phones and other devices with car navigation systems will involve global positioning systems. GPS enables car navigation systems to display a user's actual location on a map, which is of course shown on the navigation system's display. This enables much richer services and content than are currently offered in the Japanese mobile Internet. Further, as these GPS capabilities become available in phones, content providers will want to integrate the capabilities in both devices so that users can download information from their car navigation systems to their mobile phones when they leave their cars.

7.3 The Mobile Internet and Televisions

Televisions have very high ownership and viewing rates in most of the world's advanced countries, including Japan, the US, and Europe. America's couch potatoes reportedly spend as much as five hours a day in front of their televisions. This is why television represents the largest advertising medium; it dwarfs the advertising revenues of newspapers, magazines, and radio.

The relatively large screens on many televisions enable the presentation of relatively rich information, albeit the definition of richness is in the eye of the beholder. This capability to provide rich information is one of the main differences between televisions and mobile phones, where mobile phones have higher reach than televisions and can provide greater interactivity and personalization than existing television. Of course, digital television is supposed to bring us interactivity along with better resolution.

The Mobile Internet

Does the Mobile Internet Make Digital Televisions Unnecessary?
However, the integration of the mobile Internet and televisions may provide most of what digital television is supposed to offer, at a fraction of the cost. Many Japanese television stations (and radio stations) are already trying to integrate their television and radio services with mobile Internet services, starting with providing information about their television and radio programs on their mobile Internet sites. More than five national and 30 regional television stations and several radio stations were doing this in early 2001, and many of them also provide information in these sites on the products that are advertised on their television or radio programs.

It is easy to envision these television stations expanding these services and providing a large number of shopping and information services on their mobile sites. In the future, viewers may be able to acquire information about the programs, the actors and actresses, and their creators, along with the products that are both advertised and merely used in the actual programs. And they will probably pay for the information. From here, it is a simple step to provide services where viewers could respond to surveys and actually purchase products.

One of the leaders in this area is Fuji Television, which is working with one of the leading providers of entertainment content, Index. Index's involvement is critical, since it understands the mobile phone media better than the television stations. This includes content management, site management, and, to some extent, synergies between the two media. For example, in early 2001 Index started helping Fuji Television sell products that are advertised on Fuji Television's programs. These products are sold on Index's sites, since its sites have much more traffic than Fuji Television's i-mode site. For example, as of mid-March 2001, Index was selling about 200–300 bottles of perfume a month at $50 a bottle.[3] The wholesaler also sells these products on the fixed-line Internet, but the mobile Internet service is doing much better. This alliance goes beyond what people ordinarily envision in digital television. For example, Index was a late starter in the ringing tones market. But by providing songs that are created for Fuji Television's programs, it has been able to obtain more than 100,000 subscribers to its paid service. Many young people become attached to both the program and the theme song and thus download it on to their phone. This is an example of how the personalization of phones can be combined with the richer and popular media of televisions.

Multi-Channel Convergence

Testing Ground for Third-Generation Services
Many of these television stations would also like to become major providers of content for third-generation phone services. Several major Japanese and foreign television stations, such as Japan Television, ESPN, and Bloomberg, provide short videos that cover news, sports, and animation. The purpose of some of these services is to advertise television programs or movies, while some of the other television stations are hoping to develop a new channel for their programming.

For example, Index and Fuji Television began offering video contents in December 2000 when they began showing advertisements for Fuji TV programs on Japan's Personal Handyphone Service (PHS). PHS is a simplified (eg, less expensive) albeit higher-speed version (64 kilo bits per second) of cellular phone services that are primarily used by junior-high and high school students. [4] Index and Fuji Television are hoping to test their ideas for third-generation services in the PHS service.

7.4 The Mobile Internet and the Print Media

Some people, including myself at times, have argued that the Internet will put magazines, newspapers, and catalogues out of business. The fixed-line Internet has certainly failed to do so, due to a lack of reach. Many people enjoy reading magazines, newspapers, and catalogues at their kitchen table, on the couch, or in the bathroom. This is probably one reason why sales of clothing have lagged behind sales of other products on the fixed-line Internet. Many people like to look at catalogues while they are doing things other than sitting in front of a PC.

Some might argue that mobile phones have greater reach than PCs, and thus the mobile and fixed-line Internets together may do to the print media what PCs were not able to do on their own. It is potentially possible for people on the move to read the news just as effectively — and perhaps *more* effectively — on their mobile phones as in newspapers and magazines.

However, magazines, newspapers, and catalogues still provide greater richness than the mobile Internet, and thus they will probably be here for many more years. A good example of this can be found in catalogues and advertisements for products in magazines and newspapers. These catalogues and advertisements provide far greater richness than mobile phones can provide. Their pictures are larger and the color is still better than that found on mobile phone displays as of mid-2001.

The Mobile Internet

But it is the *combination* of the mobile Internet and these catalogues and other print media that is interesting. Several Japanese firms have already begun to take advantage of the potential synergies between the richness of catalogues and magazines and the reach of mobile phones. Firms have created sites where users can order products from catalogues merely by inputting the product code. Even more interesting is that many magazines have also made it possible for readers to use their phones to order products advertised in the magazine. They organize their sites by magazine title, issue, and page numbers. Thus, people can order products while sitting on their couch reading a magazine, watching television, or talking with their family or friends. The larger reach of mobile phones doesn't just mean that people can access the Internet while they are away from home; they can also access it anywhere in their house, including from their couch, bathroom, and bed!

Fixed-mobile convergence may also play an important role here. Many of these sites enable joint mobile and PC accounts so that users can register address and other information on their PC. These joint accounts also enable sites to provide contract conditions on the PC site and to have users verify them on their PC.

Two of the leaders in the Japanese market are Senshukai Co., Ltd., a mail-order house, and Itochu, which works with several magazines.[5] Senshukai offers Senshukai Bellne, a shopping service compatible with the i-mode service. Users of the Bellne service can order products shown in a printed catalog from a cellular phone by entering the order numbers for each item in the catalog. About 90% of the users registered with the service are in their twenties and thirties, just like those registered with its fixed-line PC-based shopping service, which has been in operation for many years. However, the mail-order house discovered that more than 80% of its users order only from their mobile phone. This means that, with the i-mode service, the company was able to attract new users who were either unfamiliar with personal computers or just preferred to do their shopping from their couch!

Itochu, a trading house that does not have a print media business, is also selling products on the mobile Internet through its partnership with Shogakukan, a publisher of women's fashion magazines. Itochu launched the Magaseek service in August 2000 in co-operation with Shogakukan. Users can make purchases with either their mobile phones or their PCs from among about 1,000 items of 52 brands that are advertised in two magazines, *Oggi* and *CanCam*. As of mid-March 2001, about 36,000 users had registered with the service, of which 80% had registered from their mobile phone.

Multi-Channel Convergence

Itochu was getting around 1,500 orders a month and plans to work with other magazines, as well as television programs, in the future. It is very possible that these kinds of services will be even more popular in the US and Europe than in Japan. In particular, America's large catalogue companies could very easily input these kinds of services, reducing the costs of their telephone support staff and increasing consumer satisfaction. Consumers could browse their magazines and phones while they watch TV or talk to their family and friends.

7.5 Clicks and Mortar: Convenience Stores

On-line shopping sites must solve many of the same distribution, payment, and return problems that bricks-and-mortar outlets must solve. In fact, they may have to solve more of them, in that some studies suggest that buyers return far more products purchased on the Internet than in stores or through catalogues.[6] The greater experience with solving these problems provides bricks-and-mortar companies with a critical advantage in Internet-based shopping, which is one reason why many of them have not been driven out of business by the pure Internet players.

Firms with a strong bricks-and-mortar presence, such as convenience stores, grocery stores, post offices, or other firms, could offer these services to Internet content providers. In Japan, convenience stores have started to play that role. There are more than 33,000 convenience stores in Japan; they are typically located near a train or subway station, and about 800 people a day visit the average store. They also have a very well-developed distribution system in which each store is typically visited twice a day.

This distribution system and their convenient locations have helped Japan's early providers of Internet shopping services such as Softbank Corporation and Rakuten (see below) to leap two major hurdles in Japan: payment and delivery. Japanese consumers use credit cards less than the rest of the world and, more importantly, these distribution systems enable Softbank and Rakuten to forgo the expensive investments in distribution made by firms such as Amazon.com. Fixed-line and mobile Internet shopping sites that work with convenience stores don't shoulder the costs of warehousing merchandise, since they can use the convenience stores' warehouses, and they often pay for the products only after they have been sold.[7]

The Mobile Internet

First Stage: Ticket Services

Lawson is the second-largest convenience store (7,300 stores) in Japan and a leader in integrating its point of sale (POS) systems and in-store terminals with the Internet. As discussed in Chapter 5, it is the leading provider of concert tickets in the mobile Internet. A major reason for Lawson's success in selling concert tickets is its in-store terminals, which are integrated with its mobile services. When users reserve a ticket via a regular or mobile phone, they receive a registration number, which they can input into any in-store Lawson terminal and receive a ticket. They pay for the ticket at the register. In the future, users will not have to input the registration number into the in-store terminal; instead, they will merely point their phone at the terminal and a short-range communication technology such as Bluetooth will instruct the terminal to print out the appropriate ticket.

Lawson also makes use of the printed media to simplify ticket reservations. Users can search for tickets in Lawson's ticket magazine, where code numbers are also included to simplify the reservation process. Users can then input the code number into the appropriate place on Lawson's mobile site as opposed to searching for the concert name.

Second Stage: Internet Photo Services

The second stage of Lawson's clicks-and-mortar strategy has been the uploading of photos to the Internet in co-operation with Photo Net Japan. Photo Net Japan originally provided this service in the photo developing outlets of its parent company, Plaza Create, and later in outlets owned by Kodak Japan. Together, these two developing outlets offered uploading services in 2,200 stores; users could have three photos loaded on to the Internet for less than $4. By placing these scanners in Lawson's 7,300 stores, the availability of the service has been greatly expanded. Photo Net Japan is one of the top 10 content providers in i-mode in terms of number of subscribers.

These services enable users to access photos on their mobile phones. Within four days of completing the paperwork, users receive mail telling them how to create their own website with their pictures. And with the spread of color screens and now higher-resolution color displays, it is quite possible that many mobile phone users will find it easier to have their pictures loaded on to the Internet than to carry them around — and, even more so, to remember to carry them around.

Multi-Channel Convergence

Third Stage: Mobile Shopping

The third stage of Lawson's clicks-and-mortar strategy is its creation of a company called i-mode convenience in co-operation with Mitsubishi Trading Company, Matsushita, and NTT DoCoMo in October 2000. Lawson started an i-mode service in May 2001 and users are now able to order products such as books, CDs, and travel products, and to pick them up and pay for them at Lawson stores. They plan to expand the number of these products over time.

The location of convenience stores next to train stations, and the large percentage of train commuters among high i-mode users, will probably make Lawson a major player in the mobile commerce market in Japan. It can provide delivery, pick-up, and payment services for people who spend very little time at home. Many of these mobile people are also young people, the major users of the mobile Internet. Lawson also hopes to get around some of the laws in Japan against discounting products below the suggested retail price by offering a point system. In the fall of 2001, Lawson will connect i-mode with its in-store terminals and POS registers so that users can accumulate these points, which can be traded in for discount coupons on the in-store terminals. In this way, users can save money through making their purchases with their mobile phones.

There are people in every country in the world whose homes are empty during the day. Convenience stores, grocery stores, post offices, or other firms with many outlets could provide these people with an easy way to receive, pay for, and even return their Internet orders. These kinds of services, in combination with mobile phones, would enable websites to reach a new group of customers, be they people who don't own a PC or who spend a lot of time away from their home or office. Further, applications such as the photo uploading service are uniquely appropriate to the mobile phone.

7.6 Clicks and Mortar: Virtual Shopping Malls

Rakuten and Net Price are two firms that offer virtual shopping mall services on the fixed-line and mobile Internets in Japan. Both of these firms offer tenant services where firms can pay between $200 and $500 for a place on their virtual shopping malls. They provide servers, home page formats, data analysis tools, advice, and payment and delivery systems. These services allow tenants to focus on their products, information about these products, and their prices, as opposed to the intricacies of the fixed-line and mobile Internet.

The Mobile Internet

Rakuten

Rakuten was the first firm to offer these services and is still the largest supplier. It had 6,930 stores in its PC virtual shopping mall as of June 2001, which sold more than 820,000 different products. At this time, it had more than 680,000 registered users, most of whom received delivery of these products at their home and paid for them via credit card, bank transfer, or COD (cash on delivery); around 20% picked them up at convenience stores.

Rakuten started its mobile shopping mall in August 2000 and is doing a lot of things that the content providers and portals described in Chapters 5 and 6 are doing. It has assigned six-digit codes to each mobile store, which users input on the Rakuten mobile site for immediate access to the store. It set up a membership system where members can register addresses and other information on their PC or phone so that they can access this information each time they make a purchase from any place in Rakuten's mobile shopping mall. It also sends members mail about newly added stores.

Rakuten also started a magazine in July 2001 where users can order products simply by inputting the appropriate product code at the portal site level. Thus, users don't have to find the specific site to order a product from the site. Not only does the magazine support Rakuten's virtual shopping mall, it also provides additional revenues from advertisements in the magazine. Although members don't pay to have their products listed in the magazine, they do pay to have their products featured in full-page advertisements.

Net Price

Net Price has added a unique service to its mobile shopping mall that makes use of the fast rates of communication available with mobile e-mail. Users can receive discounts by buying products in bulk, and the fast rates of communication between users with mobile e-mail enable them to pull together multiple buyers. Each week, stores offer about 20 different products, which include discounts of between 10% and 30% for multiple purchases. These products are typically high-margin, brand-name products such as clothing, ladies' handbags, watches, jewelry, and other accessories.

Users can find these products at the store sites, or they learn about them in the mail service that Net Price provides for subscribers to this discount service. By inputting the number of units they expect to purchase, subscribers can determine the discount they will receive if they are able to gather together the required number of buyers. They have one week in which to find these buyers, and their mobile e-mail plays a strong role in this search. They can easily send the mail that explains the discount to their friends. As of June

Multi-Channel Convergence

2001, Net Price was sending mail each week to about 300,000 users and it had $800,000 in sales. In the future, Net Price will expand the number of products and provide multiple product-specific mail services as opposed to the current single mail service.

It is highly likely that Net Price's product discounting service will be popular with young people the world over. Young people are very sensitive to both price and brand names, clearly an oxymoron. But a service like Net Price's can partially eliminate this oxymoron and bring added value to young people. It can also help eliminate the large numbers of unsold stock that often exist in high-margin, brand-name products.

7.7 Clicks and Mortar: Movie and Video Stores

Tsutaya is the largest provider of video rentals and sales and the second-, third-, and fifth-largest seller of CDs, books, and games, respectively, in Japan. It had more than 1,000 stores as of early 2001 and more than 14.5 million members. It also had the sixth-highest-rated website in Japan at this time, which is operated by its fully-owned subsidiary, Tsutaya Online. Its story is relevant to those bricks-and-mortar companies that would like to use the Internet to bring more customers into its stores, which Tsutaya has achieved.

Tsutaya Online's PC Internet site was opened in July 1999 and its i-mode site was opened in August 1999, six months after i-mode services began. Tsutaya was one of the entertainment companies that noticed the popularity of entertainment content such as screen savers and horoscopes on i-mode in the spring of 1999 and quickly applied for and started an official i-mode site. Its site first offered information on movies, music, books, and games. Like the content providers described in Chapter 5, Tsutaya Online quickly began offering a mail service to its subscribers to simplify their information searches. Along with opening sites with the other service providers such as KDDI and J-Phone, it has subsequently expanded the richness of its sites with discount coupons, an experimental music delivery service, and sales of music-related products.

Tsutaya Online had 1.5 million members at the end of March 2001, of which 60% were mobile phone members; the remainder were PC members. Although this number is small compared to Tsutaya's 14.5 million members, the on-line number is growing at more than 10% a month and Tsutaya expects this percentage to rise as it begins further promoting Tsutaya Online

The Mobile Internet

membership in its Tsutaya stores. Tsutaya began creating special corners in its stores to promote mobile phone membership in March 2001. It had done this for 12 stores by the end of March 2000 and expected to have done so for 200 stores by the end of March 2002.

On-line subscribers can use both PCs and mobile phones to access Tsutaya Online's sites. Typically, users search for information on the PC while they receive information on their phones through mail. Young people and music are more popular on the mobile site, while movies are more popular on the PC site. The average age of PC subscribers is over 30, while the average age of mobile subscribers is about 21. Thus, Tsutaya Online has been able to use the Internet to reach new customers with the Internet overall and the mobile Internet in particular.

Mail Service

Mail is a major part of Tsutaya Online's mobile contents. As of the end of 2000, Tsutaya Online offered 30 kinds of artist-specific mail, along with three kinds of general mail on movies, books, and games. While this general mail is free, the artist-specific mail costs about $2 a month. Tsutaya Online charges for the artist-specific mail because this mail helps users find information about the music for specific artists they are interested in without having to search for it on the small phone screens.

In March 2000, Tsutaya Online was sending six million mail messages a week, of which almost 80% were sent to mobile phones. This number of mail messages was more than 80% greater than in December 2000. Seventy percent of Tsutaya Online's subscribers also subscribe to one of the mail services. Although Tsutaya Online does not release the number of paying subscribers to these mail services, it also makes money on the free PC and, in particular, the mobile phone mail, since advertisements are included in this mail. And at $0.20 to $0.30 per mail mobile phone message, the 11.2 million messages a month represent a potential monthly advertising income of $2–3 million.

More interestingly, these mail services have increased the number of visitors to the Tsutaya stores. Tsutaya Online measured this by looking at the ratio of rentals and purchases by Tsutaya Online members (who receive mail) to the rentals and purchases by regular Tsutaya members. For example, after sending mail to Tsutaya Online members in August 1999 concerning three different movies, the ratio of rentals by Tsutaya Online members to overall

Multi-Channel Convergence

Tsutaya members for these movies rose from 1.6, 2.6, and 2.8 for each movie, to 3.8 for all three.

Even stronger results have been found with music purchases by combining the mail and a sample music listening service. Tsutaya Online started such a service on December 14, 1999 where users could listen to 45 seconds of a song. It sent mail on December 7 and 14 to its members concerning new CDs that would be released and available on the listening service on December 14, and it subsequently sent mail containing music rankings on December 21, 22, and 29. These mailouts and the trial listening service caused the ratio of purchases by Tsutaya Online to purchases by regular Tsutaya members to increase dramatically. For example, about 2.8% of the Tsutaya Online members purchased the CD versus 0.7% of the regular Tsutaya members, or a difference of 400% over the relevant two-week period.

Discount Coupons

Tsutaya Online began making discount coupons available on its Internet sites and sending them to its members via mobile phone mail in the spring of 2000. Users could redeem the coupons either by bringing a printed version of them into the store or by showing a mobile phone screen while the coupon was displayed. Although it wanted to send discount coupons for all of the products that it sells in the Tsutaya stores, it restricted them to rentals since the retail law prevents sales discounts on music, videos, and similar products.

Tsutaya Online quickly found that discount coupons that are sent in the mail have a particularly strong effect on rentals. Of 240,000 coupons that were sent between May and July 2000, 7% of them, or 16,000, were used. This is higher than the 2% rate with direct mail. In July, Tsutaya Online saw a 70% increase in their usage and, in spite of discounts, a 59% increase in rental income. By late 2000, the usage of discount coupons had experienced even further increases. It was sending 320,000 discount coupons a month, 90,000 of which were being redeemed.[8]

One can also see the strong effect of sending discount coupons by mail from looking at the relative increase in Tsutaya Online and regular Tsutaya customers once coupons are made available. Table 7.1 summarizes the increase in rental customers and sales after discount coupons were made available on its site and in Internet mail in late 2000. The number of rental customers and sales prior to making these discount coupons available has been normalized to 1.0. Although the number of customers and sales for both Tsutaya Online and regular Tsutaya customers increased after the

The Mobile Internet

discount coupons were made available, the increase was much larger (about 30%) for Tsutaya Online members. They received the discount coupons in the mail, while the other customers had to access them on the PC or mobile Internet sites. It is also interesting that the discount coupons caused the amount of total sales to increase, which suggests that Tsutaya Online has found new customers with these discount coupons. Further, although the number of sales and customers did decrease once the time limit for the discount coupons ended, it did not immediately return to the level of customers and sales that existed before the discount coupons became redeemable.

Table 7.1 Number of Customers and Sales Before, During, and After Discount Coupons are Redeemable

Time Period	Number of Customers		Sales	
	Tsutaya On-line Members	Regular Tsutaya Customers	On-line Members	Regular Customers
10/15 – 11/1 (Before)	1.0	1.0	1.0	1.0
11/2 – 11/12 (During)	1.45	1.09	1.41	1.1
11/13 – 11/26 (After)	1.08	1.11	1.11	1.14

Tsutaya Online's success with discount coupons has caused other firms to ask it to send coupons and distribute free products for them. It sends product surveys in mobile mail to its Tsutaya Online members and then sends product coupons to those people who complete the surveys. Users can redeem the coupons at the Tsutaya outlets. Twelve firms were participating as of February 2001. For example, Tsutaya Online was distributing cup noodles for Nisshin, and gasoline and car wash discount coupons for Shell Oil. Tsutaya Online receives several million Yen from each company for sending the product surveys and it expects increased sales from people who pick up free products and discount coupons at their stores.[9]

Competitive Advantage

Tsutaya Online is one of the most successful firms in the Japanese mobile

Multi-Channel Convergence

Internet. It receives income for its mail services in the form of subscription fees and advertisements in the mail. In fiscal 2000, 10% of its income was from advertisements that were placed in this mail, including the product surveys. It has also used this mail and the discount coupons to increase the number of its customers. The increased customers demonstrate the power of multi-channel convergence. Tsutaya Online has successfully combined the reach of phones with a rich selection of videos, music, and other entertainment products in its stores.

Its success with discount coupons and sales of music-related products (as described in Chapter 4) is also making its site a major portal for young people. Other firms want to distribute coupons on Tsutaya's sites and products in Tsutaya's stores due to its strong brand image with young people. Tsutaya's success with selling music-related products also suggests that it will become the center for distributing music and video clips with third-generation services.

Tsutaya's success can probably be replicated in a number of other countries and industries. Firms can combine the reach of phones with the richness of the product selections in their stores. This is particularly true for products that are popular with young people, such as music, movies, clothing, and cosmetics. The challenge is to offer an information service that helps users learn about new products and services, and to offer this information in a way that is easy for users to obtain, such as by using mail registration and site customization services. This can then be followed by discount coupons and, later, richer information and services.

Sound Bites

1. **Integration is more important than competition between channels.** The mobile Internet is not a simple substitute, but actually a complement for the fixed-line Internet, TVs, the traditional print media, and even bricks-and-mortar businesses.

2. **Firms should combine the high reach, interactivity, and personalization of mobile phones with the greater richness of other media.** Other media, such as PCs, car navigation systems, PDAs, magazines, and TVs, lack the reach and, in some cases, the interactivity and personalization of mobile phones.

The Mobile Internet

3. **The mobile Internet facilitates purchases of advertised products.** People can purchase items with a mobile phone when they see the items advertised on TV or in a magazine or catalogue.

4. **Just like the fixed-line Internet, the mobile Internet can increase the value of bricks and mortar.** Bricks and mortar are needed to provide many products and services, and the mobile Internet enables people to more easily carry discount coupons and other information into the bricks-and-mortar outlets.

Notes:

1. For example, see D. Pottruck and T. Pearce, *Clicks and Mortar: Passion Driven Growth in an Internet Driven World* (New York: Jossey-Bass, 2000).
2. Reed Stevenson, "Japan continues to embrace Net in a wireless way," *Yahoo News*, July 9, 2001.
3. The purchasers were paying for the products upon receipt of them, with Index taking responsibility for the payments. There are apparently very few returns with the cash on delivery method in Japan.
4. PHS services were started in mid-1995 by three service providers and there are now about six million subscribers to these services. The system uses lower power base stations and phones than regular cellular systems. The lower power of these base stations and phones makes it difficult for signals to enter buildings, and other simplifications in PHS mean that PHS phones cannot be used in vehicles traveling at high speeds. However, the high-speed data capabilities mean that many of the non-voice services now being offered by cellular service providers were first offered by PHS service providers.
5. Both of these examples are taken from an article that appeared on the Asia Biz Tech home page, "NTT DoCoMo's I-mode service enters its second phase," March 26, 2001.
6. Bob Tedeschi, "E-commerce report: Returns pose problem for e-tailers," *New York Times*, May 28, 2001, Technology section.
7. This is summarized from an article by Stephanie Strom, "E-commerce the Japanese way: Ubiquitous convenience stores branch into cyberspace," *New York Times*, March 18, 2000, Technology section.
8. "Mobariu wo jiku ni kurikkusu to morutaru (Clicks and mortar, the base of the mobile Internet)," *Mobile Media Magazine*, January 2001.
9. "Tsutaya onrain, netto kaiin muke ni, keitai tsukai kigyou koukoku hansoku — muryou shouhinken (Tsutaya Online is giving its members coupons for free products as advertisements for those firms)," *Nikkei News*, March 6, 2001, p. 15.

Chapter Eight:
Mobile versus Fixed-Line Content:
The Future

Business models, portals/search engines, content, and information strategies for content providers are evolving at a furious pace in the Japanese market through the positive feedback that has been created between portals and search engines, services content, users, phones, and business models. NTT DoCoMo and the other Japanese service providers created this feedback through a focus on the *initially* appropriate services, content, users, phones, business models, and portals/search engines, unlike service providers in the West. Chapter 3 used the concepts of reach and richness to describe why simple entertainment content, young users, and simple business models and portals are initially the most appropriate.

This chapter describes how this positive feedback is causing a trade-off between reach and richness to change (see Figure 8.1). Thus, this chapter is highly speculative. So far, this book has attempted to explain why things have happened the way they have in the Japanese market and how similar things may occur elsewhere. This chapter will attempt to predict what will happen next in the Japanese and then other markets, clearly a difficult and highly uncertain task.

It is the evolution of phones, other devices, and services, and their potential effect on the other items in the positive feedback — in particular, content — that is of most relevance to the trade-off between reach and richness. Phones with larger screens, better displays, larger memory, internal cameras, and other capabilities, along with Java and high-speed data services, will enable phones to access richer information. The diffusion of devices such as PDAs and car navigation systems, which already have larger screens and better displays and thus can access richer information than phones, will also

Figure 8.1 New Phones, Higher Speed Data Services & New PDAs will Continue to Change the Reach & Richness Trade-off

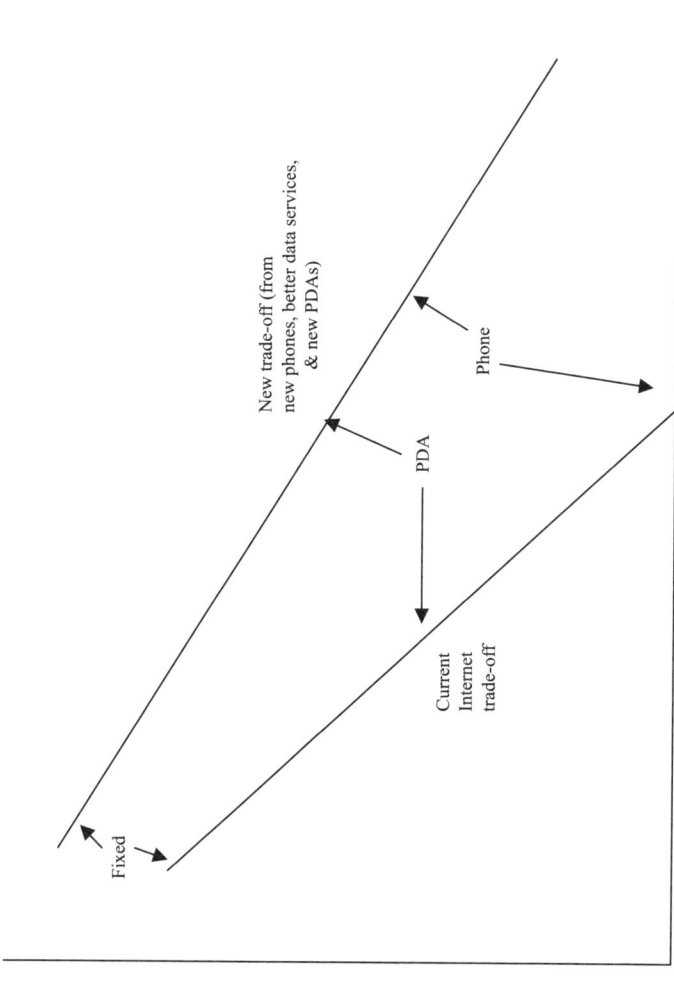

Mobile versus Fixed-Line Content: The Future

accelerate, thus increasing their reach. Finally, the concepts of phones, PDAs, and other devices will blur as manufacturers start to use the concept of wearable computing. They will break up and distribute the various phone functions into multiple devices that exchange data wirelessly. The use of multiple devices will enable manufacturers to make the input (eg, keyboards) and output devices (eg, displays) much larger and thus capable of accessing richer information. This chapter deals with each of these individually, beginning with advances in semiconductor technology and its effect on displays, computing power, and embedded cameras.

8.1 Greater Richness through Advances in Semiconductor Technology

Advances in semiconductor technology have led to reductions in the size, weight, and cost of computing, phones, digital cameras, and many other electronic products. It is generally believed that these advances will continue and thus provide manufacturers of electronic devices with the means to further reduce the size, weight, and cost of their devices.

Manufacturers of mobile phones can use these advances to reduce the size, weight, and cost of mobile phones, or to add new functions such as larger screens, better displays, or greater computing power. Most of the world's mobile phone manufacturers have pursued all of these simultaneously over the last 10 years, with a particular focus on the first two. Over the last decade, phones have become smaller, lighter, and cheaper, and it is very likely that this trend will continue for several years.

This is particularly true in Japan, where manufacturers have concentrated on reducing the size and weight of their phones. As described in Chapter 4, the high activation commissions paid by Japanese service providers have enabled Japanese manufacturers to use a greater amount of new technology, and thus to pursue weight and size reduction more than Western manufacturers. This new technology includes the latest integrated circuits, discrete components, printed circuit boards, and batteries. Sub-100 gram phones were first released in late 1996, and in 1997 more than 50% of the phones sold weighed less than 100 grams.

Larger Displays
However, the size and weight of Japanese phones had reached a point of diminishing returns by 1998. Phones weighing less than 70 grams were common, even those capable of displaying multiple lines of text. Thus, it

Figure 8.2 Evolution of Weight and Screen Size for Japanese Mobile Phones*
(Numbers refer to the year in which the phone was released)

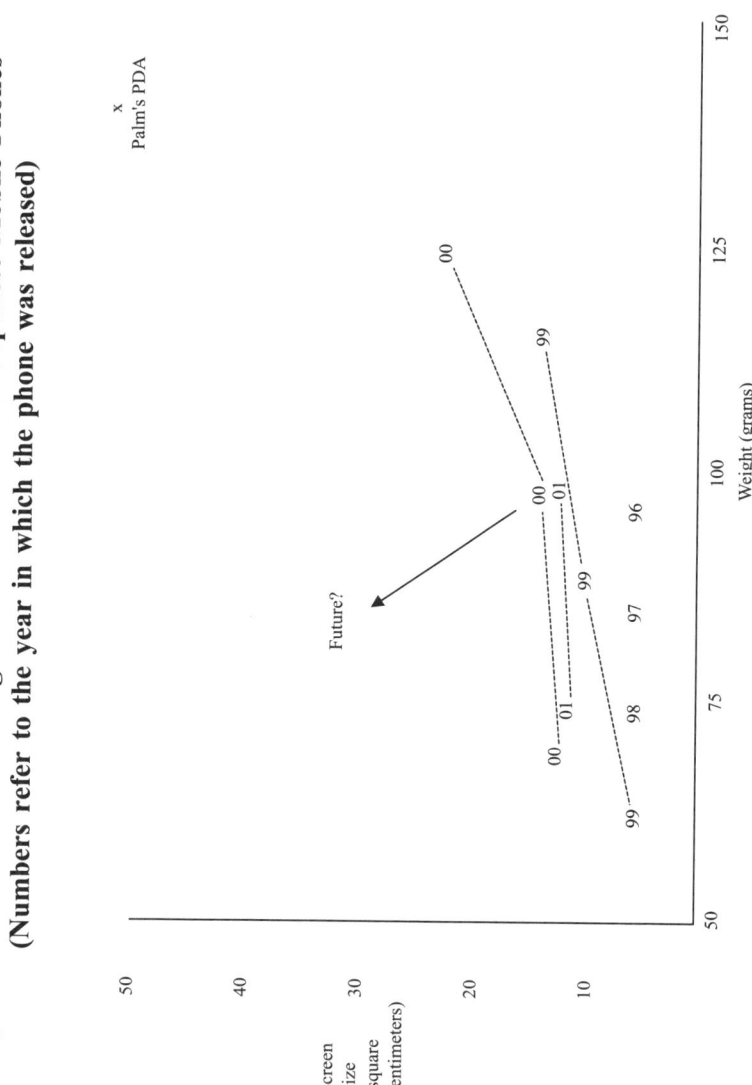

*Only phones from NEC, Panasonic, and one phone from Sharp (125 gram phone) are shown

Mobile versus Fixed-Line Content: The Future

became possible for Japanese manufacturers to add new functions such as larger screens, better displays, and greater computing power to their mobile phones just as NTT DoCoMo started i-mode services in February 1999. NTT DoCoMo's mobile phone manufacturers added these new functions by making sacrifices in the size, weight, and cost of phones.

As shown in Figure 8.2, the first group of i-mode phones, which were released in early 1999, ranged in weight from 89 grams to 115 grams. The lightest phone was capable of displaying six lines of eight Japanese characters, and the heaviest one was capable of displaying 12 lines of 10 characters. Manufacturers released a second group of i-mode phones in early 2000, ranging in weight from 69 grams to 125 grams and with an even larger variety of display sizes.[1]

Better Displays and Higher Computing Power

With the third group of i-mode phones, released in early 2001, manufacturers turned their attention to improving display quality and increasing the computing power of the phones, which caused display size to decrease slightly. Although some manufacturers had introduced color displays in their second-generation i-mode phones, all of the third-generation phones had color displays and were superior in color quality to the previous generation. For example, one of the phones is able to display more than 65,000 different colors. Further, the third group of i-mode phones also included greater computing power in order to handle Java programs.

Manufacturers are expected to continue increasing the computing power in phones to this end. The Java capabilities in the third group of i-mode phones are severely limited due to restrictions on the size of the Java Applets, which are 10,000 bytes. Greater computing power also makes it possible to play music, which Sony has done with one of its phones that is compatible with another service provider's mobile Internet service (not i-mode). This phone contains Sony's memory stick, which can be used to transfer music from a PC to the phone after the music has been downloaded to the PC from the Internet.

Embedded Cameras

Another interesting trend is small cameras in phones. In late 2000, Sharp released a phone that is compatible with another service provider's mobile Internet service (not i-mode) and includes an internal camera. The camera has 110,000 pixels and only adds six grams in weight and less than $10 to

The Mobile Internet

the cost of the phone. These phones have already created a large impact on the Japanese market, and the small cameras will probably become standard items on most phones by the year 2002, just as color displays have already become standard items. Users can add text and characters to pictures and exchange them with friends via e-mail. It is also possible to print out pictures at kiosks. At some point, the use of embedded cameras may reduce the need for hard-copy pictures, but further improvements in display technology are still needed.

Although, in the near term, entertainment sites will be the main beneficiaries of these camera phones and improved displays, it is likely that these technologies will also have an impact on other content. Internal cameras, and to some extent the new detachable cameras (along with the better displays and other technological advancements), will drive the addition of pictures to mobile Internet sites. We can envision pictures being useful for sites that rent hotels, sell used cars, provide surfing news or dating services, rent apartments, sell clothing, or promote restaurants, as well as many other sites. Thus, these new camera-compatible devices will cause an evolution from simple to rich content.

Market Competition Will Determine the Key Functions

Larger display sizes, better displays, increased computing power, and camera-compatible phones will help phones move from the high-reach and low-richness area to areas of higher richness, as shown in Figure 8.1. As to which of these items will have the largest impact on enabling phones to access richer contents, in the end, the market will decide which of the various phones best meets user needs. Although manufacturers focused on display quality, computing power, music, and internal cameras in the third group of mobile-Internet-compatible phones, it is quite possible that display size will again become an important area of competition in the future. This will probably happen once all manufacturers have introduced high-resolution color displays, embedded cameras, and sufficient computing power to utilize Java-based programs, which will probably occur by early 2002 in the fourth group of mobile-Internet-compatible phones.

Competition in display size will cause phones to again move in the northwest direction shown on Figure 8.2. As it becomes possible to make phones thinner, it becomes easier to design folding phones. So-called clamshell phones, which were first made popular by Motorola and are now very common in Japan, only include a single horizontal fold in the phone. Nokia's Communicator folds in the opposite direction, thus providing the user with

Mobile versus Fixed-Line Content: The Future

a larger screen and keyboard. It is now possible for Japanese manufacturers to design a phone with a similar-size screen and keyboard to Nokia's Communicator weighing less than 160 grams. With some sacrifices in screen and keyboard size, it is possible for some Japanese manufacturers to make a similar phone with a 40-square-centimeter display that weighs less than 130 grams. In Japan, 130 grams is still considered too heavy for consumers, so the Japanese manufacturers are not releasing such a phone. Further, content are designed for a specific horizontal screen size, so consumers would not receive the full benefits from larger displays. But in the future, such problems will be solved and phones with 40-square-centimeter displays will be available in Japan and subsequently in other markets.

It is only a matter of time before these developments reach the rest of the world. While the lower activation commissions paid by service providers in the US and Europe will slow the emergence of these devices, it is possible that the lower service charges available in the West will eventually make them more widely used than in Japan. The critical challenge is to create the positive feedback between phones, users, content, business models, and search engines/portals so that phones will evolve and become capable of accessing rich information.

8.2 Greater Richness through Higher-Speed Services and Phones

When this book was being written in the spring of 2001, there was a great deal of uncertainty about so-called third-generation services. NTT DoCoMo had delayed the start of these services, which it was calling FOMA (Freedom of Mobile Multimedia Access), from late May until the fall of 2001, and no other service provider was planning to start such services in 2001. In fact, many European service providers were planning to delay the start of services until 2003, and most US service providers were talking about 2005. These delays reflect both technical and market uncertainties.

Technical Uncertainties
New technologies generally experience problems and there is no reason to believe that third-generation mobile phone technologies such as wide-band CDMA (W-CDMA) will be any different. Second-generation GSM (the world's global standard for second-generation digital phones) services were delayed by more than a year due to a lack of handsets, a problem that is also causing delays in the start of third-generation services. For example, in March 2001, NTT DoCoMo announced that only two of 11 handset manufacturers

The Mobile Internet

that had signed contracts to provide them with third-generation phones would be ready for the launch of its services, originally scheduled to be operational in May 2001.

Also in early 2001, NTT DoCoMo regularly announced that it did not expect to sell many third-generation handsets in the first year of service, with a typical estimate being 150,000 phones. Compare this with the 40 million current-generation phones that are being sold in Japan each year. Reasons given for the low sales forecasts include the lack of phones, their high cost, and the uncertainty in applications. Devices for a new technology are often initially very expensive but become cheaper as manufacturers go down the learning curve and increase volumes. This seems also to be the case in third-generation phones, as many Japanese manufacturers claim that the new phones will initially cost about $1,500 each. Even if NTT DoCoMo continues subsidizing phones at the current levels, it will be difficult for users to acquire these new phones at a reasonable price.

Market Uncertainties
NTT DoCoMo and the rest of the world are also concerned about applications for third-generation services, due to the small screens of the phones and high data charges. The small screens may prevent users from accessing rich content even when high-speed data services are available. Although most PC users do not have access to anywhere near the speeds that are possible with third-generation services, they will probably still be able to access richer content than mobile phone users even when third-generation mobile services start. Thus, third-generation services may not become popular until mobile phone screen sizes either become larger or devices with larger screens, such as PDAs and car navigation systems, become more popular (see below).

Data charges are also an issue; they are ¥0.05 per packet (one packet is 128 bytes), or one-sixth the current level of i-mode data charges. This can be considered a very large decrease if the data charges are applicable to the small amounts of data that users currently download on i-mode. Many Japanese content providers have told me that this would be the biggest impact of Japan's third-generation services on the mobile Internet. On the other hand, many people argue that these charges are too high for the higher bandwidth applications that NTT DoCoMo plans to offer, such as video (see Table 8.1), TV phone, and music downloading services, to succeed. For example, many people have argued that data charges must be set at one-tenth their current levels for the downloading of music to be commercially viable.[2]

Mobile versus Fixed-Line Content: The Future

Table 8.1 Key Video Services in NTT DoCoMo's Third-Generation Service

Application	Service Name	Contents
Entertainment	Everywhere Video	Animation
	Japan TV	TV channel guide and pro wrestling
	Laughing Channel	Stand-up comedy
Movies & Music	Tsutaya Online	Movie rankings and previews
	Star Channel	Movie and Hollywood news
	Special Music Channel	Live concerts and interviews
News & Sports	Bloomberg News	Financial and other news
	ESPN	WorldCup, pro basketball, and other sports
	Kanetani Golf	Golf lessons
Information	Elle Navi	Information about brand products
	Doctor Navigation	Health advice and hospital guide
	Kanebo Beauty Square	Makeup, skin care, and diet advice

Source: "FOMA ga ijoiyosuta-to: Jisedai Ke-tai wa, Kirifuda ka (Are next-generation phones the key to a successful start of FOMA.services?)," *Trendy*, May 2001, pp. 30–45.

Even more controversial is whether NTT DoCoMo can make money with these data charges. Many people argue that NTT DoCoMo would be unable to make money even if it sets the charges at six times their current level![3] This suggests that business applications (such as those described below) may be the first major applications for third-generation services. This will cause third-generation services to evolve much more slowly than i-mode services have evolved, a result that could pose problems for all service providers. A slow evolution suggests long payback times, since the low phone volumes will prevent phone prices from declining and thus new content from appearing.

Uncertainty Outside of Japan

There appears to be even greater uncertainty in the rest of the world about third-generation services. One reason for this is the lack of success of the mobile Internet outside of Japan. With relatively few subscribers and even fewer actual users of current applications, it is not clear who will want to use more complex and high-speed services to download data to small phone screens. And with the high investments associated with these third-generation services, many service providers are clearly concerned about the high risks associated with implementing them. The British and German service providers who paid high fees for licenses are in the most trouble. They have no choice: they have to implement the third-generation services in order to recoup the fees that they paid for their licenses.

The rest of the world has its work cut out for it. Without a successful mobile Internet or Intranet (see the next section) service to add video and business applications, the third-generation consumer and business services in Europe and the US are likely to fail in the short term. High-speed third-generation services are nothing but a new feature for the mobile Internet, one that is even rarely used on the fixed-line Internet. The rest of the world needs to create successful mobile Internet businesses that use the current technology before implementing third-generation systems.

8.3 Greater Reach of Car Navigation Systems

The diffusion of devices such as car navigation systems and PDAs will also change the trade-off between reach and richness (see Figure 8.1). The larger and often higher-quality displays found on car navigation systems and PDAs enable these devices to display and process richer information than mobile phones. The problem with these devices is their low reach. As discussed in Chapter 3, the reach shown in Figures 3.1 to 3.3 is the *theoretical* reach of these devices. In actuality, these devices still have a very low reach everywhere except in car navigation systems in Japan.

In Japan, more than seven million car navigation systems were already being used in early 2000 and more than one million a year are sold. Car navigation

Mobile versus Fixed-Line Content: The Future

systems that can access the Internet, including i-mode content, became available in late 2000. The sales of these Internet-compatible devices are currently small and the usage is even smaller. The problem with using these car navigation systems to access the Internet is that there are fixed-line and mobile Internet content that is compatible with the size of the car navigation display. And content providers will not adjust their content until they believe users want to access them on a car navigation system.

Someone will have to create the positive feedback between this content and users. This is why Chapter 6 argues that portals can help mobile phone users deal with the different types of devices and mark-up languages that exist in the mobile phone world. Portals that adjust content to fit the size of a car navigation or PDA screen can create this positive feedback between users and content providers and probably succeed better than portals that do not provide this service.

In the case of car navigation systems, NTT DoCoMo is already playing this role. It is working with many content providers to reconfigure their content for the larger screen sizes of car navigation systems. In fact, several content providers, including providers of restaurant, map, and other local information, already claim to have reconfigured their content for car navigation system. But there is a lot of unofficial i-mode content and even more PC-based content that could be reconfigured for the size of the car navigation display. Just as the traffic to unofficial content sites has already exceeded that to official content in i-mode, similar things will probably occur in car navigation systems. Therefore, there are still many opportunities for these kinds of portals in Japan and even more opportunities in the rest of the world.

8.4 Greater Reach of PDAs

For the rest of the world, where car navigation systems have a very low level of use, PDAs offer greater possibilities for accessing rich content. They have larger screens than mobile phones and, due to their relatively small size, they potentially have much higher reach than PCs. PDAs can be used by themselves if they contain an internal communication function, or in conjunction with a mobile phone and a cable. For users who are standing while they are accessing the mobile Internet, as is often the case in Japan, short-range wireless transmissions technologies such as Bluetooth offer greater usage. Two devices that contain Bluetooth can communicate for free at short distances. For example, a user with a mobile phone and PDA that both contain Bluetooth would be able to view content with one hand,

The Mobile Internet

thus leaving one hand free for other things, such as holding on to a handle while standing in a train or bus.

The problem for PDAs is their low usage and thus low actual reach. In fiscal 2000, 13.1 million PDAs were sold worldwide (as compared to more than 400 million phones), of which the US market was the largest.[4] The reason for the currently small market is their high cost and emphasis on the business market. Currently, most PDAs cost more than $200, and the best ones are more than $400. Since most people can obtain a phone for less than $50, the current price of PDAs is still too expensive for them to be anywhere near as popular as phones. Part of the reason for their high cost is the high proportion of business functions in these phones. Further, the business orientation turns off many people who are more interested in being entertained than in checking their schedules. But this may change as firms such as Sony and Sharp begin releasing PDAs that are focused on entertainment rather than business functions.

Should Service Providers Subsidize PDAs?

A bigger issue is whether service providers should subsidize PDAs just as they do phones.[5] For example, consider the following analysis of the Japanese market. Currently, the Japanese service providers pay retail outlets between $300 and $400 to obtain a new phone subscriber and about $150 to provide an existing subscriber (greater than one year of service) with a new phone. The former subsidies are provided to attract subscribers, while the latter are provided to discourage subscribers from changing service providers. Both of these subsidies are implemented under the assumption that they will provide the service provider with about $80 a month in additional income.

The same logic can be applied to PDAs: subsidize their price in order to obtain new subscribers and discourage subscribers from changing service providers. They could offer users the option of receiving either a subsidized PDA or a subsidized new phone. The question is, what is the appropriate amount of the subsidies? This depends on the perceived importance of voice versus packet charges. Currently, NTT DoCoMo's average monthly income per subscriber is about $40 for basic, $40 for voice, and $20 for packet charges. NTT DoCoMo and the other service providers consider the basic monthly charges as voice-related charges, since people are primarily buying the phone for the voice services. Therefore, the service providers believe they are paying $150 in subsidies to protect an existing subscriber and obtain about $960 ($80/month x 12 months) in a subsequent year.

Mobile versus Fixed-Line Content: The Future

However, as the packet charges have increased and continue to increase, it is difficult to say whether people are buying them for the voice or mobile Internet services. This suggests that the Japanese service providers are really paying $150 to obtain $480 in monthly fees, $480 in voice charges, and $240 in packet charges. Since the packet charges are about half as high as the voice charges, they could just as easily pay $75 to subsidize the purchase of a PDA. And as the ratio of packet to voice charges rises, particularly in third-generation phones, the appropriate PDA subsidy will grow.

Should a Point System be Used?

Further, the subsidies for PDAs should, and can easily, be adjusted for each user. Clearly, the service providers want to retain the large users, and there is a significant difference between the big and small users of i-mode. The $20 average monthly i-mode charges mask large differences between users. The Japanese service providers could easily change their one-year subscription rule into a point system where users can acquire points as they accumulate packet charges. (This can also be done with voice and/or packet charges for phones.) For example, for every $100 in packet charges, the user acquires $15 in discounts on a PDA. This would enable large users of i-mode (more than $100 in packet charges per month) to acquire a $200 PDA in less than 14 months and a more sophisticated $300 PDA in less than 20 months for free.[6]

Similar arguments can be made in the US. In fact, it is possible that the market for PDAs is now similar to the market for phones in the late 1980s and early 1990s when the market for phones exploded. In the late 1980s, the price of phones had reached a point where activation commissions could actually have a significant impact on the price of the phone and service providers began increasing these commissions. The increase in activation commissions accelerated the decline in phone costs and prices as volumes expanded, thus causing phone costs to fall further. If service providers were now to start subsidizing the price of PDAs, it is possible that similar phenomena would occur.

It is also possible that the rapid diffusion of PDAs will make large-screen phones, such as those discussed earlier in this chapter, unnecessary. If large-screen PDAs are inexpensive to acquire and easy to use, people may stop using phones to access the mobile Internet. They can leave their phones in their pocket or handbag and look at contents, be they animated characters or a list of restaurants, on a larger PDA screen.

The Mobile Internet

8.5 Wearable Computing

A computer science and engineering field called wearable computing is developing the technology necessary to distribute the various functions in a computer among your various articles of clothing. For example, it is possible to put the batteries in your shoes, the memory in your belt buckle, other electronics in your buttons, and the display in your wristwatch, and to use short-range communication technologies such as Bluetooth to communicate between these devices. Ideally, wearable computing would enable people to access a computer and Internet while moving around and using their hands for other things. The wearable computer would include sensors that would notify you of environmental changes.[7] Although much of this sounds highly futuristic and very military-oriented, aspects of it are already being implemented.

The obvious place to start is the watch, and watch manufacturers are already introducing these kinds of innovations. They are turning watches into one-way pagers, mobile phones, e-mail readers, computers, cameras, MP3 music players, television receivers, voice recorders, automobile security keys, television and VCR remote controls, health monitors, weather stations, compasses, Global Positioning System monitors, altimeters, games, simple amusements, and passes for ski lifts.[8] Is this a long enough list to convince you that wearable computing will become a reality? These possibilities are being driven by the same advances in electronics that were discussed earlier — advances that will enable phones, and even PDAs, to access richer information.

But the more interesting issue is how to divide up the various mobile Internet functions among the phone, the PDA, the watch, and, in the future, a variety of different devices and articles of clothing. This is likely to generate far more possibilities than will be generated by just considering the watch, or even the phone or PDA. For example, it certainly is possible for the watch to display contents downloaded from the Internet. While some may argue that the display would still be small, in the future it will be possible to make folding displays or even to use holograms to view contents that are much larger than the actual physical display. Such a display would only have to be folded once in order for it to exceed the size of the largest i-mode displays, which are currently 13 square centimeters.

As with the diffusion of PDAs, the diffusion of simple forms of wearable computing such as advanced watches may make large-screen phones unnecessary. It is quite possible that phones will return to their voice-centered

Mobile versus Fixed-Line Content: The Future

function and most of the innovations in displays, keyboards (and other input methods), and entertainment functions will be realized on other devices such as watches or PDAs, or even articles of clothing such as belt buckles and shoes. Who knows, your underwear may even play an important role in the mobile Internet!

8.6 Navigation and Location-Based Services

Changes in the reach and richness curve, which will be driven by the availability of new phones and services, and the increased usage of car navigation systems, PDAs, and wearable computing, will make possible new mobile Internet services, including navigation and location-based services, mobile Intranets, business-to-business webs, and others. This section looks at navigation and location-based services, which are considered one of the most promising mobile Internet applications both in the West and in Japan. For example, NTT DoCoMo believes that the market in Japan for these services will exceed $3 billion within a few years.

Future navigation and location-based services include Internet access of local information (restaurants, bars, and stores), position information in conjunction with maps, optimal route selection, emergency services, tracking, and other firm applications. Toshiba's service, which was described in Chapter 5, is merely a harbinger of things to come. Toshiba is adding information about restaurants, bars, and stores that are near train stations to its train information service. Its early acquisition of users suggests that Toshiba will probably add this richer content faster than other firms. For the same reason, it may also succeed in adding position information, route selection, and the other services mentioned above.

There are a variety of ways to offer position information on maps. The two major ways to do this are through base station information (either the closest base station or triangulation between base stations) and GPS (General Positioning Satellites). The PHS service providers have been using the high density of PHS (summarized in section 7.3 of Chapter 7) base stations to determine the user's location to within about 100 meters. But PHS has poor coverage when compared to their cellular counterparts and is often not useful in fast-moving vehicles. Thus, cellular service providers such as NTT DoCoMo, KDDI, and J-Phone can, and to some extent do, use triangulation between the closest base stations to a user to identify their location (to an accuracy of about 1.5 kilometers, or one mile) and provide them with this

The Mobile Internet

information.[9] GPS provides even more accuracy (several meters), and this technology is used in car navigation systems. One question is how to transfer this GPS capability to phones, which have smaller screens and memories but require more detailed maps since the service is for pedestrians and not people in vehicles.

For example, NTT DoCoMo uses GPS in its "Doko Navi Service," which provides users with their location on a map that is displayed on a PDA screen. As described in Chapter 5, the problem is that the PDA screen is small, there is very little detail in the map, and the route selection searches take too long. Thus, these services require improved PDAs or phones that have better displays, more memory, more processing power, and better maps.

Maps are a central problem for location- and navigation-based services. Many firms are trying to transfer the CD-ROM, and DVD-based maps that are used in car navigation systems to the fixed-line and mobile Internets. A variety of standard-setting organizations are trying to determine the best way to represent longitude and latitude, buildings, roads, and other landmarks. But even when these device and map-related problems are solved, firms will still struggle to move the information from the Internet to the mobile phone or PDA, due to the large amount of data necessary. For example, Matsushita Communication, the leading providers of car navigation systems in Japan, argues that while the high-speed third-generation services will improve services considerably, their two million bits a second services will still be inferior to the 40 million bits a second that a DVD car navigation service can provide. Thus, a critical issue will be how to simplify the car navigation maps for PDAs and phones while providing more of the additional detail required by pedestrians.

Many firms are attempting to bypass these problems and pursue business applications for car-based users that require far less data, simpler maps, and less-sophisticated devices. For example, there are a large number of firms that would like to use mobile technology to dispatch their service personnel to locations in a more effective and efficient manner. Xerox, NTT-ME (part of the NTT Group), and others are currently using PHS-based systems to identify and dispatch the closest service person when a service call is received. This merely requires the tracking of service personnel, the identification of the closest service person, and providing that person with the proper route.

However, the coverage problems and low use of PHS have caused many firms to develop and use location and navigation systems in conjunction

Mobile versus Fixed-Line Content: The Future

with regular cellular phone systems. Firms using these systems try to identify and dispatch the closest service person when a service call is received. It is quite possible that these location and navigation services will be an important application for high-speed data services. Of course, the effective use of either the PHS or cellular-based systems requires the development of the proper computer systems and solving various organization problems, of which the latter may be the largest bottleneck.

8.7 Mobile Intranets

Mobile Intranets also represent a potentially large application for mobile Internet technology. Many employees, in particular sales and service personnel, spend a great deal of time outside the office but need access to internal information. As discussed in the last section, some of this information is as simple as the next place to visit, but in many cases employees also need customer and inventory information and work schedules and reports. It would also be useful if they could input information such as customer orders and work reports. Currently, facsimiles, telephone calls, and returning to the office are the ways in which employees obtain and input this information.

However, the trend toward placing most information on corporate Intranets, and the ability to access these Intranets from a mobile phone or PDA/laptop in conjunction with a mobile phone, opens up many new possibilities. The mobile phone offers greater reach, while the PDA and laptop offer more richness. And this trade-off will continue to evolve and drive the use of mobile Intranets. In Japan, firms are implementing Intranets that can be accessed from mobile phones, or other devices in conjunction with mobile phones, in a variety of ways. In ascending order of difficulty, they can be classified into four different applications:

- group mail;
- access schedules and customer information;
- input information into work schedules and accounting systems; and
- access and input to order management and supplier system.

The application of mail is very widespread. For example, Tomen and Sapporo Beer forward PC mail to the phones of their salespeople based on the mail's degree of importance. A package transportation company called Dot Japan takes this one step further by enabling its delivery personnel to input the outcome of the delivery. The delivery personnel receive mail telling them

The Mobile Internet

where to make their next pickup, and, by selecting a specific item in the mail, the riders can transmit the outcome of the work (eg, completed pickup or delivery) to the office.

Many firms also enable their employees to access information through their mobile phones. For example, Osaka Gas employees access schedules that are located on web pages through the input of the appropriate IDs, passwords, and URLs. Tokyu Advertising Agency uses phones to manage projects. By accessing the group's home page, users can utilize the bulletin board, schedules, and address lists. Tokyo Gas employees can obtain customer data such as maps and building information by accessing the appropriate web pages.

Many firms also enable their employees to prepare and submit simple information with their mobile phones or PDAs. Salespeople with Goldwine, a sports apparel company, are using their phones to write status reports. They access a website that includes bulletin boards and then input information gathered at retail outlets. Nurses are using their phones to transmit patient data back to their office after they have visited a patient in the field. Finally, firms such as Gifuko (a gift products manufacturer), beer manufacturers, and Osakaya (a book wholesaler) are enabling their salespeople to use their mobile phones to check inventory and place orders. For example, Osakaya's salespeople can search, and place orders, for books by title and ISBN.

Many of these projects are being driven by the creation of groupware software, which was initially developed for PCs and is now being transferred to mobile phones and PDAs. Suppliers of mobile-based groupware compete in terms of functions (eg, mail, schedules, bulletin boards, meeting reservations), compatibility with different mobile Internet services (eg, i-mode, EZ Web, J-Sky), security functions (eg, SSL), computing environment (Windows), and specific applications. And many suppliers of this groupware software focus on a specific application such as construction or medical reporting.

The difficulties of developing and implementing this type of groupware and other software are causing firms to offer these capabilities as services. For example, Japan Communications Inc., the largest mobile virtual network operator (ie, reseller of mobile phone services to companies) in Japan, provides various kinds of mobile Intranet services described above for a fixed monthly or transaction rate. Further, other firms are providing the various kinds of navigation services described in the previous section. The eventual success of these services and projects will probably depend more

Mobile versus Fixed-Line Content: The Future

on organizational than technical factors. Research on the implementation of information technology, including Intranets, has found that organizational structures, incentives, power relationships, and other organizational variables have had a large effect on the degree of project success. Similar organizational variables will probably also play an important role in the success of mobile-Intranet-related projects. [10]

8.8 Business-to-Business Webs

Business-to-business webs also represent a large potential market for mobile-Internet-compatible phones. Many transactions are conducted while people are outside the office, and many small businesses don't have PCs because they consider them too expensive for their business.

For example, a firm called Flower Auction Japan (FAJ) is trying to use the mobile and fixed-line Internets to create a business-to-business web. FAJ acts as a broker for the buying and selling of flowers. Currently, after the flower growers send descriptions of flowers to FAJ by facsimile, FAJ negotiates with wholesalers and retailers by phone and takes a percentage of the sale as commission. FAJ would like to replace this facsimile- and phone-based system with a business-to-business web that uses both PCs and phones. Phones are expected to play an important role, since much of the negotiating occurs while the flowers are being transported to cities.

Guru Navi, a leading supplier of information on restaurants (described in Chapter 4), is creating a business-to-business web for restaurants, bars, and food and beverage producers that will use both PCs and mobile phones. Food and beverage producers must have PCs to participate, while restaurants and bars will be able to place orders with either PCs or phones; apparently, few restaurants, and even fewer bars, have PCs. According to Guru Navi, most restaurants and bars pay exorbitant prices for food and beverages, since they buy small quantities often from small mom-and-pop grocery stores. By buying in bulk from Japanese and US food and beverage producers, Guru Navi hopes to provide these restaurants will lower-cost services. The participation by US firms is a potentially interesting example of Japan's mobile Internet reducing trade barriers between the US and Japan.

The Mobile Internet

Sound Bites

1. **Positive feedback is leading to richer content.** The positive feedback that has been created between content, users, phones, and business models is causing the trade-off between reach and richness to change.

2. **Advances in semiconductor technology continue to improve phones and other devices.** Displays will become bigger and better, embedded cameras will become standard items, phone memories will become larger, and other aspects of mobile phones will be improved through advances in semiconductor technology.

3. **The diffusion of complementary devices will spur the creation of rich content.** The diffusion of car navigation systems, PDAs, and wearable computing will lead to the appearance of richer content and applications.

4. **Higher-speed data services will eventually make richer content possible.** High-speed data services will become important as mobile devices with larger screens (both phones and PDAs) become available.

5. **Navigation services, mobile Intranets, and mobile business-to-business webs will change the way companies communicate and work.** It is expected that better phones, PDAs, and higher-speed data services will enable firms (and, to some extent, consumers) to use navigation and other location-based services, mobile Intranets, and mobile business-to-business webs to improve their productivity and services.

Notes:

1. The 125-gram phone from Sharp did not sell well due to various problems that are independent of the large display. Thus, we are unable to draw many conclusions from this phone.
2. "Mobairu Kontentsu no shinchouryuu (The new tide of mobile contents)," *Nikkei Communications*, September 18, 2000, pp. 102–120.
3. Personal communication with Frank Sanda, President of Japan Communications Inc. Also see Jun Nakai, *Ayaushi! Nihon no Jisedai Ketai (Apprehensions about Japan's Next Generation of Mobile Services)* (Nikkei Publishing, 2001).

Mobile versus Fixed-Line Content: The Future

4. "PDA 50% seichou tsuzuku — nihon shijou, keitai to no chigai, fukaketsu (The 50% growth continues with PDAs — in Japan, the PDA is different from the mobile phone and indispensable)," *Nikkei Industrial*, April 5, 2001, p. 3.
5. Clearly, it would only be in their interest to subsidize PDAs that can be used only with their service and not another service.
6. This is not merely an academic discussion, as the case of KDDI in Japan shows. KDDI has been losing share almost continuously for the last five years. It has even lost two percentage points in share (it had 18.7% at the end of 2000) since the achievement of its investment-intensive cdmaOne nationwide service in April 1999. It has recently attempted to recover and acquire those same large mobile Internet users through a rather roundabout student discount. It has been offering discounts to students since November 2000 that are as high as 50% in the hope that it can acquire the major users of the mobile Internet. It would have probably been much more effective to provide a point system so that it could actually acquire the large users of the mobile Internet (or the heavy voice users).
7. For example, see MIT's project on wearable computing. http://wearables.www.media.mit.edu/projects/wearables/.
8. For example, see P. H. Lewis, "Look out! New wrist devices on the loose! Watches, once used to tell time, are rapidly mutating," *State of the Art*, January 20, 2000.
9. The PHS service providers have been providing a similar service for years. The high density of PHS base stations enables these Japanese PHS service providers to use the location of the closest base station to the user to identify their location to within several hundred meters.
10. For example, see the section on organizational change in E. Byrnjolfsson and B. Kahan (eds), *Understanding the Digital Economy* (Cambridge, MA: MIT Press, 2000).

Chapter Nine:
The Challenge for the Rest of the World

Many people argue that the Internet is the most important technological development of our time (the end of the 20th and early 21st centuries), and it is clear that the mobile Internet will play an important role in the overall Internet. The mobile Internet provides higher reach than the fixed-line Internet, and eventually it will be able to handle richer contents.

The question is how to get the ball rolling and create positive feedback between content, phones, users, business models, and portals/search engines. The rest of the world, including the US and Europe, appears to be taking the long, slow road. Their current focus on business content and users, and their failure to develop a comprehensive model that supports content providers and phone manufacturers, is slowing growth in their mobile Internet. This book has argued that business users are not the initially appropriate users of most portable products and that business applications are too complex to be the first killer applications on the mobile Internet. Further, even if some business people in the US and Europe become satisfied mobile Internet users, just the fact that there are many fewer business people than regular consumers means that it will take a long time for positive feedback to take hold in the West.

The slow creation of a successful mobile Internet is a major loss to consumers and producers in the rest of the world. Consumers are not able to use a valuable service, while producers such as mobile service providers, manufacturers, content providers, and other firms are missing important opportunities. This is particularly problematic for firms that are involved with implementing high-speed third-generation systems. These systems will enable users to access richer content on the mobile Internet through the

The Mobile Internet

higher-speed services. But without a successful mobile Internet, it is unlikely that these high-speed services will succeed. Users are unlikely to suddenly access video and other expensive services unless they are already experienced mobile Internet users. People must learn how to use any new technology, and they typically first learn with simple applications. This suggests that service providers who are investing large amounts of money in third-generation systems and who may have paid high fees for third-generation licenses face financial problems unless they are able to make their second-generation mobile Internets work.

Western manufacturers are also in danger, albeit not just from the failure of third-generation systems. Although manufacturers such as Nokia, Motorola, Ericsson, and Siemens dominate the global phone market, the success of the Japanese mobile Internet provides Japanese manufacturers with a unique opportunity for success in the overseas markets. These Japanese firms may be able to use their early experience in the Japanese mobile Internet, and not their fundamentally superior technology, to succeed in the global mobile Internet market. This book has argued that it is NTT DoCoMo's and the other Japanese service providers' focus on the initially appropriate content, users, services, and business models that has enabled the Japanese mobile Internet to succeed, as opposed to the use of specific technological standards such as c-HTML. The resulting positive feedback in the system has enabled Japanese firms to develop valuable experience and new technologies for the mobile Internet at a far more rapid pace than Western firms.

Further, Japanese content and other technology providers are also hoping to use i-mode's success and WAP's failure to enter foreign markets. Japanese content providers of all types would like to use their success in the local market to provide similar services overseas. Already, content and technology providers such as Bandai, Index, Cybird, Toshiba, Access, and many others, have begun providing content, content delivery platforms, or other technologies services outside of Japan.

Interestingly, the success of mobile Internet services by Western service providers such as KPN and AT&T Wireless may cause other service providers to purchase most of their mobile Internet systems from the Japanese firms. These service providers received investments from NTT DoCoMo and they (particularly KPN) and their partially owned subsidiaries are already working with a number of Japanese firms to implement services and content that are expected to be quite similar to NTT DoCoMo's i-mode services. If they are able to acquire a significant number of users for their services, other providers may turn to Japanese firms for turnkey solutions in order to quickly achieve

The Challenge for the Rest of the World

success with their mobile Internet. This could lead to rapid share increases for Japanese phone manufacturers and other providers of mobile Internet technology in Japan.[1]

The rest of this chapter discusses why the rest of the world has misunderstood the mobile Internet (and why Japan got it right) and summarizes a blueprint for the Western firms. Interestingly, the rest of the world's misunderstandings about the mobile Internet reflect common mistakes concerning new technology. Firms often focus on complex technological solutions when they could obtain better results with a simpler approach. They often focus too much on existing users, even when the technology is more appropriate for new and different users. Firms also often modularly modify their systems when an entirely new system, including new business models, is needed. Finally, many mobile service providers are trying to create closed systems when today's economy requires openness.

9.1 Mistake #1: Initial Use of Complex Technologies and Business Models

Most of the Western world appears to believe that complex technologies and business models are critical to the mobile Internet, including its early phases, in part because they are certainly critical in the successful fixed-line Internet in the West. Broadband (ie, higher-speed networks), video and audio streaming, encryption, optical networking, and a plethora of other technologies play an important role in competition on the fixed-line Internet. Similarly, relatively sophisticated business models, such as shopping, advertising, dynamic pricing, and auctions, also play an important role.

The key role that these complex technologies and business models play in the fixed-line Internet has caused Western firms to believe that complex technologies and business models will also play a critical role in the mobile Internet. A wide variety of location-based technologies get the most attention where mobile service providers would like to send content and advertisements to users that are based on the user's location. But they are not the only sophisticated, and probably overly complex, technology that is being billed as the killer application for the mobile Internet. A casual look at the proceedings for a mobile Internet conference will find talks on dynamic bandwidth adaptation, synchronization, transcoding, and a variety of technologies for enterprise solutions such as mobile Intranets and application service providers. Sophisticated and complex business models are also often an important part of these new technologies.[2]

The Mobile Internet

Business history is littered with examples of firms who invested in technologies before their time was right. Apple's early investment in PDAs, Monsanto's support of genetically engineered foods, and America's (including General Electric's and General Motors') investments in factory automation are just a few examples of firms that invested in the wrong technologies. America's over-confidence in factory automation is the most interesting example, because it involves Japanese versus US perceptions about new technology.

Japan's Emphasis on Simplicity Beat US Complexity in Factory Management

In the early and mid-1980s, US firms initially responded to competition from Japanese manufacturers by using America's strength in computer systems to invest in sophisticated production systems such as computer-integrated manufacturing and manufacturing resource planning. General Electric invested heavily in its relatively unsuccessful factory automation business, and General Motors reportedly spent $50 billion on implementing these technologies in its factories.[3] But it wasn't until the late 1980s that most US firms realized that simpler production systems such as just-in-time (JIT) manufacturing were less expensive and more appropriate for many factories.

These systems were implemented first by Toyota and other Japanese firms. Using these systems, Japanese firms reduced inventory, improved quality, reduced set-up times on machine tools, and used *Kanban* cards to control production; they then implemented automation.[4] But many Westerners dismissed these ideas as too simple and too dependent on Japanese culture to be of interest to the West (sound familiar?). It was only when Japanese firms began successfully implementing these production systems in the United States that Western firms became interested in them.

However, even in the 1990s, many of the academic experts on production systems were still arguing that complex production systems were superior. These professors of operations research and production control were focused on complexity, because that was their personal competitive advantage. They had developed sophisticated mathematical and computing techniques for calculating the optimal lot size, determining schedules, and performing other production tasks. But simple production systems such as JIT manufacturing don't require lots of sophisticated mathematical techniques, so the so-called experts on production systems didn't like them.[5]

The Challenge for the Rest of the World

Japan's Initial Emphasis on Simplicity will Beat US Complexity in the Mobile Internet

A similar story can be told about the debate on the mobile Internet. Although the mobile Internet requires a simplified version of the fixed-line Internet, many Westerners and their firms want to supply sophisticated technology because that is where their personal and firm competitive advantage lies. They developed some of this technology for the fixed-line Internet and now they want to apply it to the mobile Internet. Their capabilities in these areas make them quick to criticize the simple content and business models that are used in the Japanese mobile Internet.

This is one way in which the lack of fixed-line Internet success has helped the mobile Internet succeed in Japan. The Japanese service and content providers did not try to apply complex fixed-line Internet technologies to the mobile Internet, since the fixed-line Internet was not that well developed when the Japanese mobile Internet was being developed between 1997 and 1999. Instead, NTT DoCoMo and the other service providers reinvented the wheel by using their comprehensive business models to encourage the development of content and phones that are appropriate for the mobile Internet. Interestingly, as the positive feedback has been created in the Japanese mobile Internet, providers of richer content have begun creating synergies between their mobile and fixed-line content and other aspects of their business.

The production system and mobile Internet stories have roughly the same beginning and it is very possible that they will have the same ending. In both cases, the Japanese started with simplicity while the US started with complexity, due to America's greater capabilities in computing systems. In the production system example, the Japanese emphasis on simplicity has enabled them to implement automation to a much larger extent in their factories than have the Western manufacturers, in spite of the West's advantage in computer systems. Similarly, it appears that Japan's initial emphasis on simplicity will result in their faster implementation of rich content. The Japanese mobile Internet is already evolving from simple entertainment to more interesting content. In fact, it can be said that the Japanese mobile Internet now has more users of sophisticated contents than the West does, in spite of the West's greater emphasis on complex technologies. As described in the last chapter, Japanese firms are developing, and people are already using, sophisticated navigation services (eg, Toshiba), mobile Intranets, and business-to-business webs on the mobile Internet.

The Mobile Internet

2. Mistake #2: A Focus on Existing Users

Western firms are focusing on business users because mobile service providers have always offered new services first to business users. The initial users of analog phones in the 1980s were, of course, business users, and subsequently these business users became the initial users of smaller phones, digital services, and roaming. These Western firms are now trying to sell the mobile Internet to business people. When they have asked business users for their ideas about new services, they have responded with location-based services, including airline and hotel reservations, and other services such as on-line banking and stock trading, mobile shopping, and mobile Intranets.

But when the mobile service providers offered some of these new WAP services to business users in 2000, the business users weren't interested. And it wasn't just because there were technological problems with WAP; it was also because the screens and keypads were, and are still, too small, and because the services were too undeveloped to be useful to business users. As of mid-2001, the mobile service providers were hoping that new 2.5-generation services would solve some of the technological problems and provide higher speeds, which would enable more sophisticated services such as video conferencing.

The mobile Internet is more appropriate for young people than business users. Young people place a larger emphasis on content with high reach and low richness than do business users, and this content is the most appropriate content for the small screens and keyboards found on mobile phones. Further, mobile phones and mobile services are now very inexpensive and easily affordable for young people. For these two reasons, young users are the main users of short message services in Europe, and they will also be the major users of the mobile Internet if the manufacturers and service providers offer them appropriate phones and content.

Disk Drive Manufacturers Focused Too Much on Existing Customers
This will not be the first time that firms have focused too much on existing customers. A seminal study by Clayton Christensen of the Harvard Business School found that many failed companies listened too much to their existing customers; an interesting result that flies in the face of Total Quality Management. Christensen's study found that the successful producers of disk drives in each generation of disk drives failed to make the transition to the next generation of smaller disk drives because their existing customers (computer manufacturers) told them they didn't need the smaller disk drives.

The Challenge for the Rest of the World

For example, producers of 14-inch disk drives for mainframe computers developed eight-inch disk drives. But when they showed these smaller disk drives to their existing customers, the mainframe producers said they didn't have sufficient memory. Being intelligent business people who listened to their customers, the disk drive manufacturers stopped their development of the eight-inch disk drives. The result was that new entrants developed the eight-inch disk drives and sold them to the small but growing mini-computer manufacturers who were more interested in small and inexpensive disk drives than those with large memories.

Interestingly, these new entrants gradually increased the memory size of the eight-inch disk drives until eventually the mainframe manufacturers were also interested in them. Thus, the 14-inch disk drive manufacturers not only did not become suppliers to the mini-computer manufacturers, but they also lost the market for mainframe computers and many of them eventually disappeared. This pattern was repeated in the move from eight-inch to 5.25, 3.5, and 2.5-inch disk drives that corresponded with the emergence of desktops, portables, and notebook computers. No independent disk drive producer made the move from one size to the next. Christensen's book, *The Innovator's Dilemma*, gives examples of this phenomenon in many other industries.

A similar thing is happening in the mobile Internet. Young people are like the mini-computer manufacturers, and business people are like the mainframe manufacturers when eight-inch disk drives were first released. The young people are willing to put up with the small screens found on mobile phones in return for greater reach, just like the mini-computer manufacturers were willing to put up with lower memory in return for smaller size and cost. And like the disk drive industry, the phones, content, and services found on the mobile Internet keep getting better and bringing in new users. In the disk drive industry, it was continuous improvement that caused the mainframe computer manufacturers eventually to buy the eight-inch disk drives, while it is positive feedback between the key items that is causing business and other people also to become mobile Internet users in Japan.

There is one key difference between the hard disk industry (and Christensen's other examples) and the mobile Internet which is making it even harder for the Western firms to focus on young users and simple content. Whereas the employees of the hard disk drive firms didn't think of themselves as customers for their own products, many employees of service providers, manufacturers, and other key participants in the mobile Internet industry

The Mobile Internet

believe they are the key customers for their product, the mobile Internet. The employees of these companies are business people, they use the Internet, and they are mobile, and thus they believe they will be the first users of the mobile Internet. Therefore, many of them seem to believe that they don't really need to ask anyone else about the appropriate services and content for mobile Internet. They merely ask themselves about the services and content *they* would find useful. I have been in many conversations with Western people about the mobile Internet where they have wanted to tell me about the services and content that they would find useful. I always tell them about the consumer products company that almost missed the market for sanitary napkins.

Many years ago there was a consumer products company that was thinking of selling the first sanitary napkins. Unfortunately, the man in charge of the business didn't think the market would grow, since he didn't see himself using the product. He mistakenly assumed that *he* was the target customer for the product. Many US and European companies seem to be making this mistake. They keep asking themselves how *they* would like to use the mobile Internet, when the question they should be asking is: "Who would *initially* find the mobile Internet to be useful given the large number of initial limitations?"

9.3 Mistake #3: Modular Improvements to the Existing System

Revolutionary technologies like the mobile Internet require firms to reinvent the wheel. They require firms to rethink their key customers, the needs of those customers, their products, and their internal processes. To do this, different organizational units must work together to question existing paradigms and create new ones. However, this does not seem to be happening, as Western service providers appear to be taking a modular approach to the mobile Internet.

The Need for Integration of New Services and Billing Systems
Two key units inside mobile service providers that need more effective integration are new services and billing systems. These two units address very different issues, they work with different suppliers, and their members typically attend different conferences. The "new services" unit analyzes the market and thinks of new services such as the mobile Internet and its associated technologies. As discussed above, they are focused on a large number of complex technologies.

The Challenge for the Rest of the World

Few people outside the industry are familiar with mobile billing systems and the key role they play in the industry. Billing systems are highly complex and sophisticated systems that reflect the service provider's business models. They determine what users pay for and what they receive for free. For example, service providers often provide free minutes in a fixed-price package, and the billing systems determine when people have used up the free minutes and must start paying for additional minutes. Real-time capability, with its sophisticated technologies, is needed to ensure that service providers charge users for the correct amount.

This emphasis on accurate billing is being carried over into the mobile Internet area where micro-payment systems, such as those offered by the Japanese service providers, are a necessary part of the new billing systems. For example, most regulators require service providers to inform pre-paid users of their remaining pre-paid time before they make a call. With a packet service, the regulators will probably require service providers to inform these pre-paid users of their remaining packets before they access a mobile Internet service. But what happens when the number of packets is insufficient to complete a specific transaction? Should these packets be given back to the mobile user? Many mobile service providers are struggling with these kinds of issues.

While these issues are important, they distract mobile service providers and their billing vendors from the real issue of creating a comprehensive business model that will lead to the emergence of appropriate content and phones. Mobile service providers need to look beyond the details of their existing billing systems and create a business model that encourages content providers and phone manufacturers to offer the appropriate content and phones. To do this, the billing people need to work with the new services people to understand exactly how the mobile Internet is different from the current voice business that is the main income for the mobile service providers. They need to discuss the issues that are presented in this book, such as who will be the initial users, what are the key initial content, and what are the critical business models.

The problem is that even if they carry out these discussions, the history of business is littered with examples of firms that were unable to escape from their existing paradigms, business models, and users. Firms often focus on incremental or modular improvements because their internal processes and procedures reinforce their existing systems and thus encourage them to make modular, as opposed to system-wide, improvements. In fact, firms often

The Mobile Internet

end up designing their organizations such that the organizations reflect, and thus reinforce, the actual structure of the product or service. [6]

New Entrants and Vertically Integrated Firms are More Likely to Focus on System Improvements

Research on these phenomena has found that new entrants as opposed to incumbents, and vertically integrated as opposed to non-vertically integrated firms, are more likely to implement necessary system-wide improvements. [7] While NTT DoCoMo and the other Japanese service providers are certainly not recent entrants to the mobile phone industry, they and others perceived Japan to be a new entrant to the Internet. They did not equate their mobile Internet services with the fixed-line Internet, nor did they see the fixed-line Internet to be an actual competitor to their services. On the other hand, the fixed-line Internet is perceived to be, and is, highly developed in the US and many European countries, and thus many service providers have attempted to equate their mobile Internet services with the fixed-line Internet services.

The Japanese service providers are also more vertically integrated than their Western counterparts. While NTT DoCoMo and the other Japanese service providers develop most of their own software systems and manage many of the equipment installations, there is a highly developed structure of vendors in the US and Europe. Turnkey equipment solutions are common in the West but rare in Japan.

For example, mobile billing vendors provide most of the billing systems in Europe and the US, while the Japanese service providers do most of this work themselves. And like most vendors, the European billing vendors believe their role is to respond to requests from service providers and not to create a comprehensive business model that supports the creation of new content and phones. In the several mobile billing conferences that I attended in late 1999 and early 2000, I heard almost no discussion of users. Further, more than one mobile billing system vendor told me that he didn't care whether young users or business people were the proper target market for the mobile Internet. The service providers believed that business users were the initial target market and thus his firm must develop a billing system that supports such a target market.

NTT DoCoMo's more centralized approach to technology and billing systems may have helped it to effectively create a comprehensive business model that supports the creation of appropriate content and phones. This does not mean that Western service providers should become more vertically

The Challenge for the Rest of the World

integrated and develop their own billing systems, since there are certainly cost disadvantages to doing this. But the Western service providers must recognize that they need to rethink their business models for the mobile Internet. They need their services people to work effectively with their billing systems people to effectively integrate their complete services and billing systems at both a strategic and operations level. And while doing so, they need to recognize that their billing system vendors are probably unlikely to propose changes to the billing system that might run counter to business models used by the vendors.

9.4 Mistake #4: Lack of Openness

Many Western mobile service providers are trying to keep their customers and content inside their so-called walled gardens. They want to provide their customers with a limited amount of "superior" content that will enable them to charge their customers extremely high rates. At one level, this makes sense. They are trying to avoid becoming "pipes" that only transmit data and thus compete solely on price; instead, they hope to become suppliers of value-added services. But in today's world, the worst way to provide value-added services is to restrict the amount of content that your customers can see.

In the old economy, broadcasting and telecommunication companies were regulated monopolies; there were only a few firms that provided television and radio programming and telecommunication services in each market. Consumers used these services not because these firms provided superior content, but because they had no other choice. The command and control management method also worked well in this world, since choice was limited and control of the limited content was the key to success. Thus, a few people at the top of these broadcasting and telecommunications companies made the decisions with respect to content and their subordinates carried out their directives.

Choice and Diversity are Critical in the New Economy
In today's economy, the amount of available information in the traditional media is increasing since technology makes it possible to provide, and consumers desire, a more diverse collection of information (eg, more television channels). Further, the amount of information available on the Internet is exploding. Thus, firms in both the traditional media and the Internet

The Mobile Internet

must provide their consumers with more choices and customized content than their competitors, in order to stay in business.

Further, the command and control management method doesn't work in a world where choice, diversity, and thus positive feedback, determine the winners. Mobile service providers cannot hope to develop the amount of necessary and interesting content by themselves. They need to receive as much content development help from content providers as they can get. In fact, the mobile service provider that creates positive feedback first and receives more help from content providers, manufacturers, and portals/search engines than its competitors will win, since it will be able to provide its users with more choice than the competition.

Choice and Diversity Come through Positive Feedback

NTT DoCoMo achieved positive feedback first, and its competitors have been chasing it ever since. KDDI and J-Phone have struggled to make their services compatible with NTT DoCoMo's content in order that their users can access that content. By mid-2001, they had achieved this to some extent in the text and images on the content pages. This means that NTT DoCoMo must continue to innovate in order to stay one step ahead of its competitors in the race to provide its users with both better content and services. This is made possible because its early creation of positive feedback enabled it to create a strong brand image with consumers and to receive more co-operation than its competitors from service providers, manufacturers, portals/search engines, and other providers of complementary technologies. NTT DoCoMo continues to be the first Japanese firm to introduce Java-based services, new payment methods, navigation services and platforms, and mobile Intranet services and platforms.

Western mobile service providers have fewer means to differentiate themselves from their competitors than NTT DoCoMo had, since they are using a common mark-up language. But this is not a reason to restrict content, since that will ensure that users won't come. And if the users don't come, content providers and other firms will be unwilling to provide the mobile service provider with exclusive content. Instead, Western mobile service providers should quickly introduce positive feedback as well as superior services that are easier to use, a better brand image, and new technologies in order to differentiate themselves from their competition. The more positive feedback they create, the more likely it is that firms will be willing to provide them with exclusive content and technologies.

The Challenge for the Rest of the World

9.5 A Proposal for Creating Positive Feedback in the Rest of the World

Western service providers can create positive feedback between services, content, users, phones, business models, and portals/search engines, just as NTT DoCoMo and the other Japanese service providers have done. But they don't necessarily need to use i-mode technologies such as c-HTML. What they need to do is focus on the *initially* appropriate services, content, users, phones, business models, and portals/search engines. This includes micro-payment and packet services, simple content, young users, inexpensive phones, a simple portal with a fixed menu, and a comprehensive business model that encourages manufacturers and content providers to develop the appropriate phones and content. This section of the chapter describes this in terms of the roles for each type of firm.

Service Providers

Mobile service providers are the key firms in the mobile Internet, since they will make the most money from it in the short run. They need to play a variety of roles and make the largest initial investments of all the participating firms. They need to offer a simple portal, packet and micro-payment services, and create a comprehensive business model that encourages manufacturers and content providers to develop the appropriate phones and content.

Mobile service providers need to take responsibility for creating positive feedback between content and users. Thus, they must be the initial providers of content on a simple portal. They need to screen content for quality and organize them into categories and sub-categories in much the same way that fixed-line portals such as Yahoo! do (or outsource the portal service to a firm like Yahoo!). They need to provide incentives for these content providers to create appropriate content for the mobile Internet, of which the best way appears to be a micro-payment system. They can collect content charges for content providers like the Japanese service providers do, or they can give content providers a percentage of their revenues (eg, packet or fixed monthly charges) from the mobile Internet service. I believe that a variety of billing approaches will emerge as European and US service providers experiment with their mobile Internet services.

Mobile Internet service providers also need to take responsibility for creating positive feedback between phones and users. They must subsidize mobile-Internet-compatible phones in order that many users, not just business users, can afford them. Further, they need to make it possible for not just new

The Mobile Internet

users but also existing users to obtain these phones inexpensively. A key part of this business model is to look for manufacturers who will produce inexpensive mobile-Internet-compatible phones for young people. As for the size of the subsidies, although they probably should not set them as high as the Japanese service providers have done, they should subsidize them to a greater extent than regular voice phones since the mobile Internet represents new income. If the Western mobile service providers do those things necessary to create the positive feedback between the key elements, they will probably make as much (in terms of percentage of voice services) as the Japanese service providers do from their mobile Internet services.

Mobile service providers should not prevent users from accessing other portals or content that are not on their portal. Also, they should not restrict linkages between sites on their portals and other sites. In fact, they should encourage the creation of other portals, search engines, and micro-payment systems, along with the creation of unofficial sites and linkages between sites, since this increases traffic and traffic is how mobile service providers make money. In the long run, the mobile service providers should probably sell their portal sites to other firms in order to stay focused on the communications aspect of their business.

Packet services are also essential to the mobile Internet. Users should only be charged for downloading data and not for looking at content. Packet services enable mobile service providers to do this. However, the relative success of J-Phone in the Japanese market suggests that service providers don't have to wait for their packet services to be implemented before they charge by the packet. If they have sufficient capacity, they can charge by the number of packets as opposed to the connect time.

Phone Manufacturers

Phone manufacturers need to produce inexpensive mobile-Internet-compatible phones that are appropriate for many users, including young people. Without phones that are affordable and appropriate for young people and the general population, the positive feedback between phones and users will not be created. But this will require the Western manufacturers to change their business model, something they don't want to do.

The Western manufacturers have set high prices for WAP phones and plan also to set high prices for 2.5-generation phones. But these high prices have little to do with higher costs, since the marginal costs of adding mobile Internet capability such as browsers and additional memory are very low.

The Challenge for the Rest of the World

The manufacturers set these high prices because they have always set high prices for phones with new capabilities, since business users have a higher willingness to pay than other users.

But these high prices will prevent young people and other ordinary users from buying the phones, thus preventing positive feedback being generated between phones and users. The Western manufacturers need to offer a wide range of mobile-Internet-compatible phones in which the high-end phones have better mobile Internet compatibility than the low-end phones. These high-end phones might include better displays and keypads and new software such as Java. This would enable them to maintain their business model and create a successful mobile Internet market. But if the leading Western manufacturers don't want to do this, the Western service providers will probably find Japanese manufacturers that are willing to do so.

Content Providers

Service and content providers need to work together to offer simple content. Simple news about the weather, sports, and the music and entertainment industry, simple mobile commerce such as sales of concert tickets and CDs, and on-line stock trading, and simple entertainment are the most popular contents in Japan because they involve high reach and low richness. Entertainment content is probably the most controversial aspect of the Japanese mobile Internet. It is hard for practical business people in Europe and the US to understand how such services can succeed in their countries. But, of course, it was also hard for most of the practical business people in Japan to believe this. This is why there were initially so few entertainment-based content providers when NTT DoCoMo started its i-mode service in February 1999.

However, they did succeed, and I believe they can also succeed in the rest of the world, because they match the reach and richness characteristics of the mobile phone and they have nothing to do with culture. For example, ringing tones are a very popular SMS (short messaging service) in many other countries because young people often want to personalize the ringing tones on their mobile phones. The mobile Internet would merely make it easier for these young people to search, select, and download ringing tones.

Second, screen savers are like ringing tones in that people can use them to personalize their phone. Thus, just as downloading ringing tones is popular in GSM, it is quite likely that downloading screen savers and other images will also be popular in Europe and elsewhere when it becomes available.

The Mobile Internet

European manufacturers are basically saying the same thing as they create an enhanced version of SMS that will enable the downloading of screen savers and other images.

Third, horoscopes and games are popular all over the world. Horoscopes can be found in most of the world's newspapers. Handheld games are also popular the world over and many of them are made by Japanese firms. The mobile Internet just makes it easier to obtain the horoscopes and games and, in the case of horoscopes, to personalize them by inputting information about your blood type, favorite color, or whatever.

Of course all of these entertainment and news services will need to be modified to match local needs. It is highly unlikely that any of the popular Japanese content will be directly transferable overseas without modifications. In the end, just as most politics are local, most content is probably local. Each country's popular ringing tones, screen savers, horoscopes, and games will reflect its popular songs, animated characters, superstitions, and mindsets.

But, of course, this is just the beginning. Once the positive feedback is started, the really interesting content begin to appear. The question is: when will the rest of the world create this positive feedback on a large scale?

Sound Bites

1. **Simplicity is the natural place to start.** Just as Japan's greater initial emphasis on simplicity in factories has led to a greater implementation of factory automation, its greater initial emphasis on simplicity in the mobile Internet is leading to the faster emergence of complex applications.

2. **New technologies often require an emphasis on new customers.** Just as hard disk manufacturers failed through their excessive focus on existing customers, the West's emphasis on their existing "key" business users in the mobile Internet will make it difficult to create the necessary positive feedback in the mobile Internet.

3. **Revolutionary technologies require completely new systems and not modular improvements.** The West needs to organizationally integrate their services and billing system groups.

The Challenge for the Rest of the World

4. **Closed systems don't work in the new economy.** While the old economy restricted choice and diversity, the new economy demands greater choice and diversity.

5. **Create positive feedback through:** an emphasis on simple content, young users, and a comprehensive business model that encourages manufacturers and content providers to develop the appropriate phones and contents.

Notes:

1. Key differences in the Japanese and other phone markets that were summarized in Chapter 4 and described in more detail in a related book of mine may make it difficult for Japanese firms to overtake Nokia and Motorola. See J. Funk, *Competition Between and Within Standards: the case of mobile phones* (London: Palgrave, 2001).
2. For example, see the schedules and proceedings for both the WAP Congress and GPRS Conference in Rome in May 2001.
3. Richard Schonberger, *Building a Chain of Customers* (New York: Free Press, 1990), p. 290.
4. The first book to describe these techniques was Richard Schonberger, *Japanese Manufacturing Techniques: Nine Hidden Lessons in Simplicity* (New York: Free Press, 1982).
5. This opinion is based on my early years in the field of technology management when I focused on production systems, including several years as a professor of business at the Pennsylvania State University.
6. For example, see Rebecca Henderson and Kim Clark, "Architectural innovation: The reconfiguration of existing systems and the failure of established firms," *Administrative Science Quarterly*, Vol. 35, 1990, pp. 9–30.
7. Ibid.

Chapter Ten:
The Challenge for Japan

Japan's early success in the mobile Internet provides it with an opportunity to export mobile-Internet-related technology to the rest of the world. This includes phones, content, and other technologies. The longer the rest of the world takes to create positive feedback between the critical items, the greater the chance that it will want to import the Japanese "solution" as an entire system.

But a far more important task for Japan is how to use the mobile and fixed-line Internet to improve Japan. Although some of Japan's manufacturing firms are world leaders, most of its services are not, and in fact many of them are grossly inefficient, corrupt, and a major drag on the Japanese economy. This goes beyond the most notable examples of banking, finance, construction, and real estate and, in terms of inefficiency, extends to retail, education, insurance, and employment and travel services.[1]

The mobile and fixed-line Internet are two ways to improve these industries. They reduce transaction costs and make information more widely available at a low cost. Further, a look at attempts to implement the mobile and fixed-line Internet in these industries reveals many of the key regulatory problems in these industries and thus suggests the key changes needed in them and in the Japanese mobile Internet. This chapter will summarize some of these challenges, which are organized into those for phone manufacturers, content providers, service providers, portal sites/search engines, mobile virtual network operators (MVNOs), and regulators.

The Mobile Internet

10.1 Phone Manufacturers

Phone manufacturers need to provide a greater variety of high-quality phones. Certainly, Japanese manufacturers are doing this, the proof being the success of the Japanese mobile Internet. The issue of variety is more complicated. Although a visitor to a Japanese electronics store would find more than 50 different phones, most of them are quite similar in shape, size, weight, and functions. The tendency of Japanese firms to copy each other, and the fact that Japanese service providers set many of the phone specifications, causes the actual variety to be quite small.

Limited variety restricts customer choice. And new technologies, which the mobile Internet certainly is, require variety and experimentation.[2] While some people may find it odd that I am critical of Japanese phones given the success of the Japanese mobile Internet, I am considering the mobile Internet in terms of its full potential and the factors that may prevent this potential from being realized. Reducing variety prevents Japanese users from experimenting with the full range of possible phones and thus prevents Japan from realizing the full potential of the mobile Internet.

For example, screen sizes are not getting bigger in the Japanese market, in spite of the clear need for larger screens. There was an initial growth in screen size in 1999 due to the popularity of NEC's first i-mode phone. But since then, manufacturers appear to have settled on a "standard size," which is roughly similar to the size of that first NEC i-mode phone. As discussed earlier, this is partly due to the standard width of content. My guess is that users would like to experiment with larger screen sizes but they are not given the choice, since service providers have an enormous influence on phone specifications. Service and content providers and portals need to solve the problem of content width, and manufacturers need to find ways to increase screen size and thus provide a variety of screen sizes.

The lack of variety is part of a bigger issue of greater independence between phone manufacturers and service providers. Historically, some manufacturers have sold phones primarily to NTT DoCoMo, while others have only sold them to one of the other service providers. This enables more than 15 phone manufacturers to exist in the Japanese market, much more than in any other country, and this is an additional reason why Japanese mobile communication costs are much higher than in the rest of the world.

The Challenge for Japan

Granted, this appears as if it is changing. Sony is the first manufacturer in the history of the Japanese mobile phone market, outside of Matsushita, NEC, Fujitsu, and Mitsubishi, to sell a significant number of phones through NTT DoCoMo. Fujitsu has announced that it will not make next-generation phones, and Denso and Kenwood are combining their operations. But still, it is hard for KDDI, J-Phone, and Tsuka to obtain the latest phones from Matsushita, NEC, Fujitsu, and Mitsubishi. Greater independence between Japanese service providers and manufacturers will most likely lead to greater variety and lower costs.

10.2 Content Providers

As discussed in Chapter 4, content providers need to introduce new business models in order for the mobile and fixed-line Internet to reach their full potential in the Japanese economy. In particular, there are problems with the information loading model and the way it is being implemented on many sites. Firms that are the leading providers of these services in the printed world run many of these sites and don't want to cannibalize their magazine sales. They set rather high fees for other firms to put jobs, cars, or rentals on their mobile and fixed-line Internet sites, thus causing the number of data points in many of these sites to be very low. For example, it typically costs a firm $6,000 to have information about a job opening loaded into the leading employment on-line site, since the on-line site and magazine pages are sold as a package and not independently.[3]

Table 10.1 summarizes the number of data points in a number of sites as of spring 2001. Back-of-the-envelope calculations suggest that these numbers of data points are probably very small as compared to the total number of potential data points. For example, there are more than 65 million cars used in Japan, of which perhaps 20% are sold each year. This 13 million figure is more than 60 times larger than the number of cars in Goo's site. Contrast the approximately 10,000 to 15,000 jobs available in Mobile An's and Recruit Furome's sites with the almost 500,000 in America's Monster.com. There are certainly many more than 5,000 hotels in Japan. There are about three million rentals that are currently not occupied and this figure is more than 15 times the number of rentals listed in the largest rental site. The highest percentage of data points may be in Guru Navi's database of restaurants in Tokyo, particularly when we consider that most restaurants are small. It had about 7% of the 100,000 restaurants (including fast-food outlets) in Tokyo in its database as of early 2001.

The Mobile Internet

Table 10.1 Number of Data Points for Selected Sites

Site's Type of Information	Site Name	Number of Nationwide Data Points	Date of Analysis
Rentals	Able	80,000 69,000	9/4/2000 5/30/2001
	Recruit's i-size	10,000 198,000 199,000	9/4/2000 1/2001 5/30/2001
	Chintai	209,000	5/2001
Hotel Reservations	JTB	>100 >5,000	11/20/2000 5/30/2001
	Countdown	19 in Tokyo 400 nationwide	11/20/2000
	Play Co.	6 in Tokyo 60 in Tokyo	11/20/2000 5/30/2001
Employment	Mobile An	11,000 9,000	9/4/2000 5/30/2001
	Recruit's Furome	12,000 14,000	9/4/2000 5/30/2001
Used Cars	Goo	175,000 214,000 220,000	9/4/2000 1/24/2001 5/30/2001
Restaurants	Recruit's i-size	8,000	1/2001
	Guru Navi	12,000 7,000 in Tokyo	1/2001

Source: Sites or interviews.

As discussed in Chapter 4, most of these firms need to adopt new and more innovative business models in order to increase the number of data points in their services. These new business models include lower loading charges, performance-based systems, disintermediation, discount coupons, and dynamic pricing. Some incumbents will introduce new business models and others will not. But since new entrants are often more likely to introduce new business models than incumbents are, there needs to be more

The Challenge for Japan

opportunities for firms to enter these industries. And since being an official site provides many advantages, there needs to be more opportunities for new entrants to become official content providers.

10.3 Service Providers

Service providers in Japan have a lot of power over who can become an official content provider, and official content providers clearly have a large advantage over unofficial content providers. Since the mobile Internet is playing an increasingly important role in the Japanese economy, this is potentially a dangerous situation since it enables service providers to determine who can enter a specific industry and who cannot. This has the potential to stifle innovation and competition in many Japanese industries that are already lacking in innovation. In particular, NTT DoCoMo has probably become the most powerful firm in Japan, and its ability to single-handedly determine the i-mode official sites makes it potentially more powerful than any government regulator.

Consider the i-mode official menu. As of spring 2001, i-mode was like a *Who's Who in Japan*. Japan's old-line firms dominate the official menu in almost every category. Japanese financial institutions represent about one-third of the firms on the official menu, and old-line firms dominate most of the other categories. There are also very few foreign firms on the menu. Whether the lack of new entrants or foreign firms is due to their lack of effort or to NTT DoCoMo's impartiality is not the issue.

The issue is that the Internet is too important to let one firm control it. NTT DoCoMo's near-monopoly control of the mobile phone market enables it largely to decide who can or cannot participate in the Japanese mobile Internet, and how they do so. For example, its micro-payment system is very restrictive and is part of the reason why many content providers are not making money in the mobile Internet.

Many of NTT DoCoMo's restrictions on its official content providers are also quite strange. For example, virtual shopping malls are not allowed on the menu unless they agree to take responsibility for the sales of their member stores, while hotel sites are not required to take responsibility for the services of their hotel members. This is in spite of the fact that many hotels that take reservations over i-mode phones use i-mode as a way to sell their worst rooms at a discount (but they don't advertise this fact). NTT DoCoMo argues

The Mobile Internet

that virtual shopping malls are different from hotel sites, since hotels have physical assets while virtual shopping malls are not physical entities.

This is one example of why many content providers are frightened of NTT DoCoMo. They realize that many of its rules are strange, but they are powerless to argue with it. In fact, many content providers are frightened to the extent that they will not become official content providers to the other service providers. This includes NTT DoCoMo's official content providers and even those who are still waiting to be approved by it. NTT DoCoMo is becoming the Microsoft of Japan.

10.4 Portal Sites and Search Engines

Independent portal sites and search engines have played an important role in the success of the fixed-line Internet. Eventually, I believe, they will also play a similar role in the mobile Internet. NTT DoCoMo and the other Japanese service providers have been unable for some time to handle the large number of applications from content providers, and this problem will only become worse. Further, it is in their best interest to promote the creation of better portals and search engines. NTT DoCoMo makes its mobile Internet money primarily from packet charges, and this traffic comes from good content, which portals and search engines are much better positioned to provide than NTT DoCoMo is. One alternative is for NTT DoCoMo to change its screening from content to portal sites and search engines. This would be a major change for NTT DoCoMo, since it would also involve the elimination of current restrictions on official sites acting as portal sites and restrictions on linkages between its official and other sites. NTT DoCoMo could create a new category on its official menu called "portals and search engines" and allow these to determine the actual sites on their menus and the linkages between them and sites, including the current i-mode official sites. Over time, we could expect most current i-mode official sites to become part of multiple portals and search engines, and the current i-mode official menu can be slowly phased out. This would also enable NTT DoCoMo to avoid the criticisms of its policies in screening content.

Allowing independent portal sites and search engines to be on service provider official menus would increase the number of alternative micro-payment systems and the chances that content will be adjusted to fit larger-screen phones, PDAs, and car navigation systems. In particular, it is quite possible that Japan's seven million users (as of early 2000) of car navigation systems would be interested in accessing content on their car navigation

The Challenge for Japan

system displays. Portals and search engines can probably help NTT DoCoMo do this faster than it could by itself.

10.5 Mobile Virtual Network Operators

Mobile virtual network operators play a much smaller role in Japan than elsewhere, in spite of the greater need for them in Japan. As mentioned in Chapter 8, Japan Communications Inc. is the largest MVNO in Japan. It resells mobile phone services to companies, including various kinds of mobile Intranet services. And this kind of MVNO will become even more important in the high-speed data services that NTT DoCoMo will begin offering in October 2001.

High-speed mobile phone services will require the creation of a number of new content and applications. Although content providers can and are developing contents that utilize these high-speed data services, applications are a different matter. Mobile Intranet platforms, navigation platforms, and business-to-business platforms require a different set of firms and technologies. And while service providers can do some of this on their own, they cannot do it all. They need to sell a large percentage of these minutes to MVNOs in order to increase the diversity of available applications. In other words, MVNOs must be made an important player in creating the new positive feedback between applications, users, and the various devices that will be used with the high-speed data services.

10.6 Regulators

Many people argue that independent firms should offer Internet and telecommunication services. This has certainly become the case in the wireline field where the near monopolies held by local telecommunication companies have made independence a necessity. In the Japanese mobile field, there are multiple service providers, but NTT DoCoMo basically has a monopoly.

The complicating factor is positive feedback. The positive feedback that NTT DoCoMo has created in the Japanese mobile Internet suggests that there are some benefits to having mobile service providers also be Internet service providers. NTT DoCoMo has been able to influence the creation of content and phones and thus spur the diffusion of the mobile Internet. Further, it is continuing to do this through co-operative development with content

The Mobile Internet

providers and other firms and the introduction of new technologies such as Java, payment systems, navigation services, and high-speed data services.

But the policies that are needed to create and expand positive feedback in a system are very dependent on the system's stage in the product life cycle. NTT DoCoMo did Japan a big favor by starting the positive feedback in the mobile Internet, which was partly through its creation of a semi-closed portal. But now that the positive feedback has been started, it is predicted that this semi-closed portal will begin to hinder competition in several industries and overall growth in the Japanese mobile Internet.

Japan's regulators have a number of options at their disposal. They could require NTT DoCoMo to open their official content sites to outside access, a move that they appear to be currently implementing albeit at a rather slow pace. They could require complete independence between mobile service and Internet service providers, a much more radical move. They could also require service providers to sell a certain percentage of their data capability in next-generation services to MVNOs. Whatever they do, I believe the regulators should implement policies that will expand the positive feedback in the system, since in the long run this will be the best policy for Japanese consumers and the Japanese economy.

Japan's regulators also need to address other issues in the mobile Internet, including deregulation in industries where the Internet is expected to play an important role. For example, laws concerning the "retail price maintenance system" prevent retail outlets from discounting certain products, particularly copyrighted products, below their suggested retail price. Naturally, a lack of discounts reduces the incentive for consumers to purchase books, videos, and music over the mobile and fixed-line Internet. There are also many laws regulating the delivery of complex products such as PCs to homes, which also raise the cost of the deliveries. Both sets of laws make it difficult for firms to implement the kind of business models that Amazon.com and Dell Computing have used in the fixed-line Internet.

One change that is expected to increase the sale of travel products over the mobile and fixed-line Internet is the relaxation of regulations that once required all travel products to include a verbal description when they were sold. These kinds of laws clearly made it difficult to sell travel products over the fixed-line and mobile Internet. Beginning in April 2001, it has become legal merely to provide these descriptions in written form on a travel agency's website.

The Challenge for Japan

These issues suggest that many of the factors that are limiting growth in the Japanese fixed-line Internet are also limiting growth in its mobile Internet. If and when Japan rewrites these regulations, the growth in both mobile and fixed-line Internet will accelerate. When this happens, we can expect to see a growth in fixed–mobile and other forms of multi-channel convergence and richer content.

10.7 Creating the Mobile Economy

Mobile phones will probably play a large number of new, as yet unknown, roles in the Japanese and other economies in the future. The large reach of phones, coupled with the increasing richness that will come with technological advances, allows us to conceive of a "mobile economy" where mobile phones impact on all industries. The achievement of this "mobile economy" will also require regulatory and other changes that are as yet unknown. As Japanese ministries are pressured to bring weak industries up to speed with the rest of the world, the mobile Internet and other outputs from the strong and vibrant part of the Japanese economy will continue to raise the stakes of deregulation. In the end, the success of the mobile economy will depend on the implementation of appropriate government policies and firm strategies and organizations, just as it has been in the fixed-line Internet.[4]

Sound Bites

1. **Create more independency between service providers and manufacturers.** This will lead to a greater diversity of phones and choices for consumers.

2. **Content providers need to introduce a wider diversity of business models.** Many industries require new business models in order to take advantage of the mobile and fixed-line Internet.

3. **Service providers need to become more open.** Current policies toward content providers restrict innovation.

4. **Independent portals and search engines should be allowed on the official menus of the service providers.** This will accelerate the entry of Japanese firms into the mobile Internet and thus enable the faster introduction of new content.

The Mobile Internet

5. **MVNOs should play a significant role in creating applications for high-speed data services.** MVNOs may play the same role in creating positive feedback between the key items in high-speed data services that content providers have played in current mobile Internet services.

6. **Regulators need to level the mobile Internet playing field and promote continued deregulation in many industries.** NTT DoCoMo has too much power, and current regulations restrict Internet usage in many industries.

Notes:

1. For example, see F. Gibney (ed.), *Unlocking the Bureaucrat's Kingdom: Deregulation and the Japanese Economy* (Washington D.C.: Brookings, 1998); L. Carlile and M. Tilton (eds), *Is Japan Really Changing Its Ways: Regulatory Reform and the Japanese Economy* (Washington D.C.: Brookings, 1998).
2. See, for example, J. Utterback, *Mastering the Dynamics of Innovation* (Boston: Harvard Business Press, 1996).
3. Personal communication with someone who paid for the service.
4. For example, see the section on organizational change in E. Byrnjolfsson and B. Kahan (eds), *Understanding the Digital Economy* (Cambridge, MA: MIT Press, 2000).